PRIVATE INTEREST &

PUBLIC GAIN: THE

DARTMOUTH COLLEGE

CASE, 1819

PRIVATE INTEREST & PUBLIC GAIN: THE DARTMOUTH COLLEGE CASE, 1819

FRANCIS N. STITES

The University of Massachusetts Press, Amherst

Preface

In March 1819, one month after Chief Justice John Marshall had delivered the opinion of the Supreme Court in *Dartmouth College* v. *Woodward,* Daniel Webster wrote his colleague Joseph Hopkinson that "Our College cause will be known to our children's children." It is doubtful if even Webster suspected that the *Dartmouth College* decision would become one of the most frequently discussed and cited in the history of the Supreme Court—a landmark in the constitutional history of the United States. Indeed, historians and jurists have examined the decision for so long and to such an extent that at first glance it appears nothing can be added without the discovery of significant new manuscripts or an attempt at sensational revisionism. Despite the abundant material, however, no single source embraces all aspects of the case.

It is often the bits of information that tip the delicate balance in historical explanations. Histories of the College slight the legal questions, and the numerous technical analyses either ignore the crucial facts of the early history of the College or attempt to evaluate the decision in the light of a well-developed body of doctrine which did not exist in 1819. There is a tendency toward quick praise or condemnation of the decision's beneficial impact on business corporations without an attempt to discover what, if anything, it meant to business corporations in 1819. The importance of *Dartmouth College* to private and public colleges and to universities is largely ignored. By examining the history of the College, the partisan intrigues and personality clashes of 1815-1816, the litigation of 1816-1819, the decision in 1819, and its subsequent modifications—in short, by pulling the many bits together, this essay hopes to supply an informative study and a fresh analysis.

Many acknowledgements are in order, but I am particularly indebted to Maurice G. Baxter for suggesting the utility of such a study and for giving freely of his time and his frank, unsparing criticism, to Robert H. Ferrell for helping to bring the manuscript to completion, to the Dartmouth College Archivist, Mr. Kenneth C. Cramer, for cheerfully responding to my distress signals, and to my wife Joan, for aiding in countless, subtle ways.

Francis N. Stites
San Diego State College, 1971

Contents

1 The Institution

Large decisions sometimes derive from peculiar and near-ir-
relevant circumstances. Such was the case with the Supreme
Court's decision in *Dartmouth College* v. *Woodward,* announced in 1819, undoubtedly one of the most important
rulings in the Court's history. When the irascible president of
Dartmouth, John Wheelock, appealed to the New Hampshire
legislature in 1815 for a final solution to his feud with the
Board of Trustees, he did not intend to produce a milestone
in the constitutional and economic history of the United
States. Responding to Wheelock's appeal, Governor William
Plumer and the Republican legislature of 1816 remodelled
the institution in hope of realizing the Jeffersonian ideal of
a state college; but they did not anticipate litigation that ultimately would restrict state power. The College trustees' decision to challenge the 1816 legislation as an impairment of
the contract embodied in the College charter resulted from
their desire to retain control of the institution in its original
form. They were unconcerned with the broader issues of
legislative tampering with vested rights and of the contract
clause as a limit on state power. Even when the case came to
the Supreme Court, that tribunal sought a constitutional protection for vested rights, not for the expansion of corporate
enterprise.

1

The circumstances of the far-reaching decision of 1819 traced
back to the College's origin, to the year 1735 when an able
young graduate of Yale, the Reverend Eleazar Wheelock, became pastor of the church at Lebanon, Connecticut and organized a tutoring school. The young minister lent eloquence
to the fervor of the Great Awakening and became a prominent figure in that movement. But the problem of supporting
his family on a meager salary seldom paid in full was not
quickly resolved. Wheelock augmented his salary by tutoring
local youth in preparation for college. This task became a
permanent part of his pastorate, and, when enthusiasm for
the revival waned, he looked to his tutoring school as an out-
let for "his ardent and active mind."[1]

Encouraged by experience with a single Indian student in the mid-1740s, he formed a plan to use his school as an instrument for converting the Indians. The new school would include not only his college preparatory students but Indian and also English youth dedicated to advancing Indian missions. To have Indians living at the school offered the twin advantages of civilizing savages and affording young missionaries an opportunity for learning the native languages and mores. Wheelock planned to support Indian and missionary students through charity; the other scholars would pay their own way.

The school gradually took on a permanent character. Another school existed in Lebanon, and Wheelock persuaded a neighbor, Joshua More, to purchase and donate the school and its two-acre tract.[2] Wheelock appointed the former owner as the master of the new school.[3] With land, buildings, and a master, Wheelock's school began to take shape, but money was still a problem. Feeling that some sort of legal status was necessary to inspire confidence in potential donors to the school, Wheelock and several associates joined More in executing a deed of indenture. More conveyed the land to them in trust "for the founding and supporting of a charity school in said Lebanon for the educating of . . . the Indian tribes in North America or other poor persons."[4] The school then formally became More's Indian Charity School. More died a year later; the trust dissolved. In 1758 More's widow regranted the land to Wheelock personally. Thereafter the school was known as Wheelock's School.[5]

The founder for a while tried to work out an arrangement to send his students to other colleges so that they could obtain special courses and also recognized college degrees. He sent the first students to what was then known as the College of New Jersey—present-day Princeton—and then he obtained a tuition concession at nearby Yale College in New Haven.

The essential trouble, of course, was that Wheelock did not have a charter. Early American colleges were, to a large degree, community artifacts, and the charter provided the link between college and community. Generally, these colonial college charters placed college government in the hands of an independent and self-perpetuating board of trustees, separate from the faculty and including prominent members of the community and government officials as ex officio members.

Ideally, such a system would benefit the college by allowing it
to operate free from the interference by warring factions
within the community certain to flow from direct legislative
control, and it would benefit the community by providing
the supervisory or visitatorial power necessary to guard
against faculty misapplication of endowments. Charters, in
short, offered independence and permanence and inspired
the confidence necessary to elicit endowments.[6] There were
disadvantages, especially for a Congregationalist missionary
undertaking like Wheelock's. A charter from the Connecticut
assembly would be inoperable outside the colony, and a royal
charter might bring royal and Anglican interference.

Without a charter the school proved a formidable task.
Aware of the risks but eager for the benefits Wheelock attempted heroically for eleven years to secure incorporation,
but in vain. "I have made repeated application to our [Con-
necticut] General Assembly," he wrote in 1767, "and often
applied home for the royal favor. I have rode many hundred
miles, and spent much time in the affair; but God has shut up
every way hitherto, notwithstanding some have loaded me
with shame that I go on without it."[7] As early as 1763, Wheelock had contemplated adding a college and removing the entire institution from Lebanon. The school would then be
"an academy for all parts of useful learning; part of it a College for the Education of Missionaries, Schoolmasters, Inter-
preters, etc., and part a School for reading and writing, etc."[8]
Lebanon's proximity to Yale and the increasing difficulty of
recruiting Indians in the area made a new location desirable
to the enlarged operation.[9] A new location meant a land grant
and Wheelock began looking in that direction. Anxious to cur-
tail the expense of boarding students at Yale, he organized a
college department at Lebanon in 1768.[10] Again the lack of a
charter proved an obstacle. Since the school could not confer degrees without legal status, the students had to continue
on the rolls at Yale to retain their standing and graduate.

On the advice of friends, Wheelock dispatched a fund-raising expedition to England and Scotland in 1765 under the
direction of Samson Occom, his Mohegan alumnus, and
Nathaniel Whitaker, a fellow pastor, and the result was a
considerable change in the school's organization. Preaching
between three and four hundred sermons in the course of
two and a half years, Occom and Whitaker collected over

eleven thousand pounds in Wheelock's name under a power
of attorney.[11] Some of the English patrons complained that a
collection in the name of a private individual afforded no assurance of its being properly spent, and continuing pressure
led to the creation of an English board of trustees, headed
by the Secretary of State for the Colonies, Lord Dartmouth.[12]
Wheelock frowned upon this arrangement since it threatened
to remove control of the school to England, an eventuality
that would not only reduce his influence but alienate his
American supporters. After deliberation, he consented in
1768 to a double trust in which the English board had responsibility for the money, but an American board, chosen
from his ministerial friends, assumed management of the
school and its missions.

   Wheelock continued to devote much time and energy to the
problem of a charter, and at last obtained one—and here, to
be sure, was the written origin of the decision of 1819.[13] It
was a delicate task, obtaining a charter, because the English
trustees, suspicious of Congregationalism, opposed incorporation and had insisted beginning in 1768 that Wheelock conduct the school without a charter. The governor of New
Hampshire, John Wentworth, eager to placate Congregational
hostility to the established church, had expressed an interest
in having the school in his colony, had promised a grant of
land, and had even implied the promise of a charter. Knowing
the English trust's opposition to incorporation, Wheelock had
deliberately kept them unaware of his moves in that direction
and had informed them only of the proposed land grant. In
1769 he sent Wentworth a draft of a proposed charter which
reflected his hope of avoiding a clash with the English board.[14]
In many respects the draft charter resembled the 1768 deed
with the Trustees, especially in its retention of the double
trust. After several amendments by both Wentworth and
Wheelock, the Governor issued a royal charter incorporating
Dartmouth College "for the education and instruction of
Youth of the Indian Tribes . . . and also of English youth and
any others."[15] The charter declared Wheelock "founder" and
president and gave him the right to appoint his successor in
his will, "so long and until such appointment . . . shall be
approved by the Trustees of said Dartmouth College." This
was another item the English trust had insisted on in 1768,
and it was to be important later. The trustees of the College
bore resemblance to the earlier American trust insofar as they
were separate from the English trustees and had the real pow-

er of governing the institution. There the similarity ended,
for the new body was self-perpetuating and possessed (if they
should wish to use it) more power than the president.[16]

Discerning in the new College charter a perversion of Wheelock's original design, the English trustees steadfastly refused
to sanction the incorporation. Their disapproval was not miti-
gated by Wheelock's *ex post facto* notification to them of the
event. Wheelock had to placate them, since the fund they controlled was his principal resource.[17] Aware that they might
not allow the College trustees to apply any of the fund and
that they might recognize him only in his private capacity,
Wheelock adroitly circumvented their displeasure. At the first
meeting of the College trustees in October 1770, he suggested
that something be done to perpetuate the name of Joshua
More. The Trustees resolved "that they had by the charter
jurisdiction only over the College, and that the School remained under the same patronage, authority, and jurisdiction
as before the charter was given."[18] In short, Wheelock had
drawn a parchment distinction between the College and
School. If incorporation touched only the College, the English trustees could allocate money to Wheelock as director
of the School, as they had done before. Their anxiety allayed,
the English trustees allowed Wheelock to draw funds.[19]

Looking toward the future of the controversy, one should
point out at this juncture a subtlety or two in Wheelock's
clever constitutional arrangements. One must note that Wheelock had sought incorporation long before he thought of a
college, and that the college had become part of his school
before the incorporation. The charter of 1769 was not an instrument for a separate institution; it was an expedient for
perpetuation of a long-standing design including a college.
Wheelock's 1770 statement that his "Indian charity school"
had become "a body corporate and politic, under the name
of Dartmouth College," is as conclusive as his practice of
using the English fund to support both institutions—that is,
the institution.[20] His personal finances were so intermingled
with those of the College and School that the distinction was
meaningless. He considered the College and School as an en-
tity. If he deceived the English trustees, one must conclude
that it was not intentional; he did so by failure to inform
them of the full scope of his undertaking, not by his application of the fund. The charter of 1769 created in fact "The
Institution Embracing Dartmouth College and Moor's Charity
School."

Eleazar Wheelock died on April 24, 1779, at the age of sixty-eight. His biographer has concluded that no father watched "over his rising offspring with more tenderness than he manifested to the School and College."[21] The tenderness was equivalent to an enlightened despotism. Wheelock had held the offices of president, treasurer, professor of divinity, and pastor of the College church. The Trustees and faculty, controlled by his relatives or friends, acquiesced with filial piety in all his proposals, acknowledged his eminence as founder, and regarded themselves as instruments for his plans. This president-trustee relation was not unusual. Trustees in the first American colleges were absentee proprietors with little time to devote to college management. They had the legal right but not the energy to govern, and the president filled this vacuum. The trustees could replace him; they could not displace him. In law they were the college, but "in the eyes of the community and often in his own eyes, the president was the college."[22] At Dartmouth, the initiative was always Wheelock's. In the cabinet of the institution there was seldom disagreement, never serious opposition.

2

It was the death of Wheelock which set in train a series of acts and events which led, a third of a century later, to this grand conflict over the College's charter and the Court's decision of 1819. The founder's death necessarily produced some changes. College affairs were in a chaotic state during the American Revolution. The English fund had been exhausted in 1775, land titles were uncertain, and Revolutionary currency depreciated the College's non-property assets. Buildings went without repair. Wheelock's close management of the institution left the Trustees with no desire to assume management. Indeed, they doubted its future. Into this troubled situation entered John Wheelock, twenty-five years old, eight years out of college, and heir by his father's will.[23] Young Wheelock had an impressive figure and an equally impressive, and unusually large, nose which was said to have formed a perfect quadrant. His punctilious manner in personal dealings repelled many individuals, and if his friends did not feel repulsed, the students eventually did. One person wrote that life with the new president was "a kind of *Roman Catholic* penance and is well calculated to mortify the *lusts of the flesh.* . . . I am convinced that this great man's erudition has bounds, but *he* is of a different opinion. He is continually tumbling over ancient and modern authors, but never finds anything new."[24] Such an appraisal neglected young Wheelock's devotion to the College, his hard work, his business sense. Otherwise it was a fair description.[25] These personality shortcomings, however, may have resulted from young Wheelock's self-conscious uncertainty about assuming the office at so young an age and with so little preparation. Only the entreaties of the Trustees brought his acceptance in 1779, and prevented his resignation the next year.[26] Unfortunately Wheelock's initial lack of confidence produced a tenacious adherence to his father's autocratic methods. Equally unfortunate, in view of the later controversy, was the early tendency of the Trustees to acquiesce as if he were old Eleazar. As the young president gained confidence and the Trustees grew independent, the pattern of these early years made friction inevitable.

Upon assuming the presidency, Wheelock devoted his energy to the depressing condition of the College finances. The Trustees gladly gave him full authority, and the state, which later would claim an abiding interest in the welfare of the College, proved of little assistance, at least before the turn of the century. The legislature did grant permission for a lottery to raise money for a new College Hall.[27] The same legislature repeatedly denied College petitions for loans and other assistance. Had the state granted these various requests, it would have had during the litigation of 1817-1819 a more valid claim to substantial support of the College—a claim that was crucial to judicial support of legislative control of the College.[28]

An example of the legislative attitude toward the College in these early years was the state's action concerning Governor Wentworth's grant of lands to the College in 1770. Promise of this grant had been a prime inducement for locating the College in New Hampshire. An earlier grant of the same township in 1764 had made Eleazar Wheelock anxious about land titles, but Wentworth assured him that the 1764 grant had become forfeit through noncompliance with charter provisions and that there was no cause for concern. The College invested considerable sums toward developing the area.[29] When land speculators, encouraged by the doubled value of the township lands by 1780, bought out the original grantees and be-

gan introducing settlers in defiance of College leases, controversy arose. The Trustees appealed in vain for legislative support of the College title.[30] Abandoning hope of securing the
title, John Wheelock in 1788 memorialized the legislature
and sought compensation. The legislature granted relief, but
by a narrow margin, in the form of 40,000 acres of undeveloped, unsurveyed land.[31] The College sold much of this "First
College Grant" even before the title was secure, and the proceeds barely equalled the losses in the earlier grant. Later
the state pointed to this "First Grant" as evidence of its support of the College. Legislative support of the College title
would have been more convincing.[32]

As it happened, the state of Vermont supplied the support
which Wheelock was unable to obtain from New Hampshire.
After the New Hampshire legislature failed to act on his petition for lands formerly assigned to an English missionary society, Wheelock had turned to the Vermont legislature, meeting in 1785 at Norwich just across the Connecticut River
from the College.[33] He petitioned for a grant of land to the
institution embracing Dartmouth College and Moor's Charity
School, and the legislature complied a week later with 23,000
acres. The governor of Vermont issued a charter incorporating the township of Wheelock in 1788. The charter, bearing
the year 1785, awarded half the grant to the College and half
to the President of Moor's School.[34] From 1799 to 1808 this
provision became the center of a storm that not only produced increasing friction between Wheelock and the Trustees
but demonstrated the relation between the College and Moor's
School—what it originally was, what it came to be. Like his
father, Wheelock had revived this distinction to obtain money
from abroad, funds Occom and Whitaker had collected in
Scotland and which were controlled by a Scotch trust.[35] An
added motive was a desire to strengthen his personal position.
The School did exist and was functioning as a grammar school
for the children of Hanover. If he could secure a separate
source of revenue, there would be no opportunity for challenge to his leadership. There were flaws in his strategy, since
no charity student was at the School after 1785, and the
School had no legal existence. Wheelock was vulnerable to
charges of personal aggrandizement, and such charges came
before the Vermont legislature in 1799.

It was a considerable tangle, the Vermont grant, and is of
concern here because it proved decisive in increasing the con-

flict between John Wheelock and the Trustees and because
the income from this grant supplied almost half of Dartmouth's funds through the first two decades of the nineteenth century. Speculators sought a revocation of the Vermont grant to Moor's School on the ground that the School
was unincorporated and, consequently, did not exist at the
time of the grant. The Vermont legislature dismissed the
petition as unsubstantiated. Wheelock immediately recruited
one white and two Indian charity students, and sought to
silence his critics by having the College trustees audit the
School's accounts.[36] A committee of the Vermont legislature,
investigating the grant after renewed charges, reported in
1806 that Moor's School had never existed as a corporation
and lamented that Wheelock was not legally accountable for
his use of rents collected from the grant.[37] Willing to compromise, the committee proposed that if the College trustees and
the President would surrender the old charter, the Vermont
legislature would grant a new charter for the township to the
Trustees of Dartmouth College for use of both College and
School.[38] Unwilling to surrender his control to the Trustees,
Wheelock now appealed to the New Hampshire legislature.
That body passed an act in 1807 incorporating the School.[39]
After some further difficulty, Vermont allowed the 1785
grant to stand. In December 1808, a relieved Wheelock wrote
that the trouble over the grant had been settled to the School's
advantage.[40] Even so, the controversy left scars, and there
would be long-run, altogether unexpected, results.

3

Gradually the tension mounted between Wheelock and the
Trustees, leading toward an open break. Three of the Trustees
were Vermont citizens: Stephen Jacob, chosen in 1802, was
the President's staunch friend and had rendered valuable assistance during the imbroglio over the Vermont grant;[41] Elijah
Paine, elected in 1806, had opposed the grant in 1785 and attempted to defeat its passage by a proposal for a college in
Vermont;[42] Nathaniel Niles, elected in 1793, had opposed the
1785 grant as a member of the Vermont Assembly.[43] Wheelock in 1800 charged Niles in an open board meeting with
having instigated the trouble. The Trustees appointed a committee to inquire into "certain reports which have been said
to be in circulation respecting measures taken with regard to

the township of Wheelock by the Hon. N. Niles unfavorable
to the interests of this institution."[44] Niles admitted that he
might have contributed to the agitation by uttering imprudent
remarks "on a sudden emergence without deliberation." Satisfied, the Trustees momentarily dropped the matter, but
Wheelock continued to blame Niles and thereafter saw his
hand in every difficulty.[45]

Although the affront which Wheelock discerned in Niles's
imprudent remarks was more imagined than real, the old sub-
servient members of the Board of Trustees were gone, and
Niles's independence, which had earned him the nickname
Botheration Primus at Princeton, characterized the new members. At first there was no open break with the President,
only an increasing tendency to discuss matters on their merits
instead of as his suggestions. Hypersensitive to any threat to
his prerogative, Wheelock interpreted this tendency as dis-
loyalty, and, when the Trustees in 1809 appointed Asa
McFarland and Charles Marsh to Board vacancies instead of
his candidates, he charged collusion to deprive him of control
of the institution.[46] His control of the faculty began to slip
in 1809.

Wheelock's control nearly disappeared when his close friend
Elijah Parish was passed over for the language professorship
in 1810. Parish had shared Wheelock's apprehensions, and on
the occasion of his personal discomfiture suggested that the
President resign but remain on the Board of Trustees. "Should
you die in office," Parish advised, "the corporation would
then follow their own inclinations as to a Successor, but
should you yield the office & remain in the Board, you would
indubitably place the man of your choice in your place. Thus
you might *virtually* be President *30 years longer*."[47]

Then a quarrel between the President and the church in
Hanover produced an impasse.[48] Wheelock's minion and Professor of Classics at Dartmouth, John Smith, had served as
pastor of the Hanover church since 1787, and had helped
smooth difficulties between that body and the President. The
Trustees in 1804 had filled the long-vacant Divinity Chair at
the College and unwittingly produced this final crisis. Service
as pastor of the Hanover church was a part of the new divinity
professor's duties. Smith had expressed his hope that a pastor-
divinity professor would be appointed so that he might be relieved of what was initially a temporary burden. The congregation, having endured Smith's monumental dullness for

years, heartily concurred. But Wheelock, for no other reason
than that his will should prevail in Hanover, now insisted that
Smith remain as pastor. Smith complied. The outraged congregation supported the new divinity professor. Wheelock repeatedly sought to enlist the support of the Trustees. They
chose not to get involved. Their "christian and independent
stand" in this struggle increasingly alienated the President
while confirming his suspicions of collusion.[49] After many efforts at compromise, the congregation in 1811 split with
Wheelock and Smith and adopted Congregationalism. The
President and a small band of followers in Hartford, Vermont,
remained Presbyterian—as much an anachronism in the New
England of that time as Wheelock's patriarchal administration.

The Trustees in October 1811 at last candidly expressed
their opinion on the Smith controversy. They refused to sanction a church dependent upon the College, and said that as
trustees they had no right to interfere in matters of conscience.
Noting that they had "long labored to restore the harmony
which formerly prevailed in this Institution, without success,"
they concluded that "if the present state of things is suffered
to remain any great length of time, the College will be essentially injured."[50]

There was this fatal impasse, nominally over the pastorate
of the Hanover church: for the first time, the Trustees stood
in formal opposition to the President. The tension between
the two sides was extreme. The Trustees in 1811 removed
Wheelock's disciplinary prerogative. In September 1814, without notice, they relieved him of his duty of instructing the
seniors at the College.[51] Unlike the failures to appoint Wheelock's candidates, these measures were blows to the President's prestige and power. The President's uncompromising
attitude, his immeasurable suspicions, his cantankerous be-
havior, his crotchetiness, without show of tact and reason, had
laid the foundation for the struggle that was to follow, a
struggle for power in this little educational institution that
was to leave the College "essentially injured" for several
decades, and change the course of American constitutional
history.

2 Wheelock Seeks Redress

"If a majority of the Legislature are not already
willing dupes to the present board of Trustees, something
will be done, as well to relieve the venerable Wheelock
from his disagreeable dilemma, as to arrest the
government of the College in a course no less destructive
to the interests of the institution, than to the
intention of its liberal founders, and its generous
patron, the State of New Hampshire."—Isaac Hill, 1815

Any religious controversy in the early republic was likely to
be swept up in the Jeffersonian surge towards democracy,
especially a sectarian squabble at a New England college. Intense partisan commitment infected every aspect of New England life as the Federalist and Republican parties vilified
each other.[1] An enduring issue was the established Congregational church, practically synonymous with New England
Federalism. Movement away from this Federalist church had
snowballed through the first decade of the nineteenth century, and, when party concerns shifted to local problems after the War of 1812, Republicans launched a campaign for
freedom of conscience and against state-supported orthodoxy.[2] Colleges, nearly all sectarian, Federalist, and impla-
cably hostile to Republican ideology, figured prominently in
this campaign. These circumstances combined to give the
quarrel over the pastorate at Hanover a peculiar importance.
When the Trustees, all Federalist except Niles, opposed Wheelock, they had apparently attached themselves and the College to the Federalist church—epitomizing Republican jere-
miads. Unfortunately none of this distracted Wheelock. The
old Federalist, chagrined by his loss of influence over the
local church and the Board of Trustees, meditated through
the autumn of 1814 and determined to fight to preserve his
control.

1

Wheelock's first move was to lay his case before the public.
For assistance in this endeavor he turned to Elijah Parish, the
arrogant, orthodox, Federalist minister in Byfield, Massachusetts, veteran of the Wheelock-trustee difficulties. That Wheelock found it necessary to rely on Parish suggests the extent

of his alienation from those persons who knew him in Hanover. Parish's interest in Dartmouth College, though encrusted with professions of devotion to the President, was principally to secure the position he had been denied in 1810.[3] Nevertheless, the choice seemed to satisfy the President, who wrote in February 1815 that his "excellent friend" would do all in his power to promote the cause, however hazardous or uncertain.[4]

The plan for public support called for anonymous publication of a simple recital of facts concerning the actions of the Trustees, and attached to this work would be another "in way of review, & in which many remarks will be made, improper to be inserted in the former."[5] Wheelock drafted the simple recital, which in final form was an eighty-eight page panegyric on his exertions, privations, and services and an indictment of the Trustees for everything from bigotry and misuse of funds to usurpation of authority and the charter rights guaranteed the President.[6] Throughout the pamphlet Wheelock disguised himself as an alert, concerned citizen warning his fellows of a conspiracy dangerous to the public welfare of New Hampshire. He forwarded the draft to Parish who then wrote a supplement and arranged for publication of the two works.

The *Review,* as the supplement was named, revealed Parish at his vitriolic best, keeping his temper and angering everyone.[7] He accomplished this, as he informed Wheelock, by "a secret, biting satire, where the author is at his ease, & seems to say only what he is compelled to say, but yet, like a soft, secret *gas* it penetrates the very bones."[8] He hoped so to arouse the public that the Trustees, that body of "wealthy individuals . . . supported by a rich and powerful corporation" and united "as to form a phalanx, formidable to the State . . . bound together by interest and roused by party passions," would fail in their venture to depose the President.[9]

In his advice to Wheelock, Parish was nothing if not thorough. He counselled the President not to expect more from this unveiling of the Trustees' ruinous policy than pressure to make the New Hampshire legislature pause. Once public interest had been aroused, Wheelock should seek redress in a memorial to the legislature. Parish sought to have the memorial prepared beforehand, so that it might be printed and, together with the *Sketches,* Wheelock's pamphlet, distributed in the principal legislative boarding houses in Concord. He urged Wheelock to "look over the list of Representatives, & select a powerful speaker in each house, & employ a trusty friend to go & consult them & to give a liberal *fee* to seize the business & give it, early, a proper direction and tone." This was no time for "half way measures, or to count cents or dollars."[10]

Parish urged Wheelock to burn damaging correspondence and disguise authorship of the two pamphlets. It was his suggestion to have the pamphlets published anonymously, and to heighten the confusion he had the works set in different type without printer's name or place of publication. He also edited the *Sketches* to remove references to individual Trustees—a tactic he defended as a "wise trick," since they were powerful and popular men and their names "might influence many high federalists to defend their cause."[11] With these refinements the two pamphlets appeared early in May 1815. Five hundred were bound together and distributed to the legislature. Another five hundred were issued separately.[12]

At this point things became thicker. Just prior to publication of the two pamphlets the Boston *Repertory* had reported difficulties at Dartmouth College "such as will probably induce the President to resign." Consequently, the "Friends of that literary institution are already fixing their eyes on a successor to Dr. Wheelock." Parish copied this report verbatim and sent it to Wheelock with assurances that only the Trustees, who were "determined to try your *stuff,* & to *overbear, & bend you to the dust,*" could have sponsored this malignant falsehood. "Who else would have so much *audacious meanness?*"[13]

This report in the *Repertory* may have been decisive in precipitating the alliance between the two Federalists and the arch-Republican editor of the Concord *Patriot,* Isaac Hill.[14] It was after its publication that Parish and Wheelock intensified their attack. Parish suggested that Wheelock "write a short piece for the Concord Democratic paper, noticing the Sketches and Review, as tho you were a Democratic writer, & say the camp of federalism is in confusion."[15] With the newspapers already commenting favorably on the pamphlets and the public reading them zealously, Parish felt that such an article would confound Wheelock's remaining enemies. Wheelock complied, and his manager congratulated him on *"that smart piece in the Patriot."*[16] The project seemed to be producing the desired effect. Even so, that "smart piece" unwittingly carried them into Hill's camp, and the quarrel transformed itself from intramural strife to a partisan roil.

Hill's entry into the fray led to complications. His *Patriot* had been assailing everything tainted with Federalism from the time he assumed direction in 1809. Alert to every opening for an attack on the monarchical Federalists and orthodoxy or both, Hill had discerned an opportunity in the Wheelock-Parish presentation of the Dartmouth difficulties. In an editorial on May 23, 1815 he told his public that he had known of a difference between the President and Trustees, but that it was beyond his "previous conception," that "the management of that College was so much a *party* concern as to persecute in a spirit of the most inveterate malignity" the venerable Wheelock. The aristocracy which the Trustees were determined to build, he argued, was more dangerous than any other because it sought to keep the people ignorant. Only one thing prevented the consummation of their design, namely, that "the President lives" and refused to resign despite efforts by the Trustees. Since these private insults—"proceedings at which even heathens and infidels might blush—had failed, the Trustees, he said in reference to the *Repertory* report, had felt compelled to insult Wheelock publicly. Their machinations were matters for public concern, since Dartmouth College had "been liberally patronized by the State," and every citizen had a concern in it. "If a majority of the Legislature are not already willing dupes to the present Board of Trustees, something will be done."[17]

By late spring of 1815, then, most of the enduring issues in the Dartmouth imbroglio were joined. The hostility between President and Trustees had produced Wheelock's determination to seek public assistance. Parish and Wheelock had portrayed the Trustees' actions as a conspiracy to undermine the state, and Hill had translated this into a political issue: the issue of Dartmouth as a public institution. Something must be done, he argued, "as well to relieve the venerable Wheelock from his disagreeable dilemma, as to arrest the government of the College in a course no less destructive to the interests of the institution, than to the intention of its liberal founders, and its generous patron, the State of New Hampshire."[18]

2

Wheelock's next step was to appeal to the New Hampshire legislature. Josiah Dunham, a fast friend of the President and editor of the Federalist *Washingtonian* at Windsor, Vermont, wrote him that Charles Marsh and Elijah Paine had been present when a copy of the *Review* arrived; and that it struck them "like a *thunder-clap*."[19] Weary and in failing health, Wheelock wrote to David McClure that, for his personal comfort and interest, he preferred to resign and leave the College to "those men to manage & apply it, as the organ of their own interest & designs, which were shaped in origin by Old Father N[ile]s." But, he said, he felt constrained by a sense of duty and an attachment to the original principles of the College "to oppose their projects, while any prospect of success remains."[20] Bound by devotion, duty, and plans in motion, Wheelock presented his memorial to the legislature at the beginning of their session in June 1815.

Wheelock thus was moving his case into politics. Referring to the legislature as the guardian of the state's institutions, he declared his duty as a concerned citizen to report that a state institution, Dartmouth College, had ceased to promote the end of its establishment, "the social order and happiness." As the guardian of republican government the legislature ought to act. Wheelock warned that the origin of the evil at Dartmouth was less important than the dangerous tendency of the Trustees' proceedings, which he saw as having but one purpose: "to complete the destruction of the original principles of the College and School, and to establish a new modified system to strengthen the interests of a party or sect, which, by extending its influences, under the fairest professions, will eventually *affect the political independence of the people, and move* the springs of their government."[21] In the general interest he implored the legislature to appoint a committee to investigate the affairs and management of the institution and, if judged expedient, to make such improvements and reforms as would guard against the disorders and their consequences.

Whereupon the legislature acted. A special committee considered the memorial on June 10, Wheelock attended, and, after explaining his case, said that his object was to enlarge the Board sufficiently to eliminate its sectarian tendencies and enable him to regain control.[22] The legislature appointed three citizens of the state, not members of the legislature, Daniel A. White, Nathaniel A. Haven, and Ephraim P. Bradford, "to investigate the concerns of Dartmouth College and Moor's Charity School, generally; and the acts and proceedings of the Trustees of said Institutions; and to report a statement of facts at the next session."[23]

What would the Trustees do? Not notified of the special hearing before a committee of the legislature, they were upset at not being able to present their side of the dispute. Five of them assembled in Concord and inserted an appeal in the Concord *Gazette* of June 11, 1815. Noting that the *Sketches* and *Review* had sought only to arouse and mislead public opinion, the new appeal asked the public to withhold judgment "until a plain statement of facts accompanied with the proper evidence appear, which will be published within a reasonable time."[24] The Trustees had hoped that their friends in the legislature would stop any investigation and that the intense feeling generated in the spring might pass.[25] But the impending investigation presaged strife, and the Trustees therefore earnestly applied themselves to preparation of a strong case.

Thomas W. Thompson, a United States Senator and prominent Federalist of Concord, took the initiative for the other Trustees. Writing to a faculty member at Dartmouth, Ebeneezer Adams, he reported a conversation with his former law student, Daniel Webster, in which he had learned of the College supporters' ardent desire that the Trustees' response to the Wheelock-Parish maneuvers "should effectually put down a *certain man*." Thompson urged that friends of the Trustees gather affidavits to demonstrate Wheelock's character "in a just point of view" and have the desired effect on the committee's report. During his own investigation Thompson had amassed proofs of how Wheelock had resorted to base means to sway opinion. The most damaging piece of evidence was *"a scrap of the envelope* of the communication to the Repertory" which showed the handwriting and led Thompson to conclude that the author was "a president's man."[26] The summer's intrigues also brought journalistic support for the Trustees, which the latter did their best to increase. The Concord and Dartmouth *Gazettes* and the Portsmouth *Oracle* examined every facet of the controversy.[27] At a private meeting in Concord early in August the Trustees laid plans for the publication of their reply to the *Sketches,* and Niles planned a series of articles defending the Trustees in the *Patriot.*[28]

What would Wheelock do? At least one of the President's friends began to doubt the wisdom of the appeal to the legislature. Judah Dana felt that since the government of New Hampshire stood in the same relation to the College as had the British Government before the Revolution, "How far it can legally and constitutionally interfere with the vested charter rights of the Trustees is not only a very nice; but a very important question to the literary Institutions of our Country." Dana thought that if such institutions were properly managed, their charters could not be materially altered without the consent of a majority of the Trustees.[29] Wheelock obviously would have to be careful. Parish strongly advised him to prepare for the committee's investigation "with an advocate . . . say Mr. W[e]bs[te]r or M[a]s[o]n." He hoped that with the aid of counsel the President might make the Trustees' conduct "*glare*" and render them more "pliable and accommodating."[30] Mason and Webster were among the state's more prominent Federalists. That Parish suggested them demonstrated not only his Federalism but also his failure to appreciate the increasing political complexion of the feud. Wheelock had already requested Daniel Webster's aid in case of legal action, and the Portsmouth attorney had assented.[31] Wheelock accepted Parish's appraisal of the gravity of the situation, and on August 5, 1815, asked Webster's assistance before the committee.[32] As it happened, Webster was absent from Portsmouth and did not receive Wheelock's request until after the investigation. Fortunately, the President had also engaged a judge of the Vermont Superior Court, Jonathan Hubbard, together with Dunham.[33]

3

For Wheelock and the Trustees the crisis—the expulsion from office of the President—was now at hand. There had been disquieting rumors through the summer that the Trustees had decided to remove Wheelock. Dunham wrote the President that Marsh had completed the Trustees' reply to the *Sketches* and that the Board would attempt to publish "the great work" just before commencement "to raise a great smoke—&, in that smoke, to smother you. They intend, I have no doubt, to attempt your removal at Commencement."[34] There was, though, some indecision within the Board. Jeremiah Mason, later counsel for the Trustees and a leader of the New Hampshire bar, cautioned against precipitate action. Since the *Sketches* had intended to attribute the College difficulties to the Trustees' personal dislike of Wheelock, removal, especially before investigation, would only confirm the *Sketches* and alienate uncommitted persons who favored the investigation. Mason believed the Trustees would be unable to compensate by a sophisticated argument that removal was in their power. "It will be said that the reasons which justify a removal (if there be any) have existed for a long time. A removal after so long a forebearance at the present time will be attributed to recent irritations."[35]

The committee chosen by the legislature convened in Wheelock's house on August 16, 1815, despite the Trustees' preference for a more public place, and continued its inquiry for the next two and a half days. Finding the records for the history of the College too voluminous, the committee decided to limit the inquiry to subjects which the President and Trustees presented. Wheelock and his counsel, Hubbard and Dunham, presented a list of charges. Trustees Marsh, Thompson, McFarland, and Smith followed with affidavits, documents, and records to answer Wheelock's charges. Their presentation made it appear that Wheelock had acquiesced in the acts of which he now complained.[36]

At this point, and but for Wheelock's obduracy, the affair might have come to an end. Marsh, McFarland, and Smith approached Wheelock through Parish in hope of a compromise and intimated that they saw no reason why he "might not be retained in office so long as he lived," provided he would somehow or other retract the *Sketches*. This move astonished Parish who felt that it stemmed from the Trustees' desire *"to save their own bacon."*[37] Long negotiations ensued. Wheelock declared for no compromise, since he was convinced of his rightness. The Trustees' *sine qua non* was a retraction of the *Sketches*. The conversations reached an impasse. One of the committee members, Bradford, anxious for accommodation for the good of the College and the public, attempted to get the conversations moving, without effect.[38]

The Trustees now abandoned caution. When the ten men

then making up the full Board—Governor Gilman holding office as an elected and an ex-officio trustee and president-trustee Wheelock absent—convened the annual meeting before Commencement, August 24, 1815, they appointed a committee to investigate whether any member of the board or faculty had helped publish and distribute the *Sketches* and *Review*.[39] Next day the Trustees' committee reported that circumstantial evidence left "no room . . . to doubt" that Wheelock was the principal "if not the sole" author of the *Sketches*. The committee noted that Wheelock in his memorial referred to the pamphlet as "a work entitled to the highest credit"; that the *Sketches* mentioned that Wheelock had furnished the facts; that the pamphlet had been treated in Wheelock's hearing as his book without refutation; that his counsel before the legislative committee had referred to the pamphlet as the President's book; that there was a "single peculiarity of style common to the 'Sketches' and the Memorial."[40] After adjourning with a motion to consider the report at eight o'clock the following morning, the committee notified Wheelock of its findings and offered the opportunity for explanation.[41]

Again Wheelock would not back down. He refused to appear before the committee and sent a letter eulogizing his efforts for the College and lamenting that of late years the "darts of calumny" had been "secretly and cautiously" hurled against him. Never, he said, had there been a single hint by the Trustees in open meeting that there was anything reproachful in his conduct, and it appeared "singular and extraordinary" that the Trustees should now bring charges. He denied them any jurisdiction to try him and concluded that since the majority of the Trustees had combined with party leaders in views wholly repugnant to his own and the legislature had undertaken to examine and remedy the evils, it would be improper for him to answer charges before them.[42]

On Saturday afternoon, August 26, the Trustees passed resolutions preparatory to removing Wheelock. They proclaimed that it was peculiarly important for corporate bodies to explain their actions to the public when the concerns entrusted to their care were dependent upon public opinion for prosperity and success. This belief had induced them to submit their actions to the scrutiny of the investigating committee, and it now prompted them to "state the reasons that led them to withdraw their further assent to the nomination and appointment of Doctor John Wheelock to the presidency of Dartmouth College."[43] After listing the charges, notably Wheelock's authorship of the *Sketches,* they concluded "from a deep conviction that the college can no longer prosper under his Presidency." This action, they argued, was not to be construed as disrespectful to the legislature because the investigating committee had been appointed to ascertain whether the Trustees had forfeited their charter, not whether they had exercised their charter powers discreetly. They accepted the committee's right to investigate and, when that body should submit its report to the 1816 session they would "cheerfully meet the issue before any tribunal competent to try them according to the principles of their Charter."[44]

That evening the Trustees voted to notify Wheelock of these resolutions and of their intent to act unless he requested a delay.[45] Informed, Wheelock said they could do what they pleased. They removed him.[46]

Two of the Trustees, Stephen Jacob and Governor John Taylor Gilman, filed a formal protest against the removal.[47] The eight majority members, "the Octagon," dispatched a letter to the Reverend Francis Brown and offered him the presidency.[48] From their viewpoint, the thirty-one-year-old Brown was an excellent choice. Not only was he an alumnus, former tutor at the College, and pastor of the church at North Yarmouth, Maine, but his scholarship, administrative talents, circumspection, and diplomacy made him Wheelock's opposite in practically every regard.[49] On Monday, August 28, the Octagon appointed Brown, and adjourned until Tuesday, September 26.[50]

Shortly after Commencement the Trustees' able refutation of the *Sketches* appeared, but several circumstances unfortunately combined to rob it of effect.[51] Writing under the irritations of the summer, Marsh had given the pamphlet a satirical tone which made the pamphlet appear as another slander against Wheelock. Marsh had believed that if the Trustees had published their reply before removing Wheelock, it would have appeared that they were seeking sanction for a contemplated action, and that Wheelock's adherents would have interpreted this as a threat and been inspired to greater exertion. The only available course was to rid themselves of the "incumbrance" under which they had labored, publish their vindication, and "trust to the correctness of conduct and to

the candor of the public for justification."[52] Unhappily the
public concluded, as Mason had forecast, that the Trustees
were more interested in demolishing Wheelock than in justify-
ing their actions. Moreover, the pamphlet cost twenty-five
cents, in contrast to the *Sketches* which was free, and people
were "more willing to remain ignorant of the merits of the
case than to purchase a 25¢ pamphlet."[53] Parish also gleefully
informed Wheelock that it was badly written. The Trustees
had seriously miscalculated. According to Parish, the book
"having been long in the birth *died*. It is *still born*. It will have
no resurrection, for it goes from the *womb* to the *grave*."[54]

The stage was set for the *Dartmouth College* case. Despite
the welter of charges and countercharges, pamphlets,[55] plots,
intrigues, and misunderstandings that rocked New Hampshire
in 1815, there was one major point at issue, the relation of
the President and the Trustees to the College. The Trustees
had stated in their *Vindication* that the President claimed to
be sole executive of the corporation of Dartmouth College;
that he claimed sole power of appointment both of faculty
and Trustees and exclusive exercise of the judicial or visitatorial power. They opposed this claim. They believed, and
rightly, that Wheelock was mistaken in claiming powers which
had evolved from his father's experience in earlier and more
tranquil times, contrary to the charter of incorporation. Wheelock, of course, refused to admit that his personal control was
subject to legally constituted authority; and his refusal carried
the controversy to the Supreme Court of the United States.

3 The Octagon on the Defensive

*" 'Hold on,' they say, 'till the last finger is
cut off.' It is the opinion of most, that the
Trustees will protest against the legality of the
measure, & will carry it to the Supreme Court of
the U. S."—Reuben D. Mussey, 1816*

Wheelock's removal presented Republicans even greater political opportunity than the events of the spring, and Hill was
not slow to seize and exploit it. He had fulminated against
the Octagon as a Federalist attempt to establish a "Law Religion" which would perpetuate their aristocracy and allow
them to manage civil government as they pleased. Determined
that the College should not be an agent of indoctrination, the
fiery editor, from September 1815 through early 1816,
stirred popular indignation against these Federalist bigots
who, looking down from the sublime height of their untouch-
able position, had removed the "venerable President" as part
of their sectarian conspiracy.[1] His warnings to sects such as
the Baptists, Methodists, and Quakers, convinced many New
Englanders that Republican government in New Hampshire
depended upon the election of 1816 which promised proper
resolution of the Dartmouth College affair. Hostility to the
College grew so intense that even Wheelock's friends worried
for its future.[2]

1

The Federalists were indeed in trouble. Their caucus had decided against the incumbent governor, John Taylor Gilman,
in June 1815, and had chosen Timothy Farrar. Unhappily,
the latter was one of the Octagon, and Hill publicized his
nomination as further evidence of a conspiracy. Embarrassed,
the Federalists abandoned Farrar and offered the nomination
to six others, all of whom declined.[3] The caucus in desper-
ation turned to James Sheafe, who had an undistinguished
career in the Sixth Congress and served but one year of a subsequent term in the Senate. Politically he was innocuous. He
had had nothing to do with the Dartmouth issue.

A respectable merchant of Portsmouth, Sheafe was the rich-
est man in the state and was said to be "so fond of gain" that
he was "rarely seen out of his Counting Room."[4] He was a declared Anglophile, who had been imprisoned for Toryism dur-

ing the Revolution, and had adamantly opposed the national government during the late war. So, while he was not liable to charges of conspiracy at the College, he was vulnerable on class and patriotic grounds. The same could not be said of his Republican counterpart, William Plumer. There was conceivably no better man in New Hampshire to run on a platform such as Hill had been setting forth.

Plumer was a former governor and former Federalist who had left the party in 1808 during the Embargo.[5] He had attacked clerical opposition to the war and stood on a platform of patriotism and religious freedom. In his opinion it was a national misfortune that political partisans refused to confine *"party malevolence to political questions"* and extended it to all subjects however disconnected from politics.[6] This did not restrain him from joining Hill in attacks on Sheafe's character.[7] These manifestations of party malevolence were in the worst traditions of contemporary journalism, even suggesting sexual misdemeanors on Sheafe's part.[8] The Federalists retaliated in kind and the state reeled under another journalistic fusillade.[9]

Wheelock's Federalist supporters were torn between practical politics and devotion to the ex-President.[10] They were fully aware of the portents embodied in the investigating committee's report and anxious to insure a legislature opposed to the Octagon, but they viewed Plumer's candidacy with alarm. Devoted to Jeffersonian educational ideas and enthusiastic about the incipient national movement toward state universities, Plumer was a leading spokesman for the Republican principle that an effective government demanded an educated citizenry—an early champion of the view that anything impeding or threatening public control of education impedes or threatens the progress of the United States. He urged instruction in agriculture, commerce, manufacture, and mechanics in addition to the classics, as a way of making the College responsive to public needs and freeing it from sectarian domination.[11] Moreover, as governor in 1812 Plumer had firmly opposed indefinite terms in charters of incorporation and had urged the legislature to insert in such charters clauses allowing repeal in the public interest.[12] If he were governor, the Republicans would make more changes at Dartmouth than Wheelock's friends desired—not to mention other Republican policies they abhorred. Finally, since Republicans were only

using Wheelock's case for political advantage, there was no assurance they would reinstate him.

To extricate themselves and still benefit Wheelock, a leading
Federalist of Hanover, Amos Brewster, together with the
medical professor at Dartmouth, Cyrus Perkins—perhaps
Wheelock's only friend on the faculty—devised a plan which
demonstrated the extent to which the Dartmouth trouble
had become political. On Christmas morning, 1815, the two
men visited Plumer and suggested that he withdraw his candidacy for a year and allow Wheelock to run for the governor-
ship on the Republican ticket. Victory would both vindicate
the ousted President and give him the political support to reform the College and confound the Trustees. Since New Hampshire held elections annually, Wheelock would return the
party leadership to Plumer the following year. Plumer, who
was only mildly interested in Wheelock and less so with con-
founding the Trustees, refused the offer and explained that,
as a public servant, he did not seek office. If the people saw
fit to nominate him, he did not feel at liberty to withdraw unless imperious necessity required it. He saw no such necessity.[13] So Wheelock Federalists had little choice but to side
with Republicans and endure charges of political apostasy
which they steadfastly denied.[14] The *Patriot* exhorted all
"honorable Federalists" to follow the example.[15] March 12,
1816 approached.

The election brought Republican truth and light into every
branch of the government save the judiciary, and that problem did not seem difficult for it was the common practice of
victorious parties to reform the judiciary. The Federalists had
reformed it in 1813. It is difficult to assess the effect of the
College quarrel on the election, but it certainly helped ele-
vate the total votes cast to the second largest in New Hampshire history up to 1816.[16] There is no difficulty assessing the
election's effect on the College controversy; important changes
resulted. The Wheelock-Octagon feud no longer excited public attention, which confirmed the Octagon's suspicions that
the Republicans had used Wheelock's distress only so long
as it promised Federalist defections.[17]

The Republicans now frankly set out their position on Dartmouth College. The *Patriot* no longer cried either for Wheelock's restoration or for religious freedom. Hill now urged the
new legislature to "correct the abuses at Dartmouth College,"

which he reinterpreted as arising not from the machinations
of the Octagon but from the College charter, that "last remaining relict [sic] of the royalty of Great Britain." The community welfare demanded correction of the despicably aristocratic features of that charter lest this self-created parasite
gnaw on the vitals of republican institutions—even if the
abusive charter had not existed, Hill argued, the state had a
duty to protect its interest in the College.[18] Hill's editorials
also explained that the governance of Dartmouth College
would be a means of "perpetuating the republican majority
in the State," if it were "judiciously managed."[19] As for the
intentions of Plumer, he had never sympathized with Wheelock, but political expediency had caused him to assure the
ex-President's supporters that he detected a "cordial disposition to do justice to the injured Wheelock," and that he
would make at least one effort to redress the "wrongs" of
the old man.[20] And Plumer's concern with the College was
even broader. His further object, "not personal" and not
limited to Wheelock's restoration, was "to establish the power
& authority of the legislature over the institution so far as to
secure to the people the real object for which it was founded,
& form a useful connexion between government & the college."[21] This purpose lay behind his request that Wheelock's
friends in Hanover devise a means both of restoring the President and of preventing the College from being exposed to
similar evils.[22]

With Republican victory achieved, the contest was simply
between the state and Dartmouth College. Dartmouth either
was or should be a state, not a private, institution. This was
the final ingredient in the *Dartmouth College* case. The Trustees had "no vested rights to any property of the College
corporation—they [were] the servants to the public." The
legislature had the requisite authority "to enlarge the number
of Trustees or to create an independent board of Visitors to
superintend the affairs of the corporation." The question of
state control of Dartmouth College became the leitmotif of
the controversy as it unfolded before the public after March
1816. The Republican press predicted that reform of the College would be the most interesting subject for legislative consideration and urged legislators to "be just, and fear not."[23]

The events of March led the Octagon to believe the legislature would go to the utmost extent of its power to reinstate

Wheelock and that more was now at stake than a simple question of restoration. The *Patriot* removed any latent doubts by
drawing the outlines of possible legislation.[24] Uncertain about
what limits to its power over the College the legislature would
recognize, the Octagon planned carefully for the June session.[25]
President Brown and the Trustees recognized that public opinion outside Hanover seemed generally unfavorable to the Octagon and feared that "false representations & erroneous impres-
sions" resulting from the zealous activity of Wheelock's friends
would assure their failure in June. As a counter measure
Brown disseminated correct information among influential
men in the state, "especially among those who are to com-
pose the Legislature." He hoped to mitigate excess by convincing these men that political considerations had played no
part in Wheelock's removal.[26] It was, after all, only an acci-
dental circumstance that some of the leading Federalists in the
state were members of the board.

Much depended on the attitude of Governor Plumer. Brown
was unsure of Plumer's feelings toward the College but had
"no doubt" that Wheelock had taken steps "to induce him to
insert a paragraph into his Speech . . . at the opening of the
Legislature, bearing on the Trustees."[27] He hoped the Governor would see fit either to omit reference to the College
quarrel or to avoid more than a general statement. The latter
was more probable since the 1815 investigating committee
was ready to report. Had Brown been privy to Plumer's actions, he would have been less hopeful. The Governor had begun preparing his address in early April, and without Wheelock's assistance. By mid-May the document was complete.
Ironically, there was no mention of Wheelock or his restoration, only an expression of hope that the legislature would
amend the College charter.[28]

2

The hopes and frustrations of a tension-filled year hung in the
balance that afternoon of June 6, 1816, when Plumer at Concord delivered the address over which he had been laboring.
After a panegyric on the peaceful, prosperous condition of
the country, and recommendations for new taxes and a new
judiciary, came the most urgent issue upon which he had to
recommend a policy: the future of Dartmouth College. He

had saved the most important until last, but to readers of the *Patriot* it must have come as a disappointment, and it assuredly did nothing to ease the anxiety of the Octagon. In round Republican phrases Governor Plumer stressed the importance of education in a republic and the consequent duty of the state to promote literature and science. New Hampshire had shouldered these responsibilities from its earliest days, he said, by providing for schools, academies, and a college. He therefore invited the legislature to consider the condition of Dartmouth, the leading educational institution of the state.

Borrowing from Hill, Plumer argued that the state's liberal contributions to the College and the public's lively interest in its welfare gave the legislature a strong right to interfere.[29] With increasingly Republican innuendoes he discussed the charter as an emanation from royalty containing, not unnaturally, "principles congenial to monarchy." The most odious of these and the one "hostile to the spirit and genius of a free government" was that allowing the Trustees *"to perpetuate the board by themselves electing others to supply vacancies."*[30] Sound policy demanded election by some other body, and also an increase in the size of the Board. The president should be required to submit an annual report on the condition of the College. Such measures would increase the security of the College, interest more men in its prosperity, excite the officers and students to conscientious effort, and give the legislature information which would enable it to act with greater propriety upon whatever related to the College.

Plumer's argument that these measures needed no defense clearly indicated his belief that Dartmouth was already a public institution. The College was, after all, formed for the public good, not for the benefit or emolument of its Trustees; and all governments, both monarchical and republican, had exercised the right of amending acts of incorporation of this nature. A few examples demonstrated such legislative authority, and Plumer trusted the legislature would make "such further provisions as will render this important institution useful to mankind."[31]

The Governor did not mention the anticipated report of the 1815 investigating committee, because the subject of that report, the Wheelock-Octagon feud, was no longer at issue.[32] He was not interested in correcting what Wheelock or the Trustees considered the evils at the College, and like a true

Jeffersonian did not feel bound by any action of a preceding legislature. "Sound policy" required that the College be more responsive to the people of New Hampshire. The Governor intended to make Dartmouth an ideal state college.[33]

When the report at last was ready it proved to have little effect upon the College's fortunes. Upon receipt of the report Plumer immediately sent it and all papers relative to Dartmouth to a joint Committee of Eighteen, formed by the two houses to consider the Governor's recommendations.[34] The report was an impartial statement of facts pertinent to Wheelock's allegations in 1815. It drew no conclusions, although its overtones were favorable to the Octagon.[35] After "calm and laborious examination," the Committee of Eighteen had concluded what everyone knew, "that an unhappy difference has of late years arisen between the Trustees and some of the officers of Dartmouth College."[36] These difficulties, in the Committee's view, had been aggravated or had even arisen "from some radical defects in the charter." The legislature was not to undertake the "invidious and unpleasant task" of arbitrating in favor of either party, because this would only inflame, not heal, the controversy. The Committee then echoed Plumer's statements about the incompatibility of the charter and republican government and concluded that the interest of the state required no further legislative action on the report.

Still it was necessary "to remove and prevent the recurrence of the great cause of complaint on the subject of Dartmouth College, by amending its charter."[37] To bring the charter in line with the form and spirit of republican government, the Committee suggested enlargement of the board of trustees with appointments by an outside body and the creation of a separate tribunal of supervisors.[38]

Other items concerning the College occupied the Committee of Eighteen. Office seekers like the "not so capable or honest" Hill and lobbyists on all sides of the College question had besieged Plumer from the day of his arrival in Concord.[39] Wheelock's managers—their ranks now swollen by William H. Woodward, Wheelock's nephew and secretary-treasurer of the College; William Allen, Wheelock's son-in-law; and the persistent Parish—were "loud and zealous."[40] Another important, if somewhat erratic, member was General Eleazar Wheelock Ripley, part-time lawyer and army officer, Dartmouth alumnus, grandson of the founder, son of the first theology professor, and Wheelock's nephew.[41] Ripley had been in contact with Hill since the previous December, and with the cooperation of Allen and other partisans, had taken Plumer's March advice and devised measures to correct abuses at the College. The General brought these changes to Concord in the form of a draft bill recommending "material changes" in the charter.[42] After adding several amendments Plumer submitted the bill to the Committee of Eighteen. This Ripley-Plumer bill proposed removing the existing board of trustees, changing the name of the institution to Dartmouth University, and creating two new boards of fifteen trustees and thirty to fifty overseers. The bill would name the original members of both boards; Governor and Council would fill vacancies in the board of overseers, and Governor and overseers those in the board of trustees. The new trustees would elect a new president at their first meeting, and Governor and Council would make a supervisory visit at least once in every five years.[43]

On June 18, before the report of the investigating committee had been printed and distributed, the Committee of Eighteen reported a version of the Ripley-Plumer bill much closer to the Governor's views than the original measure. Instead of removing the existing trustees, the bill now proposed enlarging the board by as many as nine.[44] The new trustees would not necessarily elect a new president, but they would have power "to revise, correct, confirm or annul any act of the old Trustees of the College."[45]

In the meantime, Ripley and Allen had second thoughts about the extent of their proposed changes. Despite their cries for charter revision they had no sympathy for the principle of state control. Their chief concern remained reinstating Wheelock, and once the board of trustees had been properly reconstituted, they preferred it to remain self-perpetuating. On June 11 they approached Plumer "in a delicate manner," voiced their anxiety over that section of the bill removing the power of filling vacancies from the trustees, and upbraided the Governor for his apparent neglect of Wheelock. Plumer replied that "principles ought not to be sacrificed for men"; that his purpose was to establish effective state power over the College and not simply, much less primarily, to restore Wheelock.[46]

The bill of June 18 was certainly consistent with Plumer's

principles. It clearly established Dartmouth as a state institution. Just as clearly it served as the basis for action on the investigating committee's report. It also convinced Wheelock's friends that the Republicans had abandoned the old man; Plumer reported Ripley as saying that the Republicans had *"acted like hell."*[47] Despite their initial disappointment, the former President's supporters realized that their best chances still lay with Plumer and the Republicans. Woodward, Allen, Brewster, and Perkins deserted the Federalist ranks for the Republican caucus.

What remained for the old Trustees? Plumer's address, and the action of the Committee of Eighteen, dashed their initial hope that the legislature would be satisfied with the investigating committee's report or that it might hesitate to act because of Wheelock's failing health. Webster and others had urged delay even until the next session. Webster's suggested tactic was appointment of a committee to report at the next session on the possibility of establishing a new college at Concord in hope of pleasing Plumer, but it also ruled out the bill then before the legislature.[48]

The only recourse was to encourage opposition to the bill, and House minority leader Thompson and a determined Federalist minority worked toward this. As quickly as the College party could obtain a copy of the bill, they requested a public hearing. This was denied, on the ground that they would have recourse to the courts. Undaunted, they addressed a remonstrance to the legislature which opposed the bill as printed but offered to accept one "connecting the Government of the State with that of the College, and creating every salutary check and restraint . . . that can reasonably be required."[49] This attempt at compromise suggested a board of eighteen overseers, consisting exclusively of state office-holders, with full veto power over the acts of the trustees, but it was rejected through reference to a hostile committee. Had it been accepted, the entire course of the controversy would have changed. There would have been no *Dartmouth College* case. The Octagon would not have been able to claim violation of a contract in which they had suggested changes.[50]

The hard-pressed Federalists tried parliamentary delays, and the young Senate clerk, Levi Woodbury, noted that the "yeas and nays were called on every trifling question" and on such important ones as judicial reform.[51] Some Republicans even began to doubt and motioned to postpone action to the next session and to seek the court's opinion on the constitutionality of the bill. This motion was defeated, but these maneuvers proved so exhausting that only party discipline brought the bill to a second reading. "Such is now the state of the battle," Woodbury supposed, that the legislature would rather "sit till October . . . than not act on the two great subjects of the Judiciary and the College."[52]

The turmoil threatened Plumer's entire program, so he compromised his principles as embodied in the first College bill and recommitted seven sections for amendment. These motions passed without roll call, but Wheelock Republicans probably voted with the Federalist minority in order to carry recommitment against Plumer. The chief point of dispute between them and regular Republicans, who wanted a genuine state university, had been whether the trustees would retain the power of filling vacancies in the board. One of the amended sections granted this.[53]

Incidentally, a remonstrance filed at this time was to have a considerable effect on the *Dartmouth College* case. The gist of it was that the bill, even amended, destroyed the identity of the corporation of Dartmouth College *without the consent of the corporation.* The College charter was a contract between the state and the twelve charter trustees. The Revolution did not affect this contract, but creation of a new and distinct corporation would affect it. Passage of the bill would impugn the good faith of the government and, more important, would violate the tenth section of the first article of the Constitution of the United States prohibiting states from passing laws impairing the obligation of contract.[54] This reference to the contract clause came to be the basis of the constitutional arguments of Jeremiah Mason and Daniel Webster, and the issue enabling the *Dartmouth College* case to reach the Supreme Court of the United States.

The House passed the amended bill on June 26, 1816. Dartmouth College became Dartmouth University. The board of trustees increased to twenty-one. The bill retained the old Trustees and dropped the citizenship requirement. A majority would form a quorum, and the new board would enjoy all the privileges of the old, including that of filling vacancies. Governor and Council would appoint a board of twenty-five overseers with fifteen as a quorum, with full power to "inspect and confirm or disapprove & negative" the proceedings of the trustees.[55] The state had gained important control, but the trustees remained self-perpetuating and Wheelock was not reinstated. Almost every faction had lost something during the session. Although the bill contained some salutary improvements, Plumer felt "it was not so full & complete" as he would have wished. Even so, it could be amended later, and since he "did not feel . . . at liberty to place veto upon it," he signed it on June 27.[56]

3

The Octagon wanted to resist but, other than a futile minority protest against the bill, remained perplexed about how to do it. Thompson urged Brown to call a board meeting.[57] A Massachusetts professor and friend of the College, Reuben D. Mussey, wrote Brown with pardonable exaggeration that the bill's passage had excited "universal alarm and indignation" among Federalists of his acquaintance. "Hold on," he urged, "till the last finger is cut off." There was considerable collegiate anxiety not so much about Dartmouth as about the precedent the action would establish. The movement, underway since the late eighteenth century, to make colleges more responsive to public needs had produced repeated efforts to bring colleges under some sort of government control. The legal standing of educational corporations was still unclear, and, with Republicans gaining strength, the future looked ominous. Harvard had been deeply involved in state politics since 1810, and there were rumors that Republicans, encouraged by New Hampshire's action, were planning similar moves. Kentucky Republicans were challenging Presbyterian domination of Transylvania College. Surely, Mussey wrote, the Octagon would "protest the legality of the measure" and if necessary "carry it to the Supreme Court of the U.S."[58]

The redoubtable author of the *Vindication,* Charles Marsh, had no doubt that the June, 1816, act was altogether unconstitutional, and that it would be so judged if the question could only come before a competent and dispassionate court.[59] Marsh strongly opposed any action that could be construed in any sense as cooperation with the new board. Such would appear tacit recognition of the act's legality. Legal and extra-legal opposition would subject the College to unpleasant publicity and "to very great inconveniences," but Marsh could see no alternative.[60]

Clearly the University's future hinged on the first meeting of the new board. As soon as practical after passage of the act, Plumer began appointing the new trustees and overseers, and notified Brown and the Octagon that the first meeting of the new board would convene at Hanover on August 26.[61] After receiving his notice Marsh advised Brown that in addition to their earlier plans it would now be essential to prevent the new board from obtaining a quorum.[62] By early August these intentions were, or should have been, apparent to the University party. The polite but noncommittal acknowledgements which the old Trustees sent Plumer should have been a clue.[63] Woodbury had heard rumors that the Federalists were making "desperate struggles" to thwart the act, that Brown had called a meeting of the Octagon for August 23, and that the Octagon had determined on "acting alone and resisting any fellowship with the new Board." It was difficult to believe the old Trustees had nerve enough to secede and resist, but Woodbury expressed sentiments of the University party in concluding that "men, who could conduct as they have done on other occasions, are capable of plotting and zealous to attempt any outrage however abhorrent."[64] University supporters believed that it was more important to be prepared for the first board meeting than for any subterfuge by the Octagon, and greatest reliance would have to be on Governor Plumer. With the interest of the Republican party also depending upon the meeting, Woodbury hoped that every individual would "see that every port is manned and every pass guarded."[65]

The Octagon also realized the importance of the first meeting, and the rumored meeting of the old Board on August 23 convened after all parties, including Plumer, had been notified.[66] Secretary-treasurer Woodward was absent at the opening meeting, and President Brown notified him of the session and requested that he forward the College records if attendance was inconvenient.[67] Woodward replied immediately and, while declining either to attend or to forward the records, informed Brown that he had been appointed secretary-treasurer of the University and doubted the legality of the old Board's meeting.[68] When further correspondence found Woodward still unwilling to attend, the Octagon, minus a

secretary, began discussing their opposition.[69] Brown had
sought advice from prominent attorneys in New Hampshire
and elsewhere prior to the meeting, and all had urged the
Octagon to resist and take their cause to the courts.[70] But
the Board lacked consensus on August 26, the date the University board convened at Hanover.

That meeting brought nothing but frustration for the cham-
pions of the University. Plumer arrived in Hanover on August
20 to make arrangements but when he and the new officials
went to the College library on the fatal morning of August 26
to convene the board, the door was locked. Plumer and
Brown spent the remainder of that Monday in a busy episto-
lary exchange about a place for the meeting.[71] Convinced by
five o'clock that afternoon of the Octagon's determination
to "attempt any outrage," the Governor convened the board
in Woodward's office.

University difficulties had only begun. Brown and the Octagon refused to attend, and only eight of Plumer's trustees appeared. Since eleven were necessary for a quorum, the Governor adjourned the meeting to the following morning. One
more trustee appeared, but still no quorum. Plumer hurriedly
dispatched a note to Brown asking him to preside or give
reasons for nonattendance.[72] Brown answered that he would
attend if the University trustees met under the old charter.
He and the Octagon were considering the June act, and until
they reached a decision—until they decided to abandon their
charter and accept the act—he could not attend.[73]

Commencement, scheduled for the following day, climaxed
the frustrations of Plumer and his nine associates. Professors
Adams and Shurtleff refused to furnish the University board
with a list of candidates for degrees. They, Brown, and the
Octagon held Commencement in the College chapel. They had
also politely requested the Governor's attendance at the College Commencement, but he had politely declined. At ten
o'clock that same morning the old Trustees voted not to accept the June act.[74] The University board answered this in-
souciance with a remonstrance against future actions of the
Octagon and an admonition that actions since June were null
and void. (Ironically, the same was true of their own actions
in the absence of a quorum.) In the final hours of the session
on August 28 the University board drew up recommendations,
to be ratified at a future meeting, which would furnish Dart-

mouth University with administrators, professors, a curriculum, and professional schools of theology, medicine, and law.[75] The board then adjourned until September 17.[76]

Marsh's plan succeeded: the University had no legal existence; the College was still functioning. The latter possessed the presidency, control of the faculty, the buildings, and the students' loyalty.

Further action depended on the University's next move, and, although its supporters were so frustrated and vexed as to make "the heart sick," Woodbury was certain they had determined not to despair.[77] Plumer was now aware of the shortcomings of the act of June, 1816. He had also come to doubt the legality of the University board's August recommendations, and cancelled their September meeting.[78] Yet his hopes were buoyed by the approach of a special legislative session scheduled for November. The ostensible purpose of this session was tax assessment, but it could attend to University business.

Caution now led the Governor to do what he had felt unnecessary in June—to seek the advice of the Superior Court on the constitutionality of the June act.[79] Perhaps he was less hesitant in September, for the judiciary reforms of the last legislative session had enabled him to appoint three new judges. By September he had appointed two, both Republicans.[80] On September 19 he and the Republican members of the Council formally requested the court's opinion on the legislature's authority to pass the Dartmouth bill and on the authority of the Governor and Council to fill vacancies occurring after the August meeting since there had been no quorum.[81] The Governor reasoned that the court's opinion would forestall the inconvenience and expense of a lawsuit and so benefit all interested parties.

Woodbury, still feeling that University partisans had determined to "stick by the ship while a single plank floats," regarded this move as a master stroke. If the opinion of their "new Court" were favorable, it would have an "imposing influence" in support of the University. If it were against them, University supporters would probably have to "strike colours, or retreat and reattack the foe at some other point." Federalist plotters would harass the legislature, but Woodbury was confident that body would enact any necessary or expedient amendments. Despite formidable difficulties, "a triumph of liberal principles . . . must be effected."[82]

Federalists exploited Plumer's request as evidence of the act's unconstitutionality. Adams expressed certainty that even Plumer had doubts, their belief that his constitutional authority to require the court's opinion should be restricted to cases "in which he wishes to know *how to act,* not to know whether *he has acted* as he ought."[83] William Plumer, Jr., reminded his father that the Octagon had been denied a hearing in June on the ground that they could have recourse to the courts. Now, he admonished candidly, "without giving them time to do this, you apply to the court—a court too of your own appointing, which, without hearing the other side, must settle against them."[84] The Octagon seemingly had grounds for complaint.

Fortunately for Plumer, the Superior Court justices answered the Governor's first question by announcing that after examining the constitutions of New Hampshire and the United States they were unable "even to conjecture" any ground upon which legislative authority could be questioned. No ground, they added in an important reservation, "unless it be that such alteration, if made without the consent of the corporation may possibly be construed a violation of private vested rights which are protected by those constitutions." Beyond this, the court would not hazard an opinion, since the justices did not feel constitutionally obliged to deliver an opinion on questions other than those of an altogether public nature. Questions of right between the legislature and individuals, affecting private rights, could not be decided until those individuals interested in the question had an opportunity to be heard.[85] The Court rapidly disposed of the question about the Governor's power to fill vacancies.[86] He had plenary power over the board of overseers, but could fill only such vacancies in the board of trustees as had occurred prior to their first meeting. Since no legal meeting had been held on August 26, the date fixed by statute, the Governor could not fill subsequent vacancies.

This latest reversal, together with growing popular displeasure at the doubtful legal status of the June act, the partisan circumstances of its passage, the harsh treatment of the Octagon in June, and the August fiasco, brought new confidence to the Octagon. They were unsure of Plumer's next move but suspected that "could you peep into his closet, you would see him frequently scratching his head and biting his nails, and perhaps his lips and tongue."[87] At their adjourned meeting in September, when Woodward was again the subject of controversy, the Octagon voted to retain him if he were willing to act. When his doubts again caused him to decline, they removed him and appointed Mills Olcott.[88] Olcott demanded the College records and seal, but Woodward declined with professions of intent to retain them for the rightful owners.[89] His removal and retention of the records were as portentous as the removal of Wheelock the preceding year. If nothing else, it convinced the Octagon that despite apathy and frustration the University had not surrendered.

Everything then came down to what the legislature would do at its meeting in November 1816, and Plumer had no doubt that it would do its duty for Republican principles. In his address to the opening session the Governor recited the events of August, stressed the state's humiliation, and called attention to the important question: should a law "passed and approved by all the constituted authorities of a State" be carried into effect? If so, the legislature should not permit "*a few individuals,* not vested with *any judicial authority,*" to declare that statute "*dangerous and arbitrary, unconstitutional and void.*" It should not permit a "minority of the trustees" of an institution formed for the instruction of children to "inculcate the doctrine of resistance to the law." If the legislature would not suffer these travesties, it should amend the College law "to enable the Boards to carry the law into effect and render the Institution useful to the public."[90] The Governor was not disappointed, because a bill embodying his proposals passed and became law in December.[91] In substance the law gave the Governor the powers he lacked in August, notably by reducing the quorum to nine and giving the boards authority, in the absence of a quorum, to adjourn until one could be obtained. Another bill sought to eliminate the resistance of the Octagon by punishing anyone presuming to act as an officer of Dartmouth University except under the June act or impeding the proper officers in exercise of their duty, with a fine of five hundred dollars for each offense.[92] Plumer's delight at the legislature's swift compliance was manifest in his notice of December 20, 1816, that another meeting of the University boards would convene in Concord on February 4 of the following year.[93]

4 Blasted Hopes

*"We are therefore clearly of the opinion,
that the charter of Dartmouth College is not a
contract, within the meaning of this clause in
the constitution of the United States."—Chief Justice
William M. Richardson, 1817*

1

Passage of the act of December 1816 temporarily undermined
the determination of the Octagon, the old Trustees, to resist
the legislature's changes. The safest manner of maintaining
their charter rights was a question of considerable moment.
President Brown was anxious whether, if the June act were
eventually declared unconstitutional, the Trustees could main-
tain their charter rights without incurring the penalty.[1] Five
hundred dollars was a large sum in the early nineteenth century, especially to a College heavily in debt, and multiple of-
fenses would multiply it.

The Octagon's membership, many of whom were lawyers,
floundered amid alternatives. Marsh had not yet seen the December law and could only surmise its nature and provisions,
but he felt that the best course was to "persist as tho' nothing
had happened," especially in light of the Governor's mis-
givings about the June act. He doubted any court and jury in
New Hampshire would execute the law.[2] Farrar continued to
urge a legal decision on the June act. The sooner the question
of the state's power to alter the charter was decided the better
for the College, since the same question would arise under
either act. If the legislature could not annul the charter, they
could not make it penal to retain the name, hold the property,
and conduct the business there specified.[3] Thompson did not
want the Trustees to abandon their rights, but he could not
imagine how they could neither abandon their charter nor
adopt a course which the state judiciary would not construe
into a breach of the law, "*admitting the law to be constitutional.*" The cautious Thompson suggested that while the Octagon
pressed for a legal decision the College officers should continue their work as private individuals. In this way Trustees
and faculty could assemble for protection of their corporate
rights without hindering the University or incurring the penalty.

He urged Brown to call a meeting of the Octagon to deliberate on the crisis, and circulated a letter soliciting advice from
influential New Hampshire citizens.[4]

All came to view the penal act as a bugbear which they determined to ignore, and it now remained to give this determination some definite shape, to devise a strategy.[5] Here they
were guided by the Solicitor General of Massachusetts, Daniel
Davis, who had advised Brown in August 1816 that if Woodward refused to deliver the records, the Trustees ought to
"put his bond in suit, or commence such other action or actions as the nature of the case may require." Davis was confident the law was unconstitutional, since it represented an
arbitrary legislative act which not only dissolved the corporation but gave its property, privileges, and powers to others.
A charter, he argued, was a grant of rights and privileges beyond legislative interference. Under the constitutions of New
Hampshire and the United States only the judiciary could determine whether such rights were forfeit. A legislative determination of forfeit would not only violate the New Hampshire bill of rights, but, since a grant was a contract, the contract clause of the national Constitution. Although Davis emphasized that such a suit "must *originate* in the State court,"
he reassured the Trustees that the ultimate decision on constitutionality did not rest there. Use of the contract clause
would enable them to have the issue "reexamined and reversed by writ of error in the Sup. Court of the United
States."[6]

Davis's advice outlined the College strategy. It was, though,
painfully difficult for the Octagon to move. When Woodward
declined the Trustees had contemplated suit both for the
records and to test the constitutionality of the June act. Un-
certainties bred by the legislature's November session obscured this action, but by late December 1816 the Trustees
had decided to sue Woodward. Few expected a favorable decision in the New Hampshire courts because of the controversy's political overtones, and their anxiety to frame the
pleadings to allow the case to reach the Supreme Court forced
them to confront the problem of the intricate procedural requirements necessitated by the state's use of common-law
forms. Selection of the wrong procedure could ruin their
strategy. Paine and Thompson eagerly sought Jeremiah
Smith's advice, and Olcott, as the Trustees' agent, had written

Smith in December 1816 on the policy and form of prosecution.[7] Smith hesitated to recommend any action as certain and final, but did say he thought trover for the books and records to be best. Unwilling to judge policy, he advised that if the Trustees had decided to sue before the last legislative session, he did not apprehend from what he had heard "that any reasons now existed for abandoning that intention."[8]

Political considerations led Smith, like Davis earlier, to advise against by-passing the state courts, and, given Trustee expectations about the probable outcome in state courts, this advice was a strategic mistake. The Trustees intended to argue violations of the state and national constitutions and other broad grounds and to appeal to the United State Supreme Court. Section 25 of the 1789 Judiciary Act, which outlined the appellate jurisdiction of the Supreme Court, allowed appeal on writs of error from the highest state court only when a question involving the national Constitution was involved. So the Supreme Court on appeal could consider only the alleged violation of the contract clause. That court was unlikely to review the state constitution and less likely to review a state court decision interpreting that constitution. Initial resort to the federal circuit court would have allowed federal, and sympathetic, review of all the questions. Farrar had in fact urged original action in the circuit court.[9] Perhaps procedural difficulties in the case against Woodward prevented this action, but it would have been wiser and was, indeed, later chosen in collateral cases.[10]

At last came the decision. The Trustees accepted Smith's advice, and Olcott instituted on February 9, 1817, suit against Woodward in the Court of Common Pleas of Grafton County. The suit sought the College records, books, and seal and set damages at $50,000.[11] An anomalous circumstance was that Woodward was chief justice of that court. A trial or ordinary verdict was out of the question. By agreement between the parties, the record of facts forming the basis of the case was drawn up in a special verdict and sent directly to the Superior Court. The verdict contained only a recital of the charter of 1769 and the statutes of June and December 1816 and asked the court to pass upon the constitutionality of that legislation.[12] The case was entered for the May term at Haverhill.

Plumer, meantime, kept active preparing for the first meeting of the University board under the amended acts. He wanted to avoid the "great mortification" of another defeat like that of the preceding August. So he requested his son to question Judge Richardson whether, if the University trustees met in February and the overseers in August, the trustees could remove officers at their meeting; and whether it would be necessary to give previous notice to the officer to appear and show cause why he should not be removed.[13] The Governor intended to remove the Octagon from the University board and fill their places with more congenial members. The meeting convened on February 4, 1817. A quorum was secured late on the evening of February 6, and next day the board agreed to articles in a specification of charges against President Brown, the Trustees, and faculty of the College. In substance the specification charged that the College officials had not submitted to the authority of the legislature and had injured the University by adherence to their old charter. The board cited the College officials to appear and answer charges at an adjourned meeting on February 22.[14]

It was, then, at the second meeting of the board that Plumer discovered the intractability of his opponents, their decision to take their case to court. If Plumer and the University trustees had any doubts about the response, these were removed on February 21 when Brown, Adams, and Shurtleff issued an address to the Governor and University trustees acknowledging receipt of the citations but expressing their doubts on the validity of the pertinent legislation. These doubts arose not only from their understanding of the state and federal constitutions but also from the opinion of "a great majority of the ablest law characters in this and neighboring States." The formal protest of the House minority in June 1816 and the Governor's own doubts implicit in his application to the Superior Court reinforced these doubts. The old Trustees deemed it their duty "to wait the result of an appeal to the judicial tribunals."[15]

Undaunted, Plumer moved against his opponents. Like Wheelock before his removal in 1815, Brown and Adams and Shurtleff refused either to attend the meeting or to appear and show cause why they should not be removed. The University board waited until the early afternoon of February 22, and then removed Brown as president and trustee, Farrar and McFarland and Payson as trustees, and Adams and Shurtleff as faculty members.[16]

Wheelock thereupon became president, if for a brief final
moment of his life. The old warrior was too infirm to function,
and so his son-in-law, William Allen, was appointed admini-
strator. Plumer confided to his son that Wheelock's appointment was a "mark of respect" which would "soothe his feelings, & render him more liberal of his wealth which the institution needs—& it prevented us from making a precipitate
election of a real president."[17] Wheelock's vindication was
short-lived. He died on April 4, 1817.[18]

The removal of the old Trustees impressed them with the
urgency of commanding sympathetic public opinion. So
Brown, Adams, and Shurtleff expanded their reply to the
Governor and presented it to the public through the newspapers and as a handbill.[19] The broadside declared that the
Trustees felt dutybound to explain the principles governing
their decision not to abandon the charter. The law, they said,
was fully settled and recognized that a corporation might refuse to accept any grant conferring additional powers or restricting those already possessed. The 1816 acts, then, became
"inoperative in consequence of the nonacceptance of them by
the chartered Trustees." The suit against Woodward would
settle all these matters. The authors concluded that their
course was "strictly legal" and that no other would have been
consistent with duty. The "highest judicial tribunals" would
correct any error on their part, and they would "readily com-
ply" with the decision.[20]

It appeared in February 1817 that Plumer had realized his
goal. The new state University possessed a president, trustees,
overseers, and a faculty. Its "generous patron," the state of
New Hampshire, had not seen fit in this case, anymore than
in earlier times, to provide any funds. All Plumer's supporters
needed was to take the buildings from the College. They
succeeded in this after a busy weekend spent forcing entry
into the College buildings and changing or spiking the locks.
Yet when the University opened its term on March 5, 1817,
the only people present were the president, faculty, and one
student. The College, with a loyal student body, met in a
single building still in its possession, and the spring term
found both College and University confusedly, but placidly,
functioning on the same grounds.[21]

2

Plumer, however, was not out of the woods. A university, heavily in debt and without students, presented a serious problem. More serious and immediate was the preparation of the defense in the impending suit against Woodward. At their second meeting in late February the University trustees had assumed the defense and authorized the engagement of counsel, though the latter became the principal responsibility of the defendant. When Woodward wrote Plumer that he had been served with notice of the suit, he also noted that state attorney general George Sullivan might be employed as counsel and asked the Governor to "mention the matter to him & such other gentlemen" as he might please.[22] From then until the argument in May, the Secretary continuously importuned Plumer about counsel, and his pleas grew more earnest when he became too ill to attend to it.[23] He had attempted to enlist Jeremiah Mason for the University, but had failed in part because Mason's Federalism, like that of much of the best legal talent in New Hampshire, caused him to rally to the College.[24] Plumer exhorted the ailing defendant to persevere, and Woodward engaged Sullivan and requested Ichabod Bartlett to consult Plumer.[25] The Governor thought Sullivan would do justice to the cause and had "a high opinion of the talents, probity & industry of Ichabod Bartlett."[26] Moreover, both were closely tied to the University. Sullivan was an overseer; Bartlett a trustee. It was difficult to match the talent the College could muster, and the University sought other able Republican lawyers in Massachusetts and Maine. These were not readily available, so Sullivan and Bartlett ultimately argued the cause in the Superior Court.[27]

Preparations for the Haverhill argument also occupied Brown and the Octagon. Since the Superior Court could sit for only one week in Grafton County, there was some difficulty in predicting a May decision.[28] There was, too, some confusion about who was representing the College. Writing in April, J. W. Putnam reported Mason as saying that he had not been consulted by the College, and he urged Brown to engage Mason and Webster—who, he wished, more "than any other man might argue the question."[29] Thompson reported on April 25 that Smith had been talking as if he were not retained by the College. Puzzled, Thompson urged Olcott to investigate and "take the necessary steps."[30] Perhaps this confusion resulted from the abundant legal talent the College commanded. Whatever the source, it is strange that it existed two months after the College had initiated suit. As it turned out, the necessary steps must have been taken, for Mason and Smith did represent the College at Haverhill.

The result of this initial resort to the courts was, unfortunately, inconclusive. The pleadings in May 1817 were incomplete, and, since both parties wanted further argument, the court continued the case to the September term at Exeter. Encouraged, Brown thought the result "on the whole, the best . . . that could have been." He reported a favorable impression on all present and maintained that it would be "good to have the cause argued at Exeter."[31] The University was somewhat disappointed. Although President Allen (he had replaced Wheelock in June) hoped for a decision in favor of the constitutionality of the 1816 acts, he apprehended that "the question will be carried up, in some shape or other to the Supreme Court of the U. States."[32]

Knowledgeable people on the College side did not share Brown's enthusiasm. Farrar advised that he and the College counsel were not optimistic, although they knew the judges were having difficulty.[33] Smith was uneasy because "those who are to pronounce the act unconstitutional are dependent on the party who framed it—indebted to that party for their offices & their continuance."[34] Webster, as an interested observer, noted that it "would be a queer thing if Gov. P's Court should refuse to execute his laws."[35] Farrar had entertained doubts before the May argument and had persuaded Brown to publish a pamphlet containing the documents involved in the litigation since the legal questions were so little understood.[36] He thought the pressures on the judges would severely try their integrity and that public discussion "would be a most powerful check to dishonesty or assistance to honesty." Work on the pamphlet stopped temporarily because there was insufficient time for its appearance before the court met and because the prospect of extensive litigation made money a serious concern. That "famous gentleman, the Publick," wrote Brown, "clenches his fist & turns away his eye, with a most provoking indifference, when the College begins her story of distress." But the argument and postponement granted sufficient time, and Farrar again urged this as a means of insuring a correct decision.[37]

The Court then opened at Exeter on September 19. It was a famous session in the annals of New Hampshire jurisprudence, well-attended by clergymen and lawyers, and an important session in the history of the *Dartmouth College* case.[38] Arguments of counsel before this court were unsurpassed, even at Washington, for quality and coverage of the issues pervading the legal dispute. The fundamental question in the case was the validity of the 1816 acts, especially the June act. Six-foot, seven-inch Jeremiah Mason opened for the College and argued eloquently and persuasively for two hours.[39] Mason was one of the legal giants of the nineteenth century, and his thorough study of the case was the foundation for Webster's argument before the Supreme Court.[40] Even so, his argument only elaborated the points Davis had set forth in August 1816. After arguing that if the acts of 1816 were valid and binding on the plaintiffs without their consent the old corporation would be abolished and its property transferred, Mason denied their validity on the grounds that the acts went beyond the general scope of legislative power; that they violated certain provisions of the New Hampshire constitution; and that they violated the national Constitution. Relying heavily upon the private nature of the corporation and its property, privileges, and rights, Mason argued that the constitutions of New Hampshire and the United States established separation of powers to safeguard private rights from legislative abuse. The judiciary was chiefly responsible for the enforcement of these "parchment barriers," and the Supreme Court had decided that no vested right could be taken from an individual without the agency of a court of justice.

Mason was nothing if not thorough, and nowhere was this more evident than in his discussion of corporate rights. This was crucial to the College's strategy since a corporate charter could only be established as a contract protected by the Constitution by showing that common law regarded it as a grant of private property right. Citing English cases, Mason claimed that there were two classes of corporations: civil and eleemosynary. Civil corporations were either for purposes of government or trade and commerce. They might "with propriety" be called public, and the legislature could control them to a "certain extent." Eleemosynary corporations were private and immune from interference. They originated in private bounty and shared nothing with either type of civil corpora-

tion. Hospitals, colleges, and schools, Mason argued, were always private eleemosynary corporations at common law;
their object was to execute the donor's will. And, unlike civil
corporations, they were subject to private visitation or super-
vision. So Dartmouth College was clearly an eleemosynary and,
consequently, a private corporation. As such, its rights were
entitled to the same protection as the rights of individuals.

The thrust, then, of Mason's argument was a division of
corporations into public and private. Classification as either
depended not upon the purposes for which the corporation
was created but upon the source of the endowment. He conceded that expectation of public benefit was inducement for
the creation of Dartmouth College, but this did not mean
its property and privileges were in public trust. The state
could claim only the benefits stipulated in the grant of incorporation. *Terrett* v. *Taylor* (1815), established that state
donations entitled the state to enforce only the stipulations
attached to the donation.[41] Unless all established principles
were disregarded, it was impossible to consider this corporation as a public trust and its members public officers with
nothing of the character of private rights.

Anxious to establish that chartered rights were too sacred
to be voted away at the caprice of a legislature, the able
Mason turned to the state constitution. The English Parliament, he admitted, could abolish corporations because its
power was boundless, but the King could not have repealed
a corporate charter until a court had determined that it had
become forfeit. After the Revolution, which had been a reaction against the boundless power of Parliament, the legislature
succeeded the King. Succession constituted a general restriction on legislative power, but there were special restrictions
in the state constitution, particularly Article 15 of the bill of
rights, which provided that "no subject shall be . . . *deprived
of his property, immunities, or privileges* . . . but by the
judgment of his peers, or the law of the land."[42] The 1816
acts, if valid, would deprive the corporation of property and
privileges without trial—the tyranny over private rights this
article sought to prevent. Article 15 with its "law of the
land" clause was derived from Magna Charta, had been interpreted in this light by Coke and courts in the various states of
the Union, and was essentially the same as the "due process"
clause of the Fifth Amendment to the national Constitution.[43]

According to these constructions, "the right of property is held under the constitution, *and not at the will of the legislature.*"[44]

With the principal points of his argument established Mason declared briefly that the acts violated the contract clause of the Constitution of the United States. This point followed from that on the private nature of corporate rights, and was utterly essential to the College strategy of appealing the case to the Supreme Court. Only a brief argument was necessary at this point since the state court was principally concerned with the state constitution. The charter of 1769, he asserted, was a contract in the true constitutional meaning of that term. The Supreme Court had decided that a legislative grant, either of land or privileges, was a contract, and had also determined that state legislatures could not repeal statutes creating private corporations.[45] If all grants were contracts, it made no difference whether they took the form of statutes or charters. It was impossible to have any correct idea of a corporation without considering its creation as resulting in a contract protected by the Constitution. Mason concluded by warning that if the "present bold experiment" were carried into effect, colleges and seminaries would never be free from subservience to state legislatures.

Jeremiah Smith followed Mason with a learned four-hour argument distinguished by deep research in the common law. Smith had had a long career as a legislator and judge, was one of John Adams's midnight appointments to the national courts in 1801, a justice and later chief justice of the Superior Court, and had greatly improved New Hampshire jurisprudence.[46] Like Mason, Smith knew that a determination of the nature of the corporation was "all important to a correct decision," and he complemented Mason's discussion of the types of corporations with a lengthy examination of visitatorial or supervisory power which enabled him to place the 1816 acts beyond the scope of legislative power. Blackstone and the English case of *Philips* v. *Bury,* he argued, clearly established that the visitatorial power sprang from the initial endowment, not from the grant of incorporation.[47] Since eleemosynary corporations were founded by donations from benefactors, the founder or one appointed by him had the power of visitation over those corporations. The charter spoke of the funds as arising from the donations of private individuals (the English

subscribers) through the agency of Eleazar Wheelock and
treated Wheelock as founder. It made Dartmouth a private,
eleemosynary corporation, because the property assigned to
it was private. When Wheelock died, the right of visitation de-
volved upon the Trustees. If Smith did not deny that the state
had contributed lands, he argued that it was not the first
benefactor, and only the first could be founder.

There was, though, the problem of the charter declaration
that Dartmouth had been founded "for the benefit of said
Province"—the problem of the purpose of the corporation.
Smith admitted that the extensiveness of the charity might
cause it to be labelled public and that in the sense of extensiveness most eleemosynary corporations and all colleges, regardless of the source of the endowment, were public. But extensiveness did not affect the rights of the founder, donor, or
trustees supplying their places. Nowhere, he asserted, in English law was there a "division of eleemosynary corporations
into public and private, *and a different law for each.*"[48] Dartmouth College, hence, was a private corporation immune from
legislative interference!

George Sullivan and Ichabod Bartlett responded for the
University the following day with capable arguments. Attorney general Sullivan was a capable lawyer, though prone
to rely more on eloquence than preparation.[49] The gist of his
argument was to counter Mason and Smith by proving Dartmouth a public corporation.

For Sullivan, the purpose of the corporation or the extensiveness of the objects to be benefited was crucial to a determination of its public nature. He accepted Smith's admission that in the sense of extensiveness most eleemosynary
corporations were public and cited English authorities to
prove that a corporation created for the benefit of the state
is a public corporation. The charter declaration that Dartmouth had been founded for the benefit of the province fit
his interpretation of English authorities.[50] Since the College
was a public corporation, the legislature had a clear right to
interfere, but Sullivan was unwilling to leave any ground uncovered and asserted that the same right would exist if the
corporation were private, "so far as the public good required."[51]
To deny that would be to depart from the principle of the
greatest good for the greatest number, the foundation of
every free government. So, the notion that the grant of a

charter implied a contract by the government not to alter the
charter without consent was wholly unfounded and visionary.
Sullivan argued for the "far more reasonable" principle that
a charter of incorporation implied an agreement that the
charter might be altered for the public good.

In his opinion the contract clause was a safeguard against
debtor legislation and consequently would not protect the
charter even if it were a contract. The charter was a grant,
but one of powers for public purposes. The trustees were public agents, and the College was a public charity. Even if it
were a private charity, no evidence existed to prove Eleazar
Wheelock the founder; and unless he were, he could not have
transferred the right of visitation to the trustees. The visitation of public corporations was within the province of chan-
cery courts. Since these did not exist in New Hampshire,
Sullivan contended that visitation was a legislative prerogative.

Bartlett was only thirty-one and something of a newcomer
to the New Hampshire courts, but his talents had already
earned him a nickname of Little Giant and his argument was
the best the University received, even at Washington.[52] But-
tressing Sullivan's weak points, Bartlett countered Mason's
and Smith's argument that Dartmouth was a private, eleemosynary corporation with an assertion that they had confused
the College and Moor's Indian Charity School. Sullivan had
touched this only briefly; Bartlett apparently saw it as crucial
and developed it. The charter named Wheelock as founder,
but did not prove that he donated funds to the College, only
to the School. If this were true, the state could well have been
the first benefactor of the College. The distinction between
the two institutions raised the issue of the College's origin,
the source of the funds, clouded as it was by the sketchy
early history of the College and by Wheelock's parchment
distinction between the College and School. Bartlett spoke of
the College in such terms as to eliminate the possibility of anyone but the state being the founder and referred to the Landaff grant of 1770, the second grant, the Vermont grant of
1785, and other aid as proof that the source of funds for the
College had been public.[53] Unfortunately, the factual record
in the case supported the College, and not until the appeal,
when it was too late, did the University seek to remedy this
serious and, as it turned out, fatal flaw. In addition to the
state's donations, the extensiveness of the objects set forth

in the College charter convinced Bartlett that the corporation was public and that the legislature had a right to interfere.

The state of New Hampshire was the founder, the creator, and the only party in interest. All parties to the contract, then, had assented to the legislature's alterations. Bartlett thought that if it could be shown that the trustees held privileges which could be construed as contracts, such contracts would have to imply reserved power to the state because the privileges would have been incidental to the main design. He cited *Terrett* v. *Taylor* (1815) to show that the legislature had a right to modify, enlarge, or improve public corporations, that "private rights must yield to public exigencies."[54]

Webster summed up for the College in a brief argument of little more than one hour. Having chosen not to participate in the argument at Haverhill, he had joined the cause at Smith's suggestion. No record of his argument exists, and it would be interesting in view of the case's later history to know exactly what he said in 1817, but he probably followed the outlines of Mason and Smith and enhanced these with a persuasive and moving oratory.[55] Woodward afterward informed Plumer that Brown, Adams, and their coadjutors were circulating a highly colored report that Webster's argument "drowned the whole audience in their common tears" and had caused University supporters to shed tears of repentance.[56] In his conclusion Webster compared the attack upon Dartmouth to Caesar's murder in the Senate in what the *Patriot* termed a pathetic appeal to the judges as "alumni of the College."[57] This latter became the basis of Webster's famous peroration before the Supreme Court.

3

In 1817 everything was up to the Superior Court, and it is now pertinent to inquire into the character of that tribunal. The Superior Court had a full complement of three judges, all Republicans appointed under the judiciary act of 1816 and "men of more talent & legal information" than Plumer had known on it at any one time.[58] The Chief Justice, William M. Richardson, was a Harvard graduate and had studied law under Judge Samuel Dana of Amherst. He had been a member of Congress and United States district attorney, and his work on the Superior Court for nearly twenty-two years

contributed greatly to the ordering of New Hampshire law.[59]
Samuel Bell, a Dartmouth alumnus and Dana student, had
been trustee of the College and later became governor of New
Hampshire and United States senator.[60] Levi Woodbury was a
twenty-seven-year-old prodigy. Plumer acknowledged his
youth but praised his "irreproachable" legal talents.[61] Woodbury's later career as governor, senator, cabinet member, and
associate justice of the United States Supreme Court justified
Plumer's evaluation.

The Court postponed a decision to the Plymouth term,
commencing November 4, and again there was uncertainty, or
at least a confusion of certainties.[62] Brown, after "reflecting on
the argument," had concluded that it was *almost impossible*
for the Judges to decide against [the College argument]."[63]
Plumer was equally confident of a favorable decision, especially after his son wrote that Judge Richardson had told him
"in confidence, that the court had made up their judgment
unanimously in favour of the University." After being so
assured, the elder Plumer replied that he had never doubted
the outcome once he had investigated the subject.[64]

The Governor was, then, neither surprised nor disappointed
on November 6 when Richardson delivered the opinion for a
unanimous court. The Chief Justice opened with a vigorous
discussion of the judicial process. The court, he said, would always carefully consider questions of private right, for should
today's "infringements be sanctioned by a judicial decision
tomorrow, there will be next day a precedent for the violation
of the rights of every man in the community." Even so, these
were questions of "mere constitutional right" and would not
permit the court to judge the policy or expediency of legislative acts. Then, indicating the direction of his decision,
Richardson said that if the plaintiffs' counsel had failed to
convince the court, it was owing to a "want of solid and substantial grounds on which to rest their argument."[65]

The heart of his opinion was the defense argument that Dartmouth was a public corporation. He followed Marshall in *Bank
of the United States* v. *Deveaux* (1809)[66] and defined a corporation as "an artificial, invisible body, existing only in contemplation of law." Arguing that corporations possessed
rights and property only "in form" and that "in reality"
those rights and property belonged to individuals and the public, the Chief Justice of New Hampshire demonstrated that

the old civil-eleemosynary division of corporations was un-
suited to the demands of early nineteenth century America.
He proposed a new division into public and private based upon
property rights and the objects for which corporations were
created.[67]

Private corporations, such as banks, insurance and manufacturing companies, Judge Richardson said, were created for
the immediate benefit and advantage of individuals. The
property and franchises of private corporations belonged to
individuals under the corporate form. Towns and other public
corporations were created for public purposes. Their property
and franchises were devoted to the object of their incorporation, and the corporators enjoyed no private right other than
that of being members. It was only necessary to determine in
this case whether the objects for which Dartmouth College
was created were public or private. The endowment was of no
consequence, since a corporation held property only to enable
it to answer the object of its creation, and a gift to a corporation was a gift to those interested in its objects.

Richardson examined the College charter and found that
Dartmouth had been incorporated to spread Christianity and
knowledge among the Indians and to furnish the best means
of education to New Hampshire. "These great purposes are
surely, if anything can be, matters of public concern."[68]
Since the object was public, Dartmouth College was a public
corporation, and the office of trustee was a public trust, as
much as the office of governor or judge. As public servants,
the trustees had no private right, other than that of being members of the corporation, which they could claim the June act
in final form had infringed. Indeed, only the state had an interest, and so there was no founder whose rights the trustees
could assert. Law, Richardson declared, was only the will of
the sovereign people, and the public servants, the trustees,
could not resist the master's will in a matter that concerned
the master alone. With this established, he did not think it
necessary to inquire into the legislature's right to interfere
with private corporations. But he did admit that the property
of private corporations would stand on the same ground as
that of individuals.

In answer to Mason's argument that the 1816 acts violated
Article 15 of the New Hampshire bill of rights and its "law of
the land" clause, Richardson contended that all statutes, not

repugnant to any other clauses in the constitution, "seem always to have been considered as 'the law of the land,' within the meaning of the clause." The principle that these acts were not "law of the land" because they interfered with private rights "would probably make our whole statute book a dead letter."[69] All public interests, including public corporations, were proper subjects of legislation, and every statute interfered either directly or indirectly with private rights. Richardson said that the "law of the land" clause had historically been a restraint only upon the executive, and, consequently, it embraced legislative enactments as well as judicial pronouncements.

His interpretation of the contract clause hinged upon the definition of Dartmouth as a public corporation. Arguing that the contract clause was intended to protect private rights and that the contract decisions of the Supreme Court had concerned only legislative grants of privileges or property to individuals, the Chief Justice maintained that that clause was not intended "to limit the power of the states, in relation to their own public officers and servants, or to their own civil institutions."[70] The opposite view would place public institutions beyond state control and would be repugnant to the principles of all government.

The court, therefore, was clearly of the opinion that the charter of Dartmouth College was not a contract within the meaning of Article I, section 10 of the national Constitution. The 1816 acts were clearly constitutional, and judgment was given for the defendant. Richardson concluded that he was greatly consoled by knowledge that any errors in his decision would be corrected and prevented from working any injustice. The Trustees could "carry the cause to another tribunal, where it can be reexamined, and our judgment reversed, or affirmed, as the law of the case may seem to that tribunal to require."[71]

It should be noted that Richardson's classification of corporations enabled him to imply that *private* corporate charters would be considered contracts under the Constitution.[72] All agreed that some corporations were controllable by the legislature, but there was, as the arguments in Superior Court demonstrated, disagreement about the criterion for classifying corporations as public, for permitting regulation. Richardson, like Woodward's counsel, emphasized the objects; College counsel had stressed the origins, the sources of the funds. The case would ultimately turn on that criterion.

The *Patriot* hailed the decision as one which had "done justice to Dartmouth University and to the people of this State."[73]
Parish, the old fomenter, congratulated Plumer on the decision.
"The historian," he wrote, "will date [the University's] brilliant
era from the *administration of Gov. Pr.*"[74]

Even the Federalist press reported the decision as "able, ingenious, and plausible."[75] Despite the predictable Jeffersonian
bias, there is nothing to suggest that politics robbed the opinion of any judicial integrity.

Plumer thought it was "an important and correct decision."
It was, he said, what he had confidently expected from the
first time he had heard of its commencement. His confidence
was "founded on a knowledge of the law and the talents and
integrity of the Judges," and, one must add, his sincere belief that education ought to serve the public.[76]

Supporters of the College were not surprised by the decision.
Webster wrote to Brown that he had never expected any
other decision from Plumer's court.[77] Brown was disappointed,
but suspicions of an adverse decision had induced the Trustees
to vote in August to push the suit to a final decision in the
Supreme Court of the United States, and the President immediately began preparations for that action.[78] But for some
adherents of the College—unaware of this intention, the decision seemed a disaster. Young Rufus Choate voiced the sentiments of the loyal student body that the decision had blasted
the hopes of the College.[79]

5 Argument at Washington

*"Sir, I know not how others may feel, but, for
myself, when I see my Alma Mater surrounded, like
Caesar in the senate-house, by those reiterating
stab upon stab, I would not, for this right hand,
have her turn to me, and say, Et tu quoque mi filii!
And thou too, my son!"—Webster, 1818*

The Superior Court decision was a setback. The College's finances were precarious, and the need for further litigation to
resolve the institution's legal status threatened a financial
collapse.[1] It was imperative not only to appeal the decision
but to do so swiftly and obtain a decision at the 1818 term
of the Supreme Court of the United States. That term was
to begin February 1, leaving little time to procure funds,
enter the case on the docket, and engage counsel.

1

Both sides, College and University, set to work with as much
care—and in the case of the College, speed—as possible. President Brown worked feverishly in the weeks after the Plymouth
decision. College counsel had discussed the planned appeal at
some length at Exeter, and Brown doubtless learned from
these discussions that Mason and Smith did not intend to
manage the cause at Washington. He expected Webster to
take charge.[2] In conversation with Thompson after the November decision, Webster had disclosed a suspicion that Brown
would depend upon him; but he was no longer a Congressman,
and management of the appeal would entail a special trip to
Washington. He informed Brown that, while he was aware of
the difficulty of funds, he doubted whether he could argue
the case for less than a thousand dollars. Webster also desired to associate "some distinguished counsel" with himself
and thought Joseph Hopkinson "capable of arguing this cause
as well as any man in the United States." The thousand dollars would, he said, help pay for Hopkinson's assistance.[3]

Hopkinson was a Pennsylvania lawyer-politician and a confirmed Federalist. Although he possessed considerable legal
ability, the distinguished Philadelphian had only limited experience before the Supreme Court and none on a constitutional question.[4] He was in Washington as a Congressman from

Pennsylvania and would save the College traveling expenses.
There was little else to recommend him above other members
of the Federal bar. Hopkinson had manifested an interest in
the case, but his employment was the result of Webster's initiative. Webster knew that Plumer had heard the Philadelphian
defend Justice Samuel Chase in the Senate impeachment trial
of 1805 and had formed a high opinion of his legal talents.
Fearing the University might attempt to retain Hopkinson,
Webster requested his assistance.[5]

Preparations for the appeal thus became the principal responsibility of Webster, and one must say that the Massachusetts lawyer moved into action. He desired to have the record
in the case certified and forwarded as soon as possible, and
impressed upon Brown that "the sooner the papers are sent
to Washington, the earlier the case will stand on the docket."[6]
He also was concerned about the special verdict, and rightly
so as subsequent events proved. He seemed to sense that the
University would use Richardson's opinion as the mainstay of
its argument. The burden of that opinion was that Dartmouth
had been founded for public purposes and was, consequently,
a public corporation. The opinion contained little information
about the foundation of the College. Webster saw this as a
weak point, [7] and planned to exploit it by arguing that the
foundation, not the objects of the foundation, determined
the nature of the corporation. He wanted the special verdict
to include everything demonstrating that the state did not
found the College. The briefs of Mason and Smith had covered
this point exhaustively, especially Smith's with its probing of
the common-law rule of charitable corporations. Recognizing
that their arguments and the special verdict would enable him
to refute Richardson's opinion, Webster requested their notes,
and conversed with Mason before departing for Washington.[8]

The task of preparing the special verdict fell to Judge Smith.
His initial conferences with Bartlett quickly reached an impasse because the latter, intent on demonstrating the legislature's right to interfere, had drawn a verdict specifying that
the greater part of the lands and monies received by the College had come from the state, and referring to Wheelock's 1815
memorial as a specific request for legislative modification.[9]
Smith rejected the implication that New Hampshire had been
the founder as contrary to fact and, incidentally, to the plaintiff's design. Earlier he had sent a copy of his draft to Sullivan

who proved more amenable and accepted it. The desired verdict together with the writ of error went to the Supreme Court clerk on December 25, 1817.[10] In mid-February 1818 Webster informed Brown that the cause had been entered early enough to expect an argument at that year's term. "We shall endeavor," he said, "to argue all the points."[11]

The College's opponents meanwhile prepared their side of the case. Once the appeal was verified, University supporters worked diligently to get Richardson's opinion printed and circulated—a maneuver confirming Webster's suspicions.[12] The *Patriot* reported that the opinion was too long for the columns of a newspaper and that it was necessary to give it to the public as a pamphlet.[13] Plumer wanted the opinion published and "some copies sent to Washington before the trial comes on there."[14] Richardson himself urged that University counsel in Washington provide each judge with a copy.[15]

The University trustees voted to retain as counsel a Massachusetts Congressman for the district of Maine, John Holmes, a shrewd politician sensitive to public opinion, who had deserted the Federalists during the War of 1812.[16] Woodward considered Holmes "extremely ready—of sound mind and a good lawyer inferious to D.W. only in point of oratory."[17] Plumer, too, believed Holmes's talents and information would enable him to do "ample justice" to a cause in which every state in the Union had a deep interest.[18] In spite of these endorsements, Holmes ranked low at the bar. Probably the principal considerations leading the trustees to engage Holmes did not spring from his legal eminence but from politics, the money saved by employing counsel already in Washington, and overconfidence in the strength of Richardson's opinion. Holmes accepted, and requested President Allen to send copies of all the papers necessary to a "perfect understanding of the subject."[19]

None of the University party desired Holmes to manage the cause alone, and this suggests their doubt about his ability. Cyrus Perkins expressed some doubt with his declaration that only an able argument would give the University a fair chance and that the University ought to have the "most able lawyers & advocates."[20] Even Woodward professed that, notwithstanding his opinion of Holmes, he had "ever wished some more powerful man might be associated."[21] Perkins and Woodward

suggested the eminent New York attorney, Thomas Addis
Emmet, and the recently appointed Attorney General of the
United States, William Wirt. Salma Hale, New Hampshire
Congressman and University trustee, was the most caustic
and outspoken critic of Holmes. The University trustees had
appointed Hale to supervise the engagement of counsel, and
he informed Plumer that everyone with whom he conversed
believed that Holmes alone would be inadequate.[22] "Were
you sensible," he wrote Allen, "of the low ebb of Holmes's
reputation here, you should I think hesitate to trust the
cause with him. It *might* in the end be *decided* right, but a
lawyer of high standing would be much more likely to persuade the court."[23] In addition to other shortcomings,
Holmes was not preparing energetically even though he
knew the difficulty of winning.[24]

Friends of the University in Washington supported Hale and
urged, almost insisted upon, the engagement of Wirt as
Holmes's associate.[25] At first glance Wirt supplied all of
Holmes's deficiencies. He had wide experience at the state and
lower federal bars, and was little concerned with politics. The
acknowledged leader of the Virginia bar, he was beginning an
exceptionally distinguished career as Attorney General of the
United States. In his limited experience before the Supreme
Court he had won a prize case from Hopkinson in 1817, and
he had lost a decision to Webster just prior to the College
argument.[26] But the new Attorney General, beset by calls for
opinions and the task of preparing briefs in ten other cases for
the approaching term of the Supreme Court, was unable to devote full attention to the College case.[27]

To complicate the University's difficulties, neither counsel—
Holmes nor Wirt—was familiar with the history of the case.
Hale entreated Allen and Plumer to send information and the
notes of Bartlett and Sullivan. Woodward did his best to obtain papers from the New Hampshire counsel, to no avail.[28]
Bartlett and Sullivan procrastinated. In fact, they and Allen
doubted that the state court arguments would be of any use
at Washington, since the case there was limited to the contract clause of the national Constitution. Richardson's opinion
would suffice.[29] By late February, with the Court in session,
Hale had still not received even a list of Bartlett's and Sullivan's
authorities. He did not share the view that the case would be
restricted to the contract clause. "The first point to be de-

termined," he said, "is Jurisdiction. This is narrowing the cause it is true, but that point being determined against the University, lets in all the other points." He informed Allen that this was Wirt's opinion as well.[30] No doubt, Bartlett and Sullivan would have presented a stronger case than Holmes or Wirt. The University officials had deemed it an unnecessary expense to send them to Washington, especially after the engagement of Wirt.[31]

2

Webster opened the argument in the College case on March 10, 1818, just four days before the close of the term.[32] The Court was occupying temporary quarters because of wartime damage to the Capitol, and the small audience of interested lawyers and New Englanders overflowed the chamber. Webster at this time was thirty-six years old and, like Wirt, had argued only eight cases before the Supreme Court. Even so, supported by thirteen years of experience in courts outside Washington, an impressive physical appearance, and great oratorical ability, he presented a four-hour argument which his opponents praised as the ablest ever delivered before the Court.[33] It was, indeed, one of the outstanding performances of his career.

Beginning with what Justice Story later called "decorous deference," Webster set the stage for his refutation of Richardson's opinion by stating the facts and questions of the controversy.[34] The charter declared that the College had been founded on funds donated or procured by Eleazar Wheelock. It demonstrated that Wheelock had assigned to the Trustees the ownership of property and the right of visitation. The Trustees, then, had rights, property, and power under the charter as a corporation, and as individual members of that corporation. By creating a new corporation and transferring the property of the old without the consent of the Trustees, the acts of 1816 violated these rights of the Trustees.

Smith's research on the nature and rights of corporations at common law assisted Webster in establishing his points that such violations were contrary to natural law, to the state constitution, and to the contract clause of the national Constitution. The last point alone was justiciable in the Supreme Court, since only conflicts between state statutes and the Constitution were appropriate under the Judiciary Act of 1789.[35]

Although Webster was aware of this limit to the Court's jurisdiction, he proposed that a comparison of the New Hampshire statutes with the fundamental principles introduced into state governments to limit legislative power might "assist in forming an opinion of their true nature and character."[36]

Why might such an argument assist the Court? Chief Justice Marshall was anxious about excessive state power, and did not always confine his opinions to justiciable matters. Justice Johnson was susceptible; in a concurring opinion in *Fletcher* v. *Peck* (1810), Johnson had refused to use the contract clause but had been willing to invalidate the Georgia legislation on the ground that natural law protected vested rights from legislative abuse.[37] Webster knew that the Court, regardless of its political complexion, was receptive, and probably saw nothing extraordinary in the breadth of his argument.

It was more than the Court's receptivity or adherence to Mason's outline which led him beyond jurisdictional limits. Webster was, to be sure, arguing for the sanctity of vested rights in the broadest sense. The Supreme Court had ruled that legislative grants of land and privileges were contracts within the meaning of the Constitution, but it had not ruled that corporate charters were contracts. Webster perhaps felt safer in equating corporate rights with private property and privileges which only the judiciary could declare forfeit. It was almost as if he viewed an argument from the contract clause and the New Hampshire constitution as synonymous, since both contained restrictions on state legislative power.[38] This lack of confidence in the contract clause per se had induced him to suggest that cases be initiated in the Circuit Court, "which should present *both* & all our points, to the Supreme Court."[39] He raised both these points, and it is conceivable that he was attempting to prepare the Court for these "cognate cases."[40]

The common law, Webster argued, classified corporations as either civil or eleemosynary. Colleges were recognized as eleemosynary, or private, charitable corporations constituted for the perpetual distribution of the founder's bounty. Since the right of visitation arose from this bounty, the founder could dispose of the right as he pleased. If he transferred it to the trustees, it accrued to them as a private-property right with all the legal protection afforded any private right. Government helped perpetuate the charity by granting a charter, but it was the founder's bounty and not the grant of a charter which conferred rights. The uses and advantages of such a chartered institution might be public, and the state might contribute funds or property; the corporation was still private in the tenure of its property and in the right of administering its funds. Webster's principal precedent on this point was the English case of *Philips* v. *Bury,* in which Chief Justice Lord Holt of the King's Bench ruled that, since Exeter College in Oxford was a private corporation, the visitor's acts were not examinable in court.[41] If Holt's doctrine were correct, Webster contended, the property of Dartmouth College was private. Moreover, since the charter vested the property in the trustees, they were also *"visitors* of the charity, in the most ample sense. They had, therefore . . . *privileges, property,* and *immunities,"* within the true meaning of the New Hampshire bill of rights.[42]

So, to answer Richardson's opinion that the corporation's property was public and that the trustees had no private interest, Webster argued that the trustees as individuals possessed liberties, privileges, and immunities under the charter, and as vested rights these were inviolable. In the words of Justice Chase, when a right was vested in a citizen, "he has the power to do *certain actions,* or to possess *certain things,* according to the law of the land."[43] Article Fifteen of the New Hampshire state constitution provided that no citizen should be "deprived of his property, immunities, or privileges . . . but by the judgment of his peers or the law of the land."

What did law of the land mean? A refutation of the New Hampshire opinion demanded a broadening of Richardson's interpretation of due process as only legislative acts. In an astute synthesis of Mason's points on separation of powers and the scope of legislative power, Webster stressed that "law of the land" was the embodiment of those fundamental principles restraining legislative power. To assert that legislative acts were "law of the land" would limit inquiry to the statute book and remove any constitutional restraint upon the legislature. Richardson had interpreted the clause historically as a restraint upon the executive alone. Webster needed a broader interpretation—a judicial restraint on legislative power for the protection of individual rights—and chose Coke's that "law of the land" meant *by the due course and process of law.*"[44]

His development of Coke's definition led him into what was to become the most frequently quoted definition of "substantive due process."[45] Law of the land meant the general law—"a law which hears before it condemns; which proceeds upon inquiry, and renders judgment only after trial." In short, every citizen held his life, liberty, and property under the general rules, the constitution. Any other interpretation would unite all the powers in the legislature, and there would be no general law for the courts to administer. "The administration of justice would be an empty form, an idle ceremony. Judges would sit to execute legislative judgments; not to declare the law, or to administer the justice of the country."[46] If Richardson's interpretation were accepted, there would be no need for a constitution, state or national.

Turning to the general law of the United States, Webster examined the contract clause for the protection it afforded the life, liberty, and property of individuals. The framers of the Constitution, he concluded from Madison's *Federalist* 44, had intended that clause as a constitutional bulwark against state legislative abuse of private vested rights. The Supreme Court had affirmed this doctrine in *Fletcher* v. *Peck* (1810) and *New Jersey* v. *Wilson* (1812).[47]

Terrett v. *Taylor* (1815), he contended, was of all other cases "most pertinent to the present argument. Indeed, the judgment of the Court in that case seems to leave little to be argued or decided in this."[48] This was so because, in the course of that opinion protecting the vested rights of the Episcopal church in Virginia, Justice Story had defined the legal nature of private corporations. Story would not admit that legislatures could repeal statutes creating private corporations and by such repeal transfer their property to others without consent of the corporators. This decision, Story had thought, stood "upon the principles of natural justice, upon the fundamental laws of every free government, upon the spirit and letter of the constitution of the United States, and upon the doctrines of the most respectable judicial tribunals."[49] These were precisely the grounds of Webster's argument.

It surely was a neat argument. All precedents, Webster argued, proved that a grant of corporate powers and privileges was as much a contract as a grant of land. If precedents did not prove it the fact that such grants had to be accepted to be valid did prove it. Accepted, a charter contained all the essentials of a contract: there was sufficient matter; there were parties; there were plain terms in which the agreement of the parties, on the subject of the contract, was expressed; and there were mutual considerations and inducements. So it was with the charter of Dartmouth College; and since the acts of 1816 had abrogated parts of the contract without acceptance of the trustees, they impaired the contract.[50] This point was essential to the case and was to have far-reaching effects upon American constitutional law.

Webster concluded with some remarks on the practical aspects of the case. These, he said, led the Court back to the necessity of limiting legislative power. He would not accept the defendants' argument that these acts were necessary because of abuses at the College. All such an argument would prove was that if some evil resulted from restrictions on the legislature, the restrictions ought to be disregarded. But, Webster said, the people have thought otherwise. "They have, most wisely, chosen to take the risk of occasional inconvenience for want of power, in order that there might be a settled limit to its exercise, and a permanent security against its abuse."[51] Aside from these implications, approval of the New Hampshire laws would render every college in the country subject to the rise and fall of popular parties and the fluctuations of political opinion. Such would be the consequence if the rights of the trustees were not sustained, and Webster pleaded that if the Supreme Court did not sustain them, they would be "prostrated forever."[52]

At this juncture Webster summoned all his eloquence and delivered the peroration he had used before the Superior Court. Addressing himself to the Chief Justice, he declared, "It is, sir, as I have said, a small college. And yet *there are those who love it*."

The depth of personal feeling in this remark reportedly moved Marshall to tears.

Recovering his own composure, Webster concluded: "Sir, I know not how others may feel, but, for myself, when I see my Alma Mater surrounded, like Caesar in the senate-house, by those reiterating stab upon stab, I would not, for this right hand, have her turn to me, and say, *Et tu quoque mi filii!* . . ."[53]

3

Webster had done his best, which was very good. So powerful
was the argument that General Ripley reported to Allen that
"A friend of ours after hearing it observed to me I am afraid
you have lost the case."[54] This was the consensus, and none
withheld encomiums. Hale cast a slight aspersion when he reported to Plumer that Webster's "character, his manner, & art-
ful statement of the case & introduction of political remarks,
had great weight with some of the judges."[55] This reference
to "political remarks" has occasioned a continuing controversy, but all that one can reasonably infer from the comment
is that the tone of Webster's argument was decidedly Federalist.[56] He had sought to refute Richardson's opinion on the
near omnipotence of the state legislature. Such an argument
would have struck Republicans as political, but that does not
mean Webster wished the Judges to decide on party lines.

Although Blackstone and other common-law commentators
supported Webster's argument on the private nature of the
corporation and the trustees' rights, it was vulnerable. The
Supreme Court was not bound to apply the common law.
The legislature of New Hampshire was distinct from King or
Parliament and different rules might apply. But these weaknesses were not serious. Webster had proved the private nature
of the foundation, and if that were true, even the New Hampshire court would have supported him. To refute Webster and
win, the University counsel had to prove the state as founder.

Even an argument that Dartmouth had functioned through
the years as a public institution would have failed to answer
Webster. And such an argument would have been difficult in
1818.[57] The problem was the lack of a definition of corporations that would provide a standard for determining the relation between government power and private rights. All colleges in the United States had, like Dartmouth, enjoyed peri-
odic liberal support from state legislatures. The precedents involving colleges supported Webster.[58] If defense counsel had
stressed the state grants to Dartmouth, these could have been
construed in line with *Fletcher* v. *Peck* (1810) as contracts between the state and a private individual or corporation. This
would not have supported the contention that Dartmouth had
been a public institution.

The decisive point was Richardson's declaration that the

objects of incorporation determined the nature of the corporation. Webster countered by looking to the origins, the founding.[59]

How would the opposition respond? Holmes replied to Webster on the afternoon of March 10, and concluded the following morning.[60] His argument was a sorry paraphrase of the
Superior Court opinion, and moved Hale to comment that
the "employment of Mr. Wirt appears to me every day more
& more correct."[61] Education, Holmes maintained, was a
most important object of civil government and was a power
reserved exclusively to the states. Dartmouth was, therefore,
a public institution. The contract clause did not apply because
the College charter was a grant of a public nature, for public
purposes, relative to the internal government of the state,
liable to be revoked or modified by the supreme power of
the state, the legislature. The state constitution, Holmes contended, mandated the legislature to encourage education, and
the statutes of 1816 met this constitutional provision by im-
proving and amending the charter to "encourage" education.
He declared that even if the charter were a contract, the acts
did not abrogate its essentials; they only enlarged it.

Holmes had failed to meet the plaintiffs' challenge. Webster
reported that Judge Bell could not stand Holmes's folly. "Upon
the whole, he gave us three hours of the merest stuff that was
ever uttered in a county court."[62] Webster informed Brown
that "nothing new or formidable developed."[63]

Wirt likewise proved of little value to the University. Illness
and the burden of private and official practice had rendered
him unprepared to argue at his best. The Attorney General
was reasonably equipped to argue from Richardson's opinion,
but Webster's insistence upon Wheelock as the founder had
caught him by surprise. "Yesterday," Hale wrote Allen on
March 11, "Mr. Webster was very disingenuous, & it cost me
almost the night's labor to furnish Mr. Wirt with facts & authority to put him down."[64] The effort failed, for when Wirt rose
to follow Holmes he broke down in the midst of his argument.
Apologizing for his want of preparation, he asked the Court
to adjourn and allow him to finish the following day.[65] Hale
consulted with him again that night, and next day Wirt re-
covered some of the ground lost by himself and Holmes.[66]
After a puzzling excursion into the portion of Article I, section 10 prohibiting bills of attainder, Wirt thereupon concen-

trated on the contract clause, intended to protect private rights only. Wirt declared that the attempt to apply its protection to Dartmouth College was an extension of the natural meaning of the clause, by a legal fiction, to cases "which have always been supposed to be within the control of the sovereign power."[67] Charters of public corporations were always subject to legislative alteration.

Like Richardson, Wirt attempted to prove Dartmouth a public corporation; unlike Richardson, he concentrated on the foundation, not the objects of foundation. Wirt asserted that the charter did not declare Wheelock a contributor or that the College was a private foundation by Wheelock. On the contrary, Wheelock was only the projector, who had conducted an Indian school at his own expense, but the foundation of the College removed the institution from his estate. "The honors paid to him by the charter were the reward for his past services, and of the boldness, as well as piety, of the project. The State has been a contributor of funds, and this fact is found. It is, therefore, not a private charity, but a public institution."[68]

Wirt needed facts to support the latter point, and he did not have them. The charter declared Wheelock founder, and without evidence to the contrary this declaration stood unchallenged. Unable to develop this line of attack Wirt stressed that the charters of public institutions were not contracts, and his argument here was essentially Richardson's. In conclusion, he also summoned his powers of declamation. Hale spoke of Wirt's peroration as an eloquent introduction of the ghost of Eleazar Wheelock exclaiming to Webster, "Et tu Brute!"[69]

Wirt's performance pleased the University. Hale believed that "considering his want of preparation Wirt spoke with great ability."[70] Plumer thought it a "fortunate circumstance" that Wirt closed the defense.[71]

Even so, a rumor that Wirt had informed Webster that the College's case was stronger than the University's and that the College ought to prevail later disturbed the University adherents. Hale and President Allen doubted the veracity of the rumor, but asked Wirt to contradict it.[72] Wirt replied that such had never been his opinion and he could not have expressed it. It was possible, he surmised, "that some compliment to the argument of Mr. Webster led to this statement.

He opened the cause with great ability, and I remember to have said that I wished him all the success which his cause deserved, but not all his argument merited; by which I meant to convey my impression that his argument was, in my opinion, much better than his cause."[73]

Webster's associate, Hopkinson, closed the argument in the *Dartmouth College* case. He later said to Brown that Webster's excellent preparation left "little to do but to follow his steps and repeat his blows."[74] This was the gist of his hour-and-a-half argument, but his repetition was directed toward the arguments of Holmes and Wirt. Hopkinson reminded the Attorney General that the charter named Wheelock as founder and recited facts on which the law would vest him with that character even if the charter did not declare him such. Illuminating Wirt's weak points, he argued that if Wheelock had not been founder, the result would have been the same. The foundation was still private. Whoever was founder, the charter assigned the visitatorial power to the trustees. On the question at issue it made little difference whether the founder was one individual or another. It was clear that Wheelock had a legal interest in the funds with which the institution was founded at the time of the charter grant, and this fact made the charter a contract by which Wheelock devoted those funds to the public in consideration of the state's stipulations in the charter. The New Hampshire statutes violated these charter stipulations, impairing the contract.[75] On this point the argument of the case ended.

All parties wanted a decision of the question in 1818; but it was near the end of the term when Hopkinson concluded on the afternoon of March 12, and few persons really expected a decision that year.[76] Holmes asked the Court whether a decision was probable. Marshall replied that the Court would give the question all the consideration due an act of a state legislature, and that it was unlikely a decision would be reached immediately.[77] Next day the Chief Justice announced that some of the justices were divided and other undecided and that the case would continue to the 1819 term.[78] Both the College and University were confident that postponement would work in their favor.[79] Neither was willing to trust its intuition. Both took certain steps to insure a favorable decision.

6 A Year of Suspense

*"The Law indeed hath a long arm, & when it is
violently stretched out by the Cabbalistic Juggling
of Lawyers, assisted by a few well chosen antiquated
precedents, it makes some very unreasonable grasps.
It seems we must encounter another year of turmoil."*
—Moses Eastman, 1818

In the nineteenth century, political and legal actions seem
somehow to have occasioned much higher tempers and general concern than in our time, and Marshall's announcement
of the postponement occasioned confidence and feverish
activity on both sides. Rumors had it that two of the justices
were for the College, with one of them wavering, that two
were for the University, and that three, including Story, as
yet had no opinion. Hale estimated the University's chance
of success as five to two. He explained to Allen that "personal feelings & local prejudices account for the *error* of one,
perhaps two, of the judges."[1] Judge Bell had observed that
when the Court considered the question away from the influence of Webster's eloquence, the decision would probably
be unanimous in favor of the University. Hale would not pre-
dict unanimity but assured Allen that at least six of the
justices would rule against the College.[2] The only concern at
the moment was the expense incurred by the postponement.
Money was to be a continuing problem. Tenants refused to
pay their rent until the University's legal status was established. The argument was barely finished before the attorneys
began calling for their fees.[3]

As for the College party, it was no less confident. One University supporter wrote Allen that the "old story of Mr. Webster's eloquence . . . seems to have infused new life into the
old Trustees and their coadjutors."[4] Webster confidently
assessed the division of the Court. "The chief [Marshall] and
Washington, I have no doubt are with us. Duval and Todd
perhaps against us; the other three are holding up. I cannot
much doubt but that Story will be with us in the end, and I
think we have more than an even chance for one of the others.
I think we shall finally succeed."[5]

The College trustees nonetheless worried about support for
their cause. Even before the argument they had urged Brown
to petition other colleges for assistance, since the principles
involved could affect them. Unable to contribute, Harvard

and Yale sympathized. Their awareness of danger in the controversy brought a general moral support.[6] A congress of colleges
was proposed in April 1818, and it convened at Boston late
in May.[7] Participants included Dartmouth College, Yale, Harvard, Bowdoin, the University of Vermont, Middlebury,
Williams, and Andover Theological Seminary. Three of these
institutions were represented by their clergyman presidents.
Significantly, President Allen was not invited. His absence, in
addition to the timing of the congress, proved that the College
question had become, as Brown said, "substantially the cause
of every literary establishment in the country."[8]

Widened interest in the case helped weaken Webster's initial
resistance to circulation of his argument. By late April he had
printed a few copies. "I committed this folly," he said, "on
the motion of some friends here [Boston], who were anxious
to know something of the grounds of the case, of which they
have been most deplorably uninformed."[9] One such friend
was Chief Justice Isaac Parker of Massachusetts, who read one
of the first printed copies and urged extensive circulation.
The University had continued to circulate Richardson's opinion;
and Parker reminded Webster that popular sentiment naturally
leaned toward legislative power, since it was the power of the
people. Consequently, "the people ought to be made to know
that in certain cases their rights are above the reach of the
Legislature, and thus popularity may be given to a denial of
legislative power." Moreover, "every judge of the Supreme
Court of the United States ought to have a copy of this argument."[10] Webster remained anxious about what he considered
the "indecorum of publishing the creature."[11] He had taken
the precaution of printing it without title or author, and had
included little more than an outline and citation of cases.
When he learned that a copy had fallen into the hands of some
of the College students, he urged Brown to "caution the students against publishing it, or any part of it. The printer
should also be admonished not to say anything about it."[12]
By autumn, though, there were enough copies in circulation
that Webster, feeling, as he told Story, that "something was
necessary to exhibit the other side of the question," ceased
worrying about decorum and began to talk of publication.[13]
Acting on Parker's advice, Webster sent one copy of the argument to Story in July, and another five in September.[14] He
requested Story to "send one of them to each of the judges

as you think proper," but he cautioned that this distribution
should be discreet.

University actions aimed at influencing Chancellor James
Kent of New York in the hope that he could influence the
two remaining undecided justices, William Johnson and Henry
Brockholst Livingston. The University needed both to win its
case. Kent had vacationed in the Connecticut Valley early in
August. A staunch Federalist, the Chancellor had taken this
opportunity to visit Federalist friends in the region. At Windsor, Vermont, he was entertained by Josiah Dunham, a Whee-
lock-Federalist and ardent University supporter. Dunham
traveled with Kent to Hanover and introduced him to President Allen and the officers of the University. Kent was anxious
to learn something of the College quarrel. He had often heard
it mentioned but knew nothing of its merits. He was disappointed that the subject was not discussed and that he had
been unable to meet the College officers. But despite the
absence of discussion, the University managed to place a
copy of Richardson's opinion in the Chancellor's hands.[15]
He hastily studied the opinion on his return to Windsor the
following day and concluded that "the Legislature was competent to pass the laws in question." The opinion led him to
"assume the fact that Dartmouth College was a public establishment for purposes of a general nature."[16]

Kent's conversion to the University cause alarmed the College party. They thought it imperative to convince him of
the error in Richardson's opinion, and seem to have succeeded.
Marsh first wrote Kent and included a copy of the charter and
Webster's argument. Kent replied that the "fuller statement
of facts in Mr. W. argument" gave "*a new complexion to the
case,*" and indicated that if he should now study the case, he
might be led to a different conclusion.[17] The College determined
to work on this probability, and a certain byzantine maneuvering ensued. Brown had visited Albany for his health, and also
for the purpose of raising funds and seeing Kent.[18] The President wrote Webster that as soon as Kent saw him "he began
to express his regret at what he had said at Windsor." Kent explained that he had cautioned that his opinion was not to be
relied on and had merely said that the legislature was competent to pass the laws "*if the premises assumed* by the Court
were correct." Justice Johnson had also been to Albany and
had requested a copy of Webster's argument and Kent's opin-

ion. When Brown learned of Johnson's request, he decided
that it was important not only that Kent have a proper view
of the case but that he should declare it. "This opinion, if
given, will also have great influence on Judge Livingston."[19]
Brown informed Webster of these developments so that he
could decide whether anything else might be done, such as
having Parker write Kent. Later, Brown reported that Kent
had, without doubt, been won over by the charter and the
argument. "I believe he will take every proper & prudent
measure to impart correct views to others."[20]

Just what Kent then managed to do for the College remains
nonetheless obscure; perhaps he had not been converted to
the University in the first place. In the Brown-Webster correspondence respecting Kent there is frequent reference to
the Chancellor's activities on the New York Council of Revision.[21] In particular, Brown discussed the Council's veto
of proposed amendments to the charter of New York City in
1803 and 1804.[22] Examination of these vetoes indicates that
Brown was unduly concerned about Kent's position. In the
1803 veto, Kent proclaimed it a settled and salutary principle
of government that "in all cases where the ordinary process
of law affords a competent remedy, charters of incorporation
containing grants of personal and municipal privileges were
not to be essentially altered without the consent of the
parties concerned."[23] All charters and government grants
rested on the same foundation and could be altered or re-
sumed at pleasure unless the above rule prevailed. Any other
rule would establish a dangerous precedent which would "lead
to the destruction of all chartered rights and property of this
State, for rights and property cease to be of value when the
faith of a compact does not secure them, and they are held
at the will of any man or set of men whomsoever."[24]

The New York City case is of some interest, but it is strange
that a more relevant Council veto was not discussed at Albany.
In 1807 the Council objected to a bill transferring the power
of filling vacancies in the Board of Trustees of Columbia College to the regents of the College. This power had formerly
belonged to the trustees. The Council ruled that the College
charter of 1754 had granted this right to the trustees forever
and that it was entitled to all the security which any grant or
chartered right could receive under the state constitution and
law of the land. By transferring this right without the consent

of the trustees, the bill was void because "charters of incorporation, whether granted for private or local, or charitable, or literary or religious purposes, were not to be affected without
due process of law, or without the consent of the parties concerned."[25] Only "some strong public necessity" would justify
legislative interference.

Kent used the terms "ordinary process of law" and "due
process of law" synonymously, and intended them to refer
not only to common-law rules but also to provisions of the
New York constitution and statutes. The two vetoes indicate
Kent's further conviction that corporations were entitled to
the vague protection of these provisions.[26] These points were
the foundation of both Mason's and Webster's arguments, and
should have afforded the College some consolation.

Did Kent influence Johnson and Livingston, since both
justices eventually concurred in the decision for the College?
Webster never doubted "for a moment" Kent's ultimate position and knew that his opinion would "have *weight,* where-
ever it is known."[27] But there is no evidence to suggest the extent of Kent's influence on either justice. Moreover, his influence would not have been necessary. Livingston had been a
member of the Council of Revision and had voted with Kent
on the 1803-1804 bills. In addition he was friendly with the
Vermont members of the College board.[28] Johnson's views on
vested rights were similar to Kent's, though he might have
been unwilling to use the contract clause as a basis for decision.[29]

After the Superior Court decision of 1817 a rumor circulated
that Story favored the University, and some writers have inferred from this that the activity concerning the justices was
directed toward Story as well.[30] The evidence does not support this. Brown learned in November 1817 that College supporters in Boston were apprehensive about appealing to the
Supreme Court.[31] These apprehensions produced talk, notably
in Salem, that the College might compromise on the appeal
if the University would not require abandonment of the
charter right.[32] A Dartmouth alumnus and student at Andover,
T. J. Murdock, informed Brown that this talk had begun because it had been ascertained that Story had assisted in draft-
ing the June law and had proposed the compromise.[33] Hopkinson wrote Marsh that if these charges were true he would
have no hesitation in resorting to any legal means to prevent
such an abuse of power and office. But it would prove so dis-

reputable for a judge to sit in a case in which he had been a
feed-counselor that Hopkinson inclined to doubt the charges.[34]
Apparently the rumors lacked substance, for there is no
other mention of them in correspondence of the College party.
Story's actions throughout the controversy, in particular his
handling of the Circuit Court cases, his distribution of Webster's argument, and close collaboration with Webster throughout, give every evidence to the contrary.[35] Moreover, excessive emphasis on Story tends to obscure the personal leadership of Marshall, whose nationalism and economic conservatism were also great assets for the College.[36]

In actual fact the University was more concerned with re-
arguing its case, rather than making subtle efforts to influence
the Supreme Court's membership, and it was to this tactic,
rather than maneuvers with Kent and Story, that its supporters turned after the initial argument at Washington. The
University knew that its poor showing in the argument had
resulted from a casual attitude and poor choice and inadequate preparation of counsel.[37] After hearing Webster's argument, General Ripley had frankly said so. Within weeks after
the postponement Hale sent Allen a copy of Webster's argument "for the purpose of enabling you to decide upon the
expediency of a second statement & argument of the cause."[38]
Since the postponement afforded the possibility of reargument, Allen and the other officers of the University decided
to attempt that and avoid the mistakes of the spring. At the
regular August meeting the trustees voted Allen the authority
to engage William Pinkney, the flamboyant leader of the
federal bar, for reargument.[39] Pinkney already had promised
Allen that if the trustees should apply for his services he
would gladly engage.[40] The permission was no sooner given
than Allen made the formal request. The Marylander consented and added that, since this was the cause of a learned
institution, he would not require his usual fee for arguing
cases of importance before the Supreme Court.[41]

When Pinkney came into the reargument, the University
was belatedly awakening to what Bartlett had urged right
along: that the University should emphasize the public fund-
ing rather than the public purpose of the institution. Pinkney's entrance was less important in itself, than because the
new argument appeared shortly thereafter. He had requested
Allen to inform him of the nature of the suit as soon as pos-

sible.[42] Allen hurriedly dispatched the information, including
the College charter, Richardson's opinion, the New Hampshire statutes, and an abstract of Webster's argument.[43] But
at the trustees' request Allen had also diligently searched all
the papers of Eleazar Wheelock, and this search marked a new
departure in University strategy. Webster's argument had
forced the University to abandon Richardson's opinion as the
foundation of its case—to shift from the objects of the incorporation to the origins. It was now necessary to prove
the state as founder. Allen discovered evidence in Wheelock's
papers which, he felt, proved "some facts of consequence
which put down the positions of Mr. Webster."[44]

The new tactic of the University, which coincided with
Pinkney's entrance into the case, was of some complexity,
to be sure. One of the "facts" Allen had unearthed, a distinction between Dartmouth College and Moor's Indian Charity
School, had been briefly touched upon by Bartlett in the
Superior Court. Allen admitted that Wheelock was the founder
of the School, but now hoped to document that he was not
the founder of the College. Governor Wentworth, he informed
Hale, had ignored many of Wheelock's demands in framing the
College charter; the School and College had always been separate and distinct; the College trustees had formally denounced
any connection with the School.[45]

The University side thereupon busied itself in preparation.
Hale applauded the discovery of the "new facts" in Wheelock's papers. "When I was listening to Webster's argument, I
was strongly impressed with the idea that such facts could be
found & that they would be of essential service."[46] But Allen,
remembering the March fiasco, prevailed upon him to see that
the University counsel could prove these facts. Hale informed
Allen that Pinkney would probably not be in Washington until the term of the Court commenced and would have little
time to study the cause. So he asked that someone visit Pinkney at Baltimore.[47] The University decided that Cyrus Perkins
as secretary-treasurer was best suited to confer with Pinkney.
In addition Perkins could confer with Wirt at Washington.[48]

There followed a conference in Baltimore. Perkins spent
more time there than anticipated and told Allen that Pinkney
would not dismiss him until he had supplied all the assistance
possible in explaining the papers and the history of the controversy.[49] He assured the President that "Mr. P. will come out

in the majesty of his strength & professes to feel strong in the cause—hopes that Mr. W. will appear on the floor again; from which is to be inferred that he feels ready & able to meet him on the question."[50]

After finishing his conferences with the Marylander, Perkins had to brief Wirt in Washington. The Attorney General was again occupied with other cases and informed Perkins that he would have to prepare those before giving any attention to the *Woodward* case. At Wirt's suggestion Perkins did prepare a list of references to establish the University's points.

Despite the encouraging prospect because of the new facts, all was not well. Both Pinkney and Wirt complained that the special verdict, which contained only the charter of 1769 and the 1816 acts, did not include some of the new information.[51] It would, then, be difficult to introduce that information into the argument at Washington.[52] Disagreement between Pinkney and Wirt also threatened the cause. The indomitable Pinkney had made no secret of his low opinion of Wirt's effort in the case.[53] Wirt had no wish to hear his rival argue a case which he had poorly presented, especially since the pressure of official business again made a capable refutation of Webster doubtful. Then, complicating normal professional rivalry, the pair had nearly dueled in December 1818, barely two months before the *Woodward* decision.[54]

The University's new strategy worried both President Brown and Webster. The latter surmised that Pinkney's engagement implied reargument—a prospect he regretted. Although the College cause, he felt, could only grow brighter by discussion, he did not want to argue the case a third time.[55] The President answered "very decisively" that Webster should reargue. Brown knew of Allen's examination of the Wheelock papers, and he summarized the points he expected the University to make. Allen would attempt to prove, he wrote Webster, that Wheelock "considered the College to be altogether distinct from the *School;* the *school* [sic], to be sure being a *private charity,* the College a *public* institution, & on a very different foundation." He also anticipated a distinction between English universities and the colleges founded within them. The University would admit the latter to be private charities but would point out that Dartmouth resembled the English universities in which the Parliament had a right to interfere.[56] Webster was unruffled by the introduction of the old corre-

spondence. "The Charter declares Dr. Wheelock to be *founder*
& I do not see how it can now be denied that he was such."[57]
He was still reluctant to reargue.

Still, the College party worried, if the Court granted Pinkney's request, there was no alternative to reargument. Smith
and Mason might accept the task, but what, Brown asked,
"could they say, which has not been said?" He did not expect
them to accept, and wrote Webster that "in my judgment, &
in the judgment of all the friends of the College, we must rely
chiefly on you." Brown stressed that it was unnecessary to
repeat the 1818 argument; a reply to Pinkney would suffice.[58]

7 The Deliverance of Dartmouth College

*"The opinion of the court after mature deliberation,
is, that this is a contract, the obligation of which
cannot be impaired without violating the constitution
of the United States."—John Marshall, 1819*

With preparation complete, both parties awaited the 1819
term. Pinkney had been briefed on the new facts and intended
to use them in a masterful reargument in *Woodward* and in
defense of the "cognate cases," entered on the Supreme
Court's docket.[1] Webster and Hopkinson were hopeful the
Court would not allow a reargument, though they had reluc-
tantly agreed to reply to Pinkney if necessary. It was not.
On February 2, Chief Justice John Marshall announced that
the Court had formed an opinion in the College case during
the vacation. For the next hour and a half he read the opinion which shattered the hopes the University had pinned on
Pinkney's reargument.[2]

1

Marshall's opinion was, as Webster said, "in his own peculiar
way."[3] Characteristically the Chief Justice relied upon general
political principles or natural law and the words of the Constitution rather than authorities, and he connected these principles with close-knit, persuasive logic. Declaring state statutes
unconstitutional and reversing a decision of a state supreme
court, Marshall said, was a serious matter. Even so, he maintained that the Court had a constitutional mandate to protect contracts from legislative violation. The remainder of his
opinion amplified these statements of his nationalism and his
concern for private property.

The single question for decision was the constitutionality
of the New Hampshire legislation; Marshall recognized this
and devoted his opinion to that point. "It can require no argument," he said, "to prove, that the circumstances of this case
constitute a contract." An application to incorporate a religious and literary institution had been made to the crown.
The application stated that large contributions had been
made, and would be conferred on the corporation as soon as
it was created. "The charter is granted, and on its faith the
property is conveyed. Surely in this transaction every ingredient of a complete and legitimate contract is to be found."[4]

This statement was not, as subsequent writers on jurisprudence have concluded, a bold and dogmatic assertion of what needed to be proved. No one in 1819 disputed that the charter of 1769 represented a corporate franchise, and the common law regarded all corporate franchises as contracts. Marshall was simply using this truism as a preface to his inquiry whether this contract was within the meaning of the Constitution and, if it were, whether the contract had been impaired.[5]

Both parties were, as Marshall assumed, agreed on general principles and the true construction of the Constitution in the abstract. His general interpretation of the contract clause was in harmony with Richardson's. He admitted that the framers of the Constitution did not intend to restrain the states from regulating their internal concerns. The contract clause "never has been understood to embrace other contracts, than those which respect property, or some object of value, and confer rights which may be asserted in a court of justice."[6] But there was wide difference of opinion on application of those principles to the *College* case and on true construction of the College charter (the case turned on interpretation of that charter). If Dartmouth were a civil institution, the contract clause would not apply; if it were private and eleemosynary, the clause would apply.

After reviewing the major provisions of the charter, Marshall concluded that the College funds consisted entirely of private donations. It was immaterial who the actual donors were. The legal conclusion from the facts in the charter was that Wheelock was the founder of the College. He had founded the Indian Charity School at his own expense and, on the promise of an incorporated extension of the School, other private individuals had contributed funds. The College was "an eleemosynary, and, as far as respects it funds, a private corporation."[7] Like Webster, the Chief Justice looked to origins to determine the type of corporation. Unlike Webster, Marshall did not probe common-law precedents. Despite some reliance on common-law principles in his definition of private corporations, the Chief Justice confined himself to the contract clause.

Marshall's declaration that Dartmouth College was a private corporation was the difference between his opinion and Richardson's, and it was precisely this point which made the decision important in American constitutional law.[8] Neither judge was willing to interpret the contract clause in accord with the common-law rule that all corporate charters were contracts. This raised the problem of determining which corporate charters did fall under protection of the Constitution. Richardson used the objects of incorporation as a criterion. Marshall could not accept a criterion which would place the majority of corporations at the mercy of the legislature. By looking to origins rather than objects, he was able to equate certain corporate charters with private property and its attendant rights. This was a more congenial standard, but forced Marshall to make modifications in his view of the legal nature of corporations.

Following his earlier pronouncements, Marshall defined a corporation as "an artificial being, invisible, intangible, and existing only in contemplation of law."[9] It possessed only the properties which the charter conferred, best calculated to effect the object of creation. If the purpose of creation were private, then the corporation was "no more a State instrument than a natural person exercising the same power would be."[10] The mere grant of a charter by the government warranted no interference which would change the nature of the corporation or give the government any new power over it. The right to interfere was not founded on incorporation, but on the corporation being created as an instrument of government.

The Chief Justice denied the defense assertion that a public object made the corporation an instrument of government. "The objects for which a corporation is created are universally such as the government wishes to promote." There could be no reason for implying in the charter a power "which is not only not expressed, but is in direct contradiction to its express stipulations."[11] Eleemosynary corporations did not fill a place which would otherwise be occupied by government, but one which would otherwise remain vacant.[12] Education, Marshall said, was an object of community concern and a proper subject of legislation; and he admitted that states could found institutions and place them entirely under state control. The corporate officials would then be public officers. It did not follow that Dartmouth was such an institution, that every teacher became a public officer, that donations to education became public property.

Even if the objects did determine the nature of the corporation, New Hampshire had no exclusive beneficial interest. The state participated only incidentally in the great objects of spreading religion to the Indians and educating the youth of the country. The question of the Trustees' beneficial interest was not so quickly disposed of. Marshall felt this the most difficult question in the case. Webster had argued that the Trustees did have a beneficial interest in their right of visitation, which could not be deprived except by due process of law. The Chief Justice denied this contention. Neither the founders and donors nor the students, in his view, had a beneficial interest which could be asserted in court. "The trustees alone complain, and the trustees have no beneficial interest to be protected."[13] This raised the question of whether the Constitution protected contracts in which the parties had no beneficial interest, and, in answering this question, Marshall modified his position on corporations.

Incorporation was the instrument by which Wheelock and the donors intended to perpetuate their design. The charter created a corporation which became the representative of the donors and capable of executing their will forever. It "is the assignee of their rights, stands in their place, and distributes their bounty, as they would have themselves had they been immortal."[14] Consequently, in eleemosynary corporations, "the body corporate, as possessing the whole legal and equitable trust, and completely representing the donors, for the purpose of executing the trust, has rights which are protected by the Constitution."[15] The corporation had a beneficial interest, and the charter was a contract within the spirit and letter of the Constitution.

Upholding the College while denying the Trustees' beneficial interest was a strange course, and perhaps Marshall took it because he had limited his inquiry to the contract clause and chose not to investigate the state constitution or due process of law. Whatever his reason, this course led him to give the corporation standing before the Court. Not only was he equating corporate rights with private rights; he was declaring the corporation to be a private individual with rights protected by the Constitution. This contradicted his earlier position in which he had refused to look beyond the corporators to ascertain standing.[16] Even when one admits that the cases were different, that Marshall was not primarily interested in the legal status of corporations, and that it would take years to develop the implications fully, such statements indicated a growing legal awareness of corporations.

Marshall conceded that such a contract might not have been

in the minds of the framers and that they had designed the
contract clause as protection from the debtor legislation of
the Confederation period. But, for Marshall, a written constitution only established broad and general principles for the
government of society "for ages to come."[17] So, while a particular case might not produce a rule, it must be governed by
that rule unless there were strong reasons to exclude it. It
was not enough, he maintained, to say that this case was
not in the minds of the framers—they could not have been so
imprudent to attempt to provide specific rules for exigencies
which they could not have foreseen. Expressing his belief
that a sound constitution must be flexible and adaptable to
new circumstances, Marshall argued that it was necessary to
go further, and to say that, "had this particular case been
suggested, the language would have been so varied, as to exclude it, or it would have been made a special exception. The
case being within the words of the rule, must be within its
operation likewise."[18]

The Revolution, he asserted, had effected no change in contracts or property rights. Not only would the common law
not allow the crown to alter corporate charters, but the
crown had expressly stipulated that the corporation should
continue forever. As successor to the crown, the state legislature was similarly bound. Parliament had the power to annul corporate charters. Marshall did not deny this, but sur-
mounted it by pointing out that, unlike Parliament, the
states were limited by the national Constitution. Then, too,
he alluded to the difference between theory and practice
with regard to this power of Parliament. His statement that a
parliamentary repeal of a charter would be "universally
acknowledged" as a perfidious transaction indicated, correctly,
that it had not been Parliament's practice to use this power.[19]

So, feeling supported by reason and the former decisions
of the Supreme Court, the Chief Justice ruled that the charter
was a contract, "the obligation of which cannot be impaired,
without violating the constitution of the United States."[20]

He quickly disposed of the remaining question by demonstrating that the 1816 laws had impaired the obligation. By
tranferring the governing power and the funds of the College,
the laws had substituted the will of the state for that of the
founder. These changes, Marshall proclaimed, were not immaterial, even though they might have been for the benefit

of the College in particular or of literature in general. The
founders had contracted not merely for perpetual application
of their funds but for "a system, which should, as far as human
foresight can provide, retain forever the government of the literary institution they had formed, in the hands of persons approved by themselves. This system is totally changed. The
charter of 1769 exists no longer."[21] He reversed the decision
of the Superior Court.[22]

2

The College party believed that the other judges also had drawn
opinions, and Story and Washington did file concurring opinions.[23] Livingston had written one but did not publish it, concurring in the opinions of Marshall, Story, and Washington.[24]
Johnson concurred only in Marshall's opinion. Todd was absent. Duval dissented, without giving an opinion.

Story had drawn his opinion by late December 1818, and
shown copies to select friends, including Livingston.[25] A
lengthy demonstration of his learning in the common law, it
examined the broad grounds of Webster's argument. The
bulk of the opinion was on the nature and rights of corporations at common law, and application of its principles to the
College charter. Story divided corporations into sole and
aggregate, spiritual and lay, civil and eleemosynary, in a discussion replete with references to authorities, particularly
Blackstone's *Commentaries* and *Philips* v. *Bury*. By contrast,
his discussion of the next division into public and private
corporations was devoid of documentation. It was, in fact,
unsupportable at common law. But it was in accord with his
decision in *Terrett* v. *Taylor* (1815).[26] Possibly he used this
public-private dichotomy to develop his position. More likely
he used it to clarify the terms, since Richardson had used the
same division in ruling against the College. Story insisted that
the term "public" had a popular meaning and also a purely
legal one. The popular denoted any purpose beneficial to the
public; the legal correlated the purpose with government
ownership. "The fact, then, that the charity is public, affords
no proof that the corporation is also public."[27] It was important, Story felt, to clarify these terms because a misunder-
standing would help promote the idea that if the use were
public, the government had the sole right to regulate funds

and franchises of the corporation. The implications of such an idea were appalling.

Like Marshall, Story found the element of private property, and not the object, to be crucial to any classification. A bank, he offered as an example, "whose stock is owned by private persons, is a private corporation, although . . . its objects and operations partake of a public nature." The same doctrine held true for insurance, canal, bridge, and turnpike corporations. "In all these cases, the use may, in a certain sense, be called public, but the corporations are private."[28] Story would admit a government right to interfere with a corporate charter only when the entire interest and franchises of the corporation were exclusive property of the government. If the legislature meant to claim authority to interfere with private corporate charters, it would have to reserve such authority in the grant of that charter.[29] "These principles," he declared, "are so consonant with justice, sound policy, and legal reasoning, that it is difficult to resist the impression of their correctness."[30]

It proved difficult for all parties to "resist" these principles in later years. Legislatures resorted to such reservations in charter grants. Later arguments about public and private corporations used Story's definition.

When Story applied these principles to Dartmouth College he concluded that it was, under its original charter, a private, eleemosynary corporation. *Fletcher* v. *Peck,* applied *a fortiori,* settled that this charter was a contract, but Story felt obliged to expand. Upon the face of the charter, the crown pledged that donations perpetually should be for the donors' purposes, without interference. In absence of any reserved power, this was an implied or executory contract not to alter the charter without consent of the corporation. In his judgment, since the Revolution effected no change, an act of the legislature which altered the charter in any way was a violation of that charter's obligation. So he concluded that "the acts of the legislature of New-Hampshire, now in question, do impair the obligation of that charter, and are, consequently, unconstitutional and void."[31]

Story's attempt to bring all business corporations under the Constitution perhaps provided the reason for Washington's brief opinion.[32] Like Story, Washington drew heavily upon common-law cases and authorities to prove that a charter of incorporation was a contract. But some apprehension about Story's broad application of the clause must have prompted his remark that his opinion was to prevent "any implied decision by this court of any other case, than the one immediately before it."[33]

The wide use of common-law authorities weakened both concurring opinions. No common-law commentator drew a distinction between private and public corporations.[34] The case of *Philips* v. *Bury*, upon which both justices relied in concluding that there were two classes of corporations, private and public, dealt only with the visitatorial power.[35] In this case Lord Holt was simply declaring that the king's courts did not enjoy the visitatorial power over eleemosynary corporations that they enjoyed over civil corporations; he was not attempting a classification of corporations. The other precedent of *The King* v. *Passmore*, which both justices used to demonstrate the contractual nature of a royal grant, involved the charter of a borough, a civil or public corporation in Story's classification.[36] Justice Buller was referring to all corporate charters, in his ruling that corporate charters were franchises with which the king could not interfere once they had been granted.

Their precedents, their failure to adapt English common law to a new American setting, a different form of government, and a different economic and social environment, placed Story and Washington in an awkward position. Their authorities contradicted their declaration that public corporations did not have contract rights in their franchises. Yet they could not follow the common law and rule that all charters were immune from legislative interference because established practice in the United States allowed the legislatures full control over municipal corporations. Neither could they say that all corporations were subject to the legislative control, for that was tantamount to affirming the Superior Court's decision.

By avoiding common-law precedents Marshall escaped this dilemma. He was not ignorant of those precedents, but aware of their shortcomings and limited applicability under the Constitution. Marshall relied on the common law's general principles and, consequently, was able to classify corporate charters as contracts without becoming entangled in the lexical dispute over the terms "public" and "private." The Chief

Justice made no reference to public corporations, and it is conceivable that he was not interested in the classification. His concern lay with the distinction between private *property* and public *institutions*, since this better suited his principles and interpretation of the Constitution and the nation's needs.

3

Contemporary reaction to the decision was predictable. Both Webster and Hopkinson wrote Brown on the day of the decision and assured the beleaguered President that the College would return to its rightful owners.[37] Correspondence between College supporters through February evidenced continued jubilation at the "deliverance of Dartmouth College."[38] Webster urged moderation and told Farrar he wanted "no flourish of trumpets" to usher in the announcement of the College victory.[39] He did not want to alienate public opinion from the struggling College.

He need not have cautioned; the University furnished all the fanfare through its stalwart champion, the *Patriot*. In a long letter informing President Allen of the decision, Perkins complained of a "most strange arrangement in this business; some monkery which perfectly astonishes all our friends here."[40] Later he urged that Hill be made aware of this monkery—the College counsel "taking new ground at the U.S. Court, where our counsel could not be furnished with the necessary facts to put down the impudent falsehoods which were palmed on the Court."[41] Hill needed no prompting. The *Patriot* on February 16 launched an attack on the decision that was to continue until June.[42] Exclaiming that the doctrine of the case was "unworthy of the dark ages," Hill argued that it only made intolerance and high handed party persecution permanent. Worse yet, the decision established that funds of Dartmouth College, contributed by the people of New Hampshire, were the private property of eight men who had never contributed a cent to the institution. The only recourse, Hill proposed, was for the people to demand that the legislature *"tax this private property to the full extent of the law."*[43]

To illustrate the portents in the decision, Hill called attention to "Facts" which he felt should be published with the opinion "as a KEY by which some may, perhaps, better understand the case." There was, to begin with, Todd's absence,

Duval's dissent, and Marshall's and Washington's sympathy
with the Octagon. More revealing were the facts that Harvard
and Princeton had granted both Livingston and Johnson an
LL.D. between the argument and decision; that Story had
been elected to the Harvard Board of Overseers in April 1818;
and that Princeton had granted honorary degrees to Webster
and Hopkinson. These proved, Hill lamented, "that the governments of certain Colleges did not rely simply on the merits
and justice of the case; but took pains to 'travel out of the
record,' to procure a decision in their favor."[44]

Plumer's disappointment was equally keen—he remained
convinced that the legislature's action was strictly constitutional and that Richardson's opinion was the correct judicial
pronouncement. Marshall's reasoning appeared to the Governor as another illustration of the Court's alarming tendency
toward restricting the powers of the states, and the haste in
which the Court disposed of the case confirmed his suspicion.[45]
Republicans in Washington shared his alarm at this aspect of
the decision. Hale wrote that even the nationalistic John
Quincy Adams had expressed sympathy with these sentiments.[46]

Despite the setback, Plumer continued confident the Court
eventually would reverse the decision.[47] This glimmer of hope
resulted from Pinkney's determination to introduce the "new
facts." Initially Plumer had hoped the Court would be unable
to enter a judgment in the *Woodward* case, since the defendant
had died on August 9, 1816.[48] Webster reminded the Court
that, since the case involved a writ of error for arrest of the
Superior Court judgment, the defendant's death was irrele-
vant, and asked for a judgment *nunc pro tunc,* as of the last
term.[49] Pinkney prevailed upon the Court to defer judgment
until the "cognate cases" had been tried, but on the fateful
February 23 the Court had entered a judgment against Woodward in accord with Webster's motion.[50]

Undaunted, but vexed by the inadequacy of the special verdict in the other cases, Pinkney sought to take advantage of a
stipulation in the verdict that new facts might be added with
the consent of counsel.[51] Webster informed Mason that if the
new facts were admitted, the Court would rule that they did
not alter the result and that the charter was conclusive on the
facts therein.[52] Besides, as he observed to Brown, the other
causes had not come to the Supreme Court for judgment,

"but for a direction what judgment to give on the verdict" in the Circuit Court.[53] Perkins thought the case in its present shape hopeless and feared that Webster would not admit the new facts. He preferred to close the contest and felt that it was better to "run the risque of dieing by the sword in gallant conflict than die of vexation & famine in hopes of better armour."[54] Webster did refuse to admit the new facts, and Marshall remanded the cases back to Story's Circuit on February 25.[55]

8 Aaron's Rod

*"It is our misfortune that our cause goes to
Washington on a single point. . . . I have been thinking
whether it would not be advisable to bring a suit,
if we can get such parties as will give jurisdiction
in the circuit court of New Hampshire."—Webster, 1817*

1

Litigation in the Dartmouth College controversy involved not
only the major case, *Dartmouth College* v. *Woodward,* but
also three minor cases, and their story is important to a full
understanding of the main action. They originated with the
College's appeal from the Superior Court decision of November 1817. College counsel disliked the shape of the appeal.
In argument in the Superior Court, they had claimed that the
legislation of 1816 violated the principles of natural law, the
common law, the state constitution, and the contract clause
of the national Constitution. They were aware that section
twenty-five of the Judiciary Act of 1789 made an alleged
violation of the Constitution a requisite in appeal to the
Supreme Court from state tribunals. So the College argument
on appeal narrowed to a consideration of the contract clause.
But either because they lacked confidence in that clause or
preferred a more comprehensive opinion, College counsel
sought a method of bringing all four of their objections before
the Supreme Court.[1]

Webster in December 1817 had written Brown, Marsh, and
his colleagues before the Superior Court, Mason and Smith,
and suggested other suits against the University which they
could initiate in the Federal Circuit Court of New Hampshire
or Vermont and which would raise all the points to the
Supreme Court. The only requirements for such an action were
diversity of state citizenship and a minimum claim of five hundred dollars. These could easily be met through a lease of some
College land to a citizen of Vermont, such as Marsh, or a College suit against one of its Vermont tenants. Webster preferred
the New Hampshire circuit of Justice Story who had encouraged these new actions by "sundry sayings," but in either
manner the entire question might get to Washington.[2] This
maneuvering would have been unnecessary had the *Woodward*
case been brought originally in the Circuit Court. But in the
uncertain situation in August 1816, Brown had been advised

not to bypass the state court and to rely on the contract clause in an appeal to the Supreme Court.[3]

Brown's initial confidence in the *Woodward* action was a minor obstacle, and in a conference with the President in early January 1818, Webster succeeded in convincing him that it was expedient and also necessary to commence new action without delay. Brown then directed the College secretary, Mills Olcott, to investigate the condition of the College lands and to get in touch with Marsh about a lease.[4] Mason, who assumed management of the new action at this point, conferred with Farrar to determine what actions were most likely to succeed in raising the College question in the Circuit Court.[5] Farrar communicated Mason's recommendations to Brown for the consideration of the College trustees, who decided in mid-February to commence several suits without delay.[6] After overcoming difficulties about the form of the suits, the Trustees determined at the end of February 1818 to lease some College lands and to bring three actions in ejectment—which in England and the United States was a method of trying land title.[7]

The cases collateral to the major *Woodward* case were built by the College on a peculiar but perfectly respectable and convenient technicality. In cases of ejectment the plaintiff was always a lessee and sought damages resulting from his ouster. Since he could recover only damages, it was a personal action and differed from a real action in which the title to the land was at stake. Even so, recovery on a plea of ejectment involved establishing the lessor's title, and that was the real object of the action. It was a convenient method of suit. In England it usually involved fictitious leases and lessees, so it was true, as critics of the College were quick to point out, that these cases were fictitious.[8] Yet they were quite legal and not the least collusive. As Webster suggested, they provided the most convenient form of bringing a suit in the Circuit Court, based on diversity of state citizenship.[9]

The first of these minor actions was *Hatch* v. *Lang*.[10] A citizen of New Hampshire, Richard Lang, had leased two College lots in 1807. The lease required him to pay an annual rent of thirteen dollars. Nonpayment would end the lease and cause the land to revert to the Trustees. When the legislature reorganized the College, Lang paid the rent to the University trustees, whom he considered the legal owners. Following Olcott's investigation, the College trustees declared Lang's rights forfeit through nonpayment and repossessed the land on February 28, 1818.[11] The College then leased the land to a physician of Norwich, Vermont, Horace Hatch, who claimed that Lang on March 5 had dispossessed him and continued to withhold his lands. Hatch on March 9 entered a plea of ejectment in the Federal Circuit Court of New Hampshire. In this and the other cases Dartmouth College was the true party in interest. The question was the effect of the act of June 1816 on the College title to its lands—the validity of the legislation of 1816.

The second case, *Marsh* v. *Allen,* was similar in all but minor details.[12] The College on March 25, 1818, leased to a citizen of Woodstock, Vermont, Trustee Charles Marsh, the College buildings and the land on which they stood. Marsh claimed that on the same day William Allen, Henry Hutchinson, and Ahimaaz B. Simpson, acting on orders from the University trustees, dispossessed him. He entered a plea of ejectment on March 27.

The final case, *Pierce ex dem. Lyman* v. *Gilbert,* was the most interesting from the standpoint of the legal fictions involved in ejectment.[13] On March 24, 1818, the College leased the Commons Hall to Job Lyman of Woodstock. The next day Lyman leased the property to David Pierce, also of Woodstock. Pierce claimed that Benjamin J. Gilbert of Hanover had dispossessed him on March 26, and entered a plea of ejectment dated March 27. Gilbert was an ardent College supporter and did not actually dispossess Pierce. He was only lending his name so that the action against the University trustees, the real defendants, could begin. His role in this action of ejectment was that of casual ejector—the nominal defendant in ejectment because by a legal fiction peculiar to that action he accidentally or casually came upon the premises and ousted the tenant. As required by law in actions of this sort, Gilbert informed the University trustees that they should appear at court and have themselves made defendants in his stead, since only they had title to the property. If they failed to appear, he would have judgment rendered against him by default, and they would be turned out of their property.[14]

Mason had also advised a suit involving a Vermont citizen in a *bona fide* sale of the College library through an agent of the College trustees. If the University prevented the purchaser's entry, he could sue in the Circuit Court for his property.

Brown worked diligently to arrange the sale, and Marsh actually called upon President Allen on March 25, 1818.[15] His object, Allen wrote Plumer, was to gain admission to the library "to sell the books as an agent of the old Trustees, in compliance with advice, to lay a proper foundation for a suit."[16] Allen continually refused admission; and, when no buyer could be found, the old Trustees abandoned the project.

2

Webster was unaware of initiation of these suits when argument opened in *Woodward.* He had grown even more anxious about the new actions since the late opening of the *Woodward* case made a decision in 1818 unlikely. He was relieved when Brown informed him of the suits.[17] Earlier he had assured Brown that he would inform the Court that such actions were contemplated if it became necessary.[18] After the postponement, he informed Mason that he had given the Court reason to expect that a case, "raising the question in the amplest form, will be presented at the circuit court."[19] In addition, there was the worry that Woodward might die before the 1819 term and so prevent a decision in that case.[20]

The College hoped for a prompt disposal of the cases in the Circuit Court, to get them before the Court at Washington. Marsh anticipated that the University would attempt delay and possibly abatement. Webster and Mason were confident Marsh had miscalculated. "There is very little business in the Circuit Court in New Hampshire," Webster wrote Brown, "and I have no great doubt the cause will be disposed of in some way within the first three days of the term."[21] Story, Webster observed, was expecting a case which would present all the questions, and would send the case up in the most convenient manner. "If the district judge will agree to divide [in the judgment] without argument, *pro forma,* I think Judge Story will incline so to dispose of the case."[22]

How did the University respond to the new action? Its first hint of the suits came when Marsh visited the library and told President Allen that the College would "commence immediately three or four suits before the Circuit Court, not to multiply suits, but to plant a good action." Allen had no doubt these actions would be adopted, and the prospect was disquieting, especially since the precise nature of the suits was unknown and University finances were depleted.[23] Superior Court clerk Moses Eastman advised that the most prudent and economical course was to allow the cases to go before the Supreme Court without trial. At least, Eastman urged, the University could attempt to continue them in the Circuit Court until the decision of the main question which, "like Aaron's Rod, will swallow up all the spurious serpents engendered by those uneasy spirits aided by the chicanery, or the fictions of the Law."[24] Allen, confirming Marsh's earlier suspicions, decided to attempt delay or abatement.

The cases came before the Circuit Court at Portsmouth on May 1, 1818. Richard Fletcher represented the University in *Hatch* v. *Lang;* Bartlett was counsel in the other causes.[25] Mason again represented the College. University counsel brought the Court's attention to the fictitious nature of the suits, but Story dismissed the objection. Marsh reported that the Court "seemed disposed to pursue the most liberal course in respect to the actions." Story was particularly pleased by the action of ejectment in the English form and thought it the best means of trying the rights of parties in disputes over real property.[26] Having failed to secure an abatement, the University moved for a continuance to the October 1818 term, and the Court complied. But Story strongly advised the defendants to prepare for that term and suggested that, if necessary, the Court would hold an adjourned session in November to expedite forwarding the cases to the Supreme Court in time for the 1819 term. "The Judge intimated," Marsh observed, "that this was of great importance as the action now there [*Woodward*] did not perhaps present all the questions that would naturally arise out of the controversy and as it was time the controversy should be finished."[27]

By autumn 1818 the University had changed its view of the Circuit Court cases. Mason learned from the Circuit Court clerk in early September that the "University folks" had had a meeting at Concord and had decided not to prevent trial of the actions on their merits.[28] Webster also suspected some new University strategy and urged Brown to have Marsh attend the trial "as things may arise . . . which strangers may not be able to explain."[29] These "things," as Brown learned, were the new facts which Allen had uncovered in his search of Eleazar Wheelock's papers.[30] Knowing there would be an appeal to

the Supreme Court no matter how the case was decided, Allen
sent these papers to his counsel. In the event of an appeal
much depended on the statement on which the cases went to
Washington.[31] The University had determined to get these
new facts before the Supreme Court either through Pinkney's
reargument in *Woodward* or through the circuit cases. It had
seized what was originally a College maneuver—the circuit
cases—and converted it to its own use.

When the Court convened at Exeter on October 1, the old
adversaries again confronted each other. Mason and Smith
represented the College, and Bartlett and Sullivan the University. Both sides agreed to enter special verdicts into the
records of the cases.[32] In addition to the charter of 1769
and the legislation of 1816, these verdicts would contain
copies of the leases, entries thereunder, and the ejectments.
Counsel also agreed that the sole question to be tried before
the Supreme Court was the New Hampshire legislation. Moreover, with consent of either Court, counsel could add or ex-
punge facts deemed necessary to a decision of the case.
Story and the district judge, John Sherbourne, signed a *pro
forma* certificate of division, and the cases went to the Supreme Court. Agreements were also signed which admitted
certain Wheelock papers as authentic. The use of these papers
became a matter of some contention before the opening of
the 1819 term.[33]

The College was satisfied that "all things succeeded to a
charm at Exeter."[34] The University, Marsh observed, hoped
to prove through the addition of new papers that John Wheelock was appointed president under the charter and Eleazar
Wheelock's will; that as the founder's heir Wheelock could
have approved the 1816 acts; and that the College and Moor's
Charity School had always been distinct institutions.[35] But
Marsh assured Brown that the addition of new facts could
not alter the principles on which the cases would have to be
decided.[36]

As in *Woodward,* the task of preparing the special verdicts
was entrusted to Smith, who began revising them almost immediately on his return from Exeter. He attempted to give
these revised verdicts to Sullivan "to examine, & correct, &
say what additions D.U. proposed," but Sullivan was not
available until November 27. Smith then gave him the verdicts
and assured Farrar that Sullivan had sent them on to Bartlett.[37] Mason was satisfied with Smith's verdicts and reported

that Bartlett had brought thirty papers which he was most anxious to have admitted to the verdicts.[38] Both University attorneys presented these papers to Smith on December 17, 1818, but neither Smith nor Mason anticipated any difficulty in disposing of them. Both assured Brown that he need not fear any sacrifice of the College's interest "by *neglect* of your counsel."[39] By early January, the verdicts were complete, and the cases certified to the Supreme Court.[40]

3

The University was confident that the new facts would enable counsel to frame a better verdict than in *Woodward*, but success depended—unfortunately, as events proved—upon counsel's exertions.[41] College confidence in the face of the new strategy sprang from the casual manner of the University counsel. Bartlett was again unwilling to devote himself to the task. Since Story had agreed to the stipulation that new facts could be introduced at Washington, Bartlett was content to let the matter rest there. He was willing to include a schedule of papers, containing the facts, in the verdict, as his discussions with Mason and Smith demonstrated.[42] Hale wrote angrily to Allen that he wanted the facts and not a schedule of papers included in the verdict. The statement of the case, he added, should not be the burden of Pinkney and Wirt. If the facts were included, they would have something to argue from. "The regular course is to have everything prepared at the Court below, & certainly it can be much better done there [in New Hampshire] than here. Pray what excuse can our counsel have for neglecting what is peculiarly their duty?"[43]

The verdicts went to the Supreme Court without the facts, though containing the schedule of papers which contained the facts, and recriminations over this continued for months. Allen was unable to explain the neglect. He had sent the papers to Sullivan two weeks before the Exeter hearing. They were not used there, and, he wrote to Hale, two months later "no use had been made of them, & Mr. B[artlett] declined looking at them, thinking it best to refer the introduction of them . . . to the counsel at Washington." Even after pressing requests for introduction of the new facts, the most that could be accomplished was Bartlett's introduction of the schedule of papers.[44]

After the decision in *Woodward*, Perkins joined the chorus.

He feared that Webster would not admit the new facts into the
verdicts, facts "which ought to have been found by the jury in
New Hampshire—& I know could have been with such documents as we had at Concord." It was imperative to establish
that the charter had created a new institution, a College, distinct from the Charity School and that the state had been the
principal donor. In short, Perkins believed that if the University
could not persuade the Court that Dartmouth was a public institution, it would lose the case. An alternative was almost as
bad. The University might "persuade the Court to send it
back to New Hampshire to see if our Counsel will do their
duty on the third trial—that is make the jury find the facts."[45]
Pinkney favored sending the causes back for a special verdict
that would embrace all the facts and, at Perkins' request,
agreed to draw it himself.[46] Perkins had grown weary and
wrote Allen that, if the Court should not think the facts
material, he hoped they would not remand the cases "for the
sake of merely making their opinion appear somewhat better
supported by the actual facts in the case."[47]

Plumer did not share Perkins's depression, even after the
cases had been remanded to the Circuit Court. "I am confident," he wrote Hale, "that the fact of the State's being the
principal donor can be proved so as to remove the doubts of
even an *unwilling judge*," that is, Story. Anxious to present a
good account at the Circuit Court, he urged that the papers
be taken to Portsmouth again so that counsel could investigate them thoroughly and prepare another special verdict.
The Governor wanted "no pains or expense" spared.[48]

Webster had initially hoped to get a certificate in the cases
that would "enable Judge Story to know what to do with
them in May."[49] But Story's concurring opinion in *Woodward* covered the questions so thoroughly that, after reading
it, Webster did not see that a certificate would accomplish
anything.[50] Besides, he was aware of the University's difficulty and consternation concerning the new facts. A day or
two before the Supreme Court was to consider these cases,
Webster asked Pinkney and Wirt if they intended arguing one
of the circuit cases. "This brought on a conversation between
Bench & Bar," he reported to Smith, "which finally terminated
in this that the causes should be remanded by consent; that
Defts might, in Circuit Court, move to set aside this verdict
if they should be so advised, when the opinion of the judges

in Woodward's case should be read & known."[51] With the
facts not found in the special verdict, this was the best course,
and Webster adopted it at once. Otherwise, he informed
Brown, the University would state one fact, and the College
would counter with a repugnant or inconsistent fact. "What
judgment can be formed on such materials?" The Circuit
Court might give the University the opportunity of altering
the verdicts, but Webster doubted there would be further
discussion on them. He was confident the Court would decide for the College, and, if the defendants did not like the
decision, they could appeal it.[52]

Webster sent the records in the cases to Mason and inquired
whether Sullivan and Bartlett intended a prolonged contest.
He thought it "advisable to give them immediate notice that
we shall endeavor to bring the causes to judgment at May
term. Let them try it, & see what they can make of their
new facts."[53] The Court, he assured Mason, would see the
propriety of a speedy decision of all remaining questions,
"if there be any remaining questions."[54] After conversations
with Story on April 12, 1819 Webster grew even more confident. "You may depend on it that there will be difficulty
in getting a delay in that case, without reason."[55]

What was the University planning? Acting on Mason's and
Webster's advice, Marsh informed President Allen on April 8,
1819 that the College would insist upon a trial in May. Allen
still did not know his counsel's intentions and replied that he
had not expected a May trial.[56] Pleading that the papers had
been left at Washington and could not be received in time for
adequate preparation, he asked Marsh not to insist on a May
trial. Marsh was unmoved and informed Allen that the special
verdict in *Woodward* "embraced all the facts which ever
ought or even can have any effect in deciding the real matter
in controversy between the College and the University and
between those claiming rights or property under them re-
spectively." He could not believe that Allen would be unconcerned about the expense of a continuance to the October
term, and would not consent to any delay. Allen either had
to proceed to trial or apply to the Court for a continuance.
If the University chose the latter, Marsh insisted that the
affidavit specify the nature of the papers whose absence was
the basis for a continuance.[57]

The cases came before the Circuit Court at Portsmouth on

May 1, 1819, and the University requested a continuance until they could present new facts. Story granted a continuance to May 15 at Boston. Even so, he rendered a provisional judgment for the College in an opinion that was "very learned and able and covered all the facts that had been raised in the case."[58] Counsel for both parties agreed that this judgment should stand unless the University by June 10 presented its facts to Story in an affidavit and convinced him that these took the "case out of the principle settled at Washington."[59] On May 27, James T. Austin read the papers containing the new facts to the Court. Story, Webster reported, intimated that the *"new facts* had no bearing on any part of the Court's opinion," but in a gesture of fairness took the papers to examine them for a day or two before giving final decision.[60] Webster informed President Brown that final judgment and execution in the College cases could be expected on June 10, "as by arrangement at Portsmouth."[61]

Upon learning that the new facts were not likely to vary the judgment of the Court, Hill commented: "Thus ends the third act of the drama!"[62] The first act, he reminded his readers, had been the trouble instigated by the Octagon at Wheelock's expense. The second had been the action of the legislature and court of New Hampshire—the "people"—to redress the grievances. In the third act, a "foreign power," the Federal courts, had declared in favor of "Eight" men as opposed to the people.

"The fourth act," he added, "is yet to come—*the drama is not* ended."[63] But it was. The University had already been dispossessed; it was burdened with debt, and legislative assistance was improbable.[64] In this condition it acquiesced in the Court's decision and ended not only its own existence but the College controversy.

9 Conclusions

"The doctrines of Trustees of Dartmouth College *v.*
Woodward, *announced by this court more than sixty
years ago have become so imbedded in the jurisprudence
of the United States as to make it to all intents
and purposes a part of the constitution itself."*
—*Chief Justice Morrison R. Wait, 1880*

Despite modification through reservation clauses in corporate
charters, strict construction of such charters, and the state
powers of eminent domain, police, and taxation, *Dartmouth
College* v. *Woodward* stands as one of the most important
precedents in the history of the Supreme Court. It infused
the doctrine of vested rights into the contract clause of the
national Constitution. It restricted state power, and rendered
the corporation serviceable to the needs of a developing
national economy. Reverence for property rights and concern that state legislatures might infringe those rights caused
the Marshall Court to expand the contract clause into a constitutional shield for vested rights.

1

The *Dartmouth College* rule that corporate charters were contracts protected by the Constitution was a statement on property that gave legal form to the social and economic axioms
of America. Attachment to property represented not a reaction-
ary devotion to the status quo at public expense, but a conviction that restriction on government power was necessary to
protect the most valuable right of the individual, the right "to
acquire property, to dispose of that property according to his
own judgment, and to pledge himself for a future act."[1] The
liberal individualism of John Locke and its concern with natural law and social contract formed a climate of opinion that
society existed to preserve the rights an individual possessed
before he entered society and the corollary that society benefited or prospered in direct proportion to the protection
afforded individual rights. Protection of the basic right, property, either of private individuals or groups of private individuals would encourage the productive labor necessary to open
the continent and develop the economy. Nineteenth-century
American law absorbed this belief in the tie between individual

rights and public welfare. From a conviction that the legal order should protect and promote this productive energy and that it should help create an environment that would increase opportunity and limit circumstance, legislatures passed laws concerning canals, turnpikes, banks, and railroads, and courts built a body of doctrine—the doctrine of vested rights—founded on judicial support of the sanctity of private property.[2] The Marshall Court was no exception.

Marshall's proclamation in *Dartmouth College* that the contract clause of the national Constitution protected vested rights climaxed the expansion of that clause initiated in *Fletcher* v. *Peck* (1810), and it is this that constitutes the importance of the *College* case in 1819. The Chief Justice, imbued with a belief in eighteenth-century natural law and a conservative distrust of state legislatures, continually sought to protect private property by using the contract clause to limit state interference.[3] *Fletcher* v. *Peck* represented the first step toward employing the contract clause to protect vested rights. In that case Marshall enlarged the idea of contract by declaring that public contracts, those to which a state is a party, were as much within the limitations of the contract clause as private contracts. He failed to base the decision on a specific constitutional provision, ruling that state interference with a grant was voided "either by general principles [natural law] . . . or by the particular provisions of the Constitution."[4] There was no such subtle or ambiguous blend of natural law and constitutional provisions in *Dartmouth College*. Charters of incorporation, Marshall declared in unequivocal terms in 1819, were contracts, "the obligation of which cannot be impaired, without violating the constitution of the United States."[5]

Corporations were important to the decision not as the principal beneficiaries but as the species of private property that epitomized the wedding of individual rights and public welfare. *Fletcher* v. *Peck,* as even the New Hampshire court admitted in 1817, left little room to doubt that charters of incorporation were contracts. There was no need to establish that and there was no pressing need to single out business corporations from other types. Marshall's definition of a corporation as "an artificial being, invisible, intangible, and existing only in contemplation of law" applied to all.[6] Moreover, it highlighted the close relation between state and corporation

—the fact that this association of individuals owed its existence to the state and had to organize and conduct itself as the state required. Marshall realized that every corporation of the period, whether bank, turnpike, or college, was tinged with a public interest. Preambles to corporate charters suggested that a claim to public usefulness was important, and there was a contemporary belief that the corporate form should not be resorted to unless the public interest were involved.[7] So, when he said that the objects of incorporation were "universally such as the government wishes to promote," he was expressing his belief that the goals of the community were essentially the same as those of the individual and his concern that the New Hampshire court's use of the objects of incorporation as a standard for determining justifiable legislative meddling could affect all corporations and impede progress. In overturning that standard and ruling that the charter of Dartmouth College, in which the state had a considerable interest, was private property, Marshall was saying that a public interest in the objects, the uses, of private property was insufficient ground for state interference.[8] Protection of private vested rights would better serve the public interest.

The consequences of the decision in 1819 were for the moment confined to the College. Dartmouth University, never more than embryonic, collapsed. President Allen became president of Bowdoin College, where he got involved in a strikingly similar controversy and successfully invoked the *Dartmouth College* decision for redress.[9] President Brown, whose feeble health had been weakened by his exertions during the controversy, died in July 1820.[10] The College, saved from the reorganization embodied in the legislation of 1816, continued to suffer from financial difficulties incurred during the litigation.[11]

There was little notice of the decision in the public press outside New England, but this scant notoriety indicated contemporary appreciation of Marshall's purpose.[12] Although newspapers reflected indignation at the blow to state power, they never mentioned the decision's effect on business corporations. Even as a restriction on state power, the other two landmark cases of 1819, *McCulloch* v. *Maryland* and *Sturges* v. *Crowinshield,* overshadowed *Dartmouth College* v. *Woodward.*[13] The obscurity was doubtless due to the insignificance of colleges and business corporations in 1819, at least in comparison with the Bank of the United States and bankruptcy legislation.[14]

Some of the principals in the case did realize its importance. Early in the controversy the College had decided to publish a report of the conflict to attract public moral and financial support. Work on the project did not proceed in earnest until after the decision in 1819, and Farrar and Webster assumed major responsibility.[15] Story also assisted in the preparation; and when the book appeared in August 1819, he asked Kent to review the work in hope that the Chancellor might impress upon the public "the vital importance to the well being of society, and the security of private rights, of the principles on which that decision rested." Story was confident those principles would "apply with an extensive reach to all the great concerns of the people, and will check any undue encroachments upon civil rights, which the passions or the popular doctrines of the day may stimulate our State Legislatures to adopt."[16] Kent declined, but in his *Commentaries* concluded that the decision was the most important step in securing all rights and franchises derived from a government grant and in making solid and inviolable the "literary, charitable, religious and commercial institutions of our country."[17]

The emphasis on the importance of *Dartmouth College* to business corporations has obscured its impact on higher education.[18] Before 1819 the most practical way to introduce a measure of public responsibility into colleges had been for states to bring existing colleges under some sort of government control, either by exercising visitatorial rights or by amending college charters. The increasing probability of state interference was of considerable concern to the denominational colleges, and the *College* decision provided some assurance of immunity. After 1819, if a state wanted to control institutions such as colleges, it would have to found them. There was no middle ground. The *College* case, then, suggested the alternative of state colleges. It is impossible to determine the extent to which the decision contributed to the growth of state colleges. It might, though, have actually retarded educational development in the United States by providing a legal base for the proliferation of small private and denominational colleges which characterized mid-nineteenth-century America.[19] After state colleges developed, the decision raised the question whether these institutions were even corporations, and if so, of what species. In some cases they were held to be private corporations; in a few instances they were regarded as non-corporate departments of state government. Most of the time they were regarded as strictly public corporations.[20] Finally, in defending the Trustees, faculty, and students against legislative encroachment, the Supreme Court was unwittingly erecting a symbol of academic freedom.[21]

The *Dartmouth College* decision did not, as critics have charged, rob the states of all regulatory power over corporations.[22] It established some restriction on state power with its rulings that certain powers must be granted a corporation to enable it to function and that a donor has the right to prescribe the uses of his charity. Beyond these, the state was free to set whatever limits it deemed appropriate. Neither state nor federal courts had the power to grant corporate charters. The granting of rights and privileges which constituted a corporate franchise was entirely a legislative prerogative. Dicta in the *College* case stressed this, declaring that if the legislature meant to amend corporate charters so as to control or restrict corporate power, it would have to reserve the authority in the charter grant.[23]

The Court in *Dartmouth College* was simply reminding the legislature that the wisdom of grants was not a matter for judicial determination. This was no innovation. State courts had ruled similarly as early as 1806, and legislative practice in reserving powers dated back to 1784.[24] Beginning with a New York statute in 1827, it became common practice to insert reservation clauses in general statutes or in state constitutions and so make them applicable to corporations generally.[25] Improvident legislative grants, not the *Dartmouth College* rule, robbed states of regulatory power.

The first important modification of the *Dartmouth College* doctrine came also in 1827 when the Court in *Ogden* v. *Saunders* decided that state laws in existence at the time a contract was entered into became part of the obligation of contract.[26] This decision is generally understood as the turning point in Marshall's contract clause decisions because it undermined the logic of his position that the obligation flowed from natural instead of positive law. It was also pivotal for the *Dartmouth College* doctrine since the Court, by extension, was also saying that reservation clauses in state constitutions and general statutes became part of the contract and that subsequent exercise of that power would not impair the contract obligation.[27] Reserved powers became part of constitutional law.

After 1827 the Marshall Court took additional steps toward modifying the implications of the *Dartmouth College* rule. The most significant was *Providence Bank* v. *Billings* (1830).[28] The Bank was chartered in 1791, and in 1822 the Rhode Island legislature enacted a general tax on banks. Arguing that the Bank's charter implied an exemption from taxation, counsel for the Bank pleaded an impairment of contract. Marshall had said in *McCulloch* that the power to tax involved the power to destroy, and the Bank's counsel argued from this that if the federal supremacy clause had deprived Maryland of the power to destroy the Bank of the United States, the contract clause, as interpreted in *Dartmouth College* v. *Woodward,* should deprive Rhode Island of the power to destroy the Providence Bank.[29]

Marshall considered the taxing power vital to government and said the relinquishment of such a power could never be assumed. He could not say, without overruling *New Jersey* v. *Wilson,* that the power could not be relinquished. But "as the whole community is interested in retaining it undiminished; that community has a right to insist that its abandonment ought not to be presumed, in a case in which the deliberate purpose of the state to abandon it does not appear."[30] The state, Marshall said, granted charters of incorporation to confer the characteristics of individuals on collective bodies. Except for the stipulations in their charters, corporations were the same as individuals. They were members of the body politic, and legislative power, including taxation, operated on all members of that body. The individual's right was never so absolute that it exempted him from sharing the public burdens—a share for the legislature to determine. The corporate individual possessed only those privileges conferred by its charter. Marshall found no "express contract" for tax exemption in the Bank's charter and ruled that the state's tax law did not impair the contract's obligations.[31]

This was an important decision because, without discussion, Marshall was applying the *Dartmouth College* doctrine to business corporations, although not until *Planters' Bank* v. *Sharp* (1848) did the Court strike down a statute as an unconstitutional impairment of the contract in a commercial charter.[32]

Moreover, the Chief Justice was announcing that, at least in some regards, corporate charters must be strictly construed in favor of the state. He admitted a state's right to contract away part of its sovereign power by "express grant," but he left the states free to determine what portion, if any, they would dispose of. Corporate rights were not to be extended beyond the obvious meaning of their charters. With the legislatures thus free from any implied expansion of corporate power, it is difficult to blame the *Dartmouth College* rule for the failures of public policy that led to widespread abuse of corporate immunity in the late nineteenth century. Not even Marshall was willing to see corporate power larger than state power.

2

Corporate vested rights presented more difficult problems to the Taney Court than to Marshall, not only because of the more complex character of corporate enterprise but because the Court's personnel reflected the individualism and economic and political egalitarianism of the Jacksonian era. Like his colleagues Taney was not an implacable foe of corporations, only of monopoly and special privilege. His concern for the security of private property and his disdain for state legislative interference with what he viewed as legitimate property rights led him to accept the philosophy underlying Marshall's interpretation of the contract clause, although an equally strong concern for state's rights caused him to restrict that interpretation on occasion. From 1837 to 1863 the number of contract cases increased rapidly and the proportion of cases in which state legislation was invalidated remained the same as in the Marshall period.[33] This extended use of the contract clause manifested increasing state concern about corporations and the Jacksonian imperative to enlarge individual rights, in this case property rights. The Taney modifications of the *Dartmouth College* rule also indicated these concerns.

The Taney Court had to allow the state authority to cope with changing economic conditions, such as the building of railroads parallel to old canals. At the same time, it had to preserve precedents with which it was in essential agreement. This could only be accomplished in contract cases by denying the validity of the contract—declaring that the state was not free to contract away certain sovereign powers. In some cases, like those involving eminent domain, this strategy succeeded because there were no Marshall precedents. In others, notably the taxing-power cases, there were irksome precedents. Where it was impossible to deny the contract, the Taney Court relied upon strict interpretation of corporate charters in favor of the state.

The classic statement of this dilemma facing the Taney Court was strikingly similar to Marshall's *Providence Bank* decision. In *Charles River Bridge* v. *Warren Bridge* (1837)[34] Taney relied on strict construction in ruling that a charter to build and operate a toll bridge did not imply an exclusive grant which would prevent the erection of another bridge nearby. The words of the charter did not convey an exclusive right, and the Court would not infer such a right. The growing economy of the United States, he maintained, daily demanded "new channels of communication." If the country were not to be shackled to improvements of the last century for the benefit of old canals and turnpikes, public grants must be strictly construed. Nothing should pass by implication and any ambiguities should be interpreted in favor of the state. "While the rights of private property are sacredly guarded," the Chief Justice said, "we must not forget that the community also have rights, and that the happiness and well being of every citizen depends on their faithful preservation."[35] Despite heavy criticism from old vested-rights stalwarts, the decision was not a blow to the doctrine of vested rights. Quite the contrary, it manifested concern for the rights of the new group of private investors which an implied monopoly would have restricted. There were few cases during the Taney period applying the *Charles River Bridge* rule.[36] One of these, decided in his last term, carried the rule further by holding that even express grants of monopolies would not be interpreted as granting anything by implication.[37]

For its effect on the *Dartmouth College* doctrine, counsel's discussion of eminent domain—a subject Marshall's contract cases did not mention—in the *Charles River Bridge* case was more important.[38] Marshall had been unwilling to admit the inalienability of some state powers. He did say the contract clause was never intended to restrain the states in regulation of their internal affairs or to embrace contracts other than those respecting property rights.[39] But, for Marshall, regulation of internal affairs meant civil institutions adopted for internal government, and a grant to such an institution was a grant of political power such as that found in charters to municipal corporations. He saw no reason to infer that, because a contract involved an exemption from some state power, it was concerned with political power, not property rights.[40] The most he would say was that the grant of state powers should not be assumed.

Counsel for Warren Bridge argued that eminent domain could not be bargained away. Webster, for the Charles River Bridge, maintained that when the national contract clause and the state's power of eminent domain conflicted, the contract clause would be superior. Taney did not see fit to rule on the question, and postponed any judicial pronouncement on the subject to 1848. In *West River Bridge* v. *Dix* (1848) a near unanimous Court held that all contracts were subject to the power of eminent domain.[41] Even so, the Court upheld the *Dartmouth College* precedent. It did not deny the contract, but asserted that into all contracts "there enter conditions which arise out of the literal terms of the contract itself; they are superinduced by the preexisting and higher authority of the laws of nature, of nations, or of the community." Every contract is made subordinate to them. The exercise of those conditions "does not impair the contract . . . but recognizes its obligation to the fullest extent, claiming only the fulfilment of an essential and inseparable condition."[42] The Court was still using Marshall's equation of individual and corporate rights within society. This precedent has stood unchallenged ever since.[43]

Probably the most perplexing problem for the Taney Court's application of the *Dartmouth College* decision was the taxing power. Logically, if eminent domain were inalienable, the taxing power should have been also. But there were troubling Marshall precedents. In *New Jersey* v. *Wilson* (1812) the Court had sustained an express tax exemption under the contract clause. The *Dartmouth College* case made this precedent applicable to corporations, which proved to be the principal beneficiaries. Finally, *Providence Bank,* though emphasizing the necessity of the taxing power, upheld the state's right to bargain it away.[44] The Taney Court refused to abandon these precedents. The question of the inalienability of the taxing power first came up in *Piqua Bank* v. *Knoop* (1853).[45] In

striking down a state tax as an impairment of the charter
obligation Justice McLean ruled that the question of taxes
and tax exemptions was one of state policy and not state
power. If the state chose to grant a tax exemption, it was exercising and not surrendering its sovereignty. The same rule
applied through the century, though not without vigorous
dissents.[46] Justice Miller's dissent in *Washington University*
v. *Rouse* (1869)[47] argued that no legislature had the right
to alienate its taxing power any more than eminent domain
and reprimanded the Court for being "slow to perceive that
what were claimed to be contracts were not so, by reason
of the want of authority in those who profess to bind
others."[48] But Miller was too harsh, for the Court still ad-
hered to strict construction and held that tax exemptions
had to be clear.[49]

3

The post-Civil War years witnessed the gradual decline of the
contract clause and the *Dartmouth College* doctrine. Prior to
1865 the Court completed the doctrinal expansion of the contract clause and modified the *Dartmouth College* doctrine.[50]
State legislatures began to regret their liberal grants to corporations and to seek methods of avoiding the implications of
that doctrine. From 1888 to 1910, under Chief Justice Melville W. Fuller, the contract clause declined and was replaced
by the more comprehensive protection for vested rights found
in the due process clause of the Fourteenth Amendment. The
most interesting and important modification of the *Dartmouth
College* doctrine came in these years with the doctrine of the
inalienability of the police power—the state's power to provide for the protection of the lives, health, and property of
citizens, and the preservation of good order and morals.[51]

In this era the Vermont supreme court provided a precedent on the police power which the Court at Washington often
cited with approval.[52] In *Thorpe* v. *Rutland & Burlington R.R.
Co.* (1854)[53] Judge Isaac Redfield admitted that there would
be no question of such power were it reserved in a charter or
the general laws of the state. What if the legislature exercised
this power without reservation and after the date of the charter? Citing *Dartmouth College* with approval, Redfield noted
that Marshall's statement that the charter privileges which

could not be abrogated were those expressly conferred by the charter or incidental to the charter's existence did not settle the question. He referred to the *Providence Bank* decision and the rule that the corporation, like the individual, must share the public burden, and Taney's *Charles River Bridge* declaration of the need to protect the rights of the community. These precedents, he felt, justified his decision that the state police power was sufficient for regulation of corporations, so far as necessary to prevent injury to persons or property, without regard to charter provisions.[54]

The Supreme Court took an important step toward using the police power to regulate corporations in *Munn* v. *Illinois* (1877).[55] Like Taney, Chief Justice Waite faced the problem of reconciling the community's need to cope with changing economic conditions and precedents upholding vested rights. His solution was the rule that when private property is "affected with a public interest," it is subject to public regulation. This "public interest" doctrine repudiated the *Dartmouth College* decision. Although Waite had expressed adherence to that precedent and insisted that the two doctrines were compatible, the "public interest" doctrine abandoned Marshall's rule that the origin of the corporation determined its character and adopted Richardson's rule concerning the objects of incorporation.[56] Waite was occupying the middle ground that Marshall in 1819 would not admit. He created a new class of corporations, the quasi-public corporation whose franchise and property were private but whose business was "affected with a public interest" and subject to regulation. Most corporations receiving public franchises were of this character. With legislative regulation possible in the public interest, the implication of *Munn* was application of the police power to the many important beneficiaries of the *Dartmouth College* decision. Within three years the Court had applied the police power to uphold state regulation of corporations.

The leading case here is *Stone* v. *Mississippi* (1880).[57] There were other cases between 1877 and 1880, but *Stone* was the first where the police power was the only ground for sustaining the state statute.[58] In 1867 Mississippi had chartered a lottery company. In a revised constitution, the state then prohibited the lottery business and passed an act subjecting that business to prosecution. The lottery protested that the statute impaired the obligation of contract. Waite began his opinion with a statement on *Dartmouth College*. It was too late, he said, to contend that a charter was not a contract. That doctrine announced by the court more than sixty years ago had "become so imbedded in the jurisprudence of the United States as to make it to all intents and purposes a part of the constitution itself."[59] He maintained that instead of protecting the corporate charter, the Constitution protected only contracts contained within the charter. No one, he said, could doubt that a charter existed. The existence of a contract, however, depended upon the authority of the legislature to bargain away the subject of the grant. Property rights were valid and proper subjects of contract; government rights were not. Pointing to Marshall's *Dartmouth College* declaration that the contract clause was not intended to restrain the states in the regulation of their internal affairs, Waite contended that no legislature was free to bargain away public health and morals. He admitted the police power lacked definition, but asserted that it extended to matters affecting public health and morals. Consequently, when a corporate charter was granted subject to this power, there was no contract, only a suspension of government rights which was subject to withdrawal at will.[60]

These decisions on eminent domain, police power, and taxation affirmed the Court's adherence to the *Dartmouth College* doctrine, while they reserved to the Court the power to determine in every case the nature of the corporation and the validity of the legislation. There was little apparent difference between the property rights inherent in a college and those in a brewery and as much alienation of state power in a tax exemption as in a license to conduct a lottery. Yet these inconsistencies only demonstrated the magnitude of the problem facing the Supreme Court in reconciling private rights and public welfare, not to mention the judicial dilemmas produced by adherence to precedents in the face of a drastically changed environment.

Many viewed these modifications, especially the Granger cases and the police power, as taking the life out of the doctrine of vested rights as embodied in the *Dartmouth College* decision. It seemed that the protection given corporations had been removed and that it would be a rare case in which a decision could be obtained voiding any conceivable legislative interference. As one critic phrased it: "this historic cause has been embalmed in spices, and laid carefully away upon a shelf, like the corpse of an Egyptian king."[61]

While there was some truth in these assertions, the Court had by no means abandoned either corporations or vested rights. Accompanying this mummification of the *Dartmouth College* doctrine was gradual application of the due process clause of the Fourteenth Amendment to corporate vested rights. An important move in this direction was the 1886 decision that corporations were persons within the meaning of that clause—a decision facilitated by the long-standing equation of individual and corporate property rights initiated in *Dartmouth College*.[62] Not long after, the Court invalidated state regulatory measures on due process grounds.[63] Often in these due process cases the *Dartmouth College* decision continued to exert influence through a corollary that the charter of a private or quasi-public corporation implied a contract by the state to allow the corporation to enjoy the reasonable exercise of its franchise. In *Smyth* v. *Ames* (1898) this corollary was one of the grounds on which the Court struck down a state statute regulating freight rates. When a railroad had been incorporated and had built its road in a proper manner and at reasonable cost, the Court said, the state violated the implied contract if it regulated rates to the point of denying the corporation a reasonable return on its investment.[64] More important for the decision was the Court's declaration that such regulation deprived the corporation of property without due process.

While *Smyth* v. *Ames* left no doubt that a corporation could not be deprived of its property without due process of law—the position of both Mason and Webster before the Superior Court in 1817—the police power continued to whittle away at the *College* doctrine as protection for public grants. In *Home Building and Loan Association* v. *Blaisdell* (1934) the Court used the police power to sustain the 1933 Minnesota Mortgage Moratorium Law, a temporary and conditional interference with contracts to offset the effects of the Great Depression, and sounded the knell for the application of the contract clause and due process as protection for corporations.[65] Chief Justice Charles Evans Hughes justified the statute as an exercise of the reserved police power of the state. All contracts, he said, are subject to the future exercise of the state's regulatory power. "The policy of protecting contracts against impairment presupposes the maintenance of a government by virtue of which contractual obligations are worth while,—a government which retains adequate authority to se-

cure the peace and good order of society."[66] The state was
not free to destroy the obligations of contract, but in times
of severe economic distress it could employ the police power
to prevent the immediate and literal enforcement of that obligation. In short, the remedy could certainly be modified as
the national wisdom directed without impairing the obligation.[67]

Ironically, this decision upheld a statute of the sort the
framers of the contract clause had intended to prohibit, and
did so in a case involving not a contract to which a state was
a party but one between private individuals. The idea of the
police power, which it had used, had developed after 1787
in large measure as a response to Marshall's expansion of the
contract clause to embrace public contracts. Yet the reasons
for the *Blaisdell* decision were substantially the same as those
guiding the framers in 1787, Marshall from 1810 to 1819, and
later Courts. The history of the Court's contract decisions,
Hughes said, demonstrated a "growing appreciation of public
needs and of the necessity of finding ground for a rational
compromise between individual rights and public welfare."
The question was "no longer merely that of one party to a
contract as against another, but of the use of reasonable
means to safeguard the economic structure upon which the
good of all depends."[68] John Marshall could have made that
statement.

Few Supreme Court decisions have had more influence
through American history than *Dartmouth College* v. *Woodward,* and it deserves serious consideration on at least that
ground. Originating in a small college president's forlorn venture into local politics in 1815, the case enhanced the reputation of the Marshall Court, restricted the power of the states,
confirmed the rights of private colleges and the academic
freedom of their faculties, and provided the leading precedent regulating the scope of legislative power over corporations through the nineteenth century. Its principal importance lay more in its relation to private property than to corporations. Other decisions have equal claim to stimulating
the growth of corporate enterprise.[69] Marshall's equation of
individual and corporate rights not only shifted the doctrine
of vested rights from the vague ground of natural law, but it
enabled later Courts to modify the *College* doctrine and to
provide the more comprehensive protection of the due process
clause of the Fourteenth Amendment.

The constitutional safeguards for vested rights provided by the *Dartmouth College* doctrine and the Fourteenth Amendment grew less important as widespread abuse of corporate privilege at the turn of the twentieth century caused belief in the sanctity of private property to give way to increased demands for government regulation. So the *Dartmouth College* case, though never overruled, has been tucked away. Yet the concern for the protection of individual rights, which the Marshall Court expressed in the *Dartmouth College* case, continues. The concern has shifted from individual rights of property to individual rights of free speech and other personal freedoms, but the emphasis is the same. That much of the *College* case still operates in the American constitutional system.

Notes

Notes for Chapter One

1. David McClure and Elijah Parish, *Memoirs of the Reverend Eleazar Wheelock* (Newburyport, 1811), 18. This is the only biography of Wheelock. For additional information see William Allen, "Eleazar Wheelock, D.D.," William Sprague, ed., *Annals of the American Pulpit*, 9 vols. (New York, 1857), 1:397; Frederick Chase, *A History of Dartmouth College and the Town of Hanover, N.H. to 1815*, 2nd ed. (Brattleboro, 1928); Leon Burr Richardson, *History of Dartmouth College*, 2 vols. (Hanover, 1933), 1.

2. "More" was the donor's spelling. The variant used later was "Moor."

3. Chase, *Dartmouth College*, 10, says the land was purchased from Moses Barrett, "late schoolmaster in Lebanon"; and since Moses Barrett was the first master of the new school, "we are led to conjecture that Wheelock's school was . . . consolidated with a pre-existing school of the Barretts."

4. A copy of the deed dated July 17, 1755 is in the Dartmouth College Archives (hereafter cited as DCA), 755417.1; for Wheelock's concern about legal status, see William Smith, Sr. to Eleazar Wheelock, Aug. 6, 1755, DCA, 755456.

5. Wheelock resurrected More's name in 1770 as an expedient, but he never referred to Moor's School after 1756. In a letter to an English patron, Denis DeBerdt, July 22, 1758, DCA, 758422, Wheelock mentioned More's death and added "that the school may bear any name which may be thought proper; perhaps *The Indian Charity School in America.*" Those familiar with the undertaking always referred to it as Wheelock's School, John Smith to Wheelock, May 18, 1764, DCA, 764318.2.

6. Elmer Ellsworth Brown, "The Origin of American State Universities," *University of California Publications in Education*, 3 (1903), 1-45; Richard Hofstadter and Walter P. Metzger, *The Development of Academic Freedom in the United States* (New York, 1955), 120-51.

7. Wheelock to William Smith, Jr., April 20, 1767, DCA, 767270. For his efforts with the Connecticut Assembly and in England see Richardson, *Dartmouth College*, 1:34-35.

8. "A Proposal for Introducing Religion, Learning, Agriculture, and Manufacturing among the Pagans in America," July 27, 1763, cited in Chase, *Dartmouth College*, 32-33. Included in this proposal was an elaborate plan for removal to the Indian country. Wheelock sent the plan to England in hope of obtaining a charter and the necessary land grant.

9. See Wheelock to Hon. Hugh Wallace, Sept. 30, 1769, DCA, 769530.1 for the problems created by Yale's proximity.

10. McClure, *Memoirs of Wheelock*, 47.

11. An interesting account of this expedition is in Leon Burr Richardson, *An Indian Preacher in England* (Hanover, 1933); see also Richardson, *Dartmouth College*, 1:49-67.

12. William Legge, Second Earl of Dartmouth, was a torchbearer of the Great Awakening in England. It was his influence which secured a grant of two hundred pounds from the King. The money collected in Scotland was placed in a separate Scotch Trust.

13. To reinforce his movement at home and abroad, Wheelock outlined the history and purpose of the school in *A Plain and faithful Narrative of the Original Design, Rise, Progress, and present State of the Indian Charity School at Lebanon, in Connecticut* (Boston, 1763). The pamphlet succeeded in eliciting suggestions and offers of both sites for the school and money as an inducement to settle. In 1763 Governor Benning Wentworth offered a 500 acre tract in New Hampshire, and in 1765 the inhabitants of Lebanon raised 567 pounds to keep the school in Lebanon. There were numerous other offers. The first *Narrative*'s success led to later editions in 1765, 1766, 1767, 1769, containing a list of the subscribers to the English fund, 1771, 1772, 1773, and 1775. Together these furnish a complete history of the school and its missionary activities.

14. Wentworth made these promises to Occom and Whitaker in England and, after an inquiry by Wheelock in late 1767, promptly reasserted his willingness to fulfill them. Lawrence Shaw Mayo, *John Wentworth, Governor of New Hampshire, 1767-1775* (Cambridge, Mass., 1921), 106; Wheelock to Wentworth, Dec. 28, 1767, DCA, 767678.3. Wheelock's draft charter was sent to Wentworth Aug. 22, 1769, DCA, 769472.2.

15. The charter was dated Dec. 13, 1769, DCA, 769663.1. A copy of the charter is in 4 Wheaton 519-37.

16. The charter of 1769 took notice of the English trust by providing that "it shall be the duty of the President . . . to transmit to the Right Honorable and Worthy Gentlemen of the Trust in England . . . a faithful account of the improvements and disbursements of the several Sums he shall receive from the Donations and bequests made in England through the hands of said Trustees . . . so long as they shall perpetuate their Board of Trust."

17. Other than the English fund, the College's resources were almost exclusively in undeveloped land. Governor Wentworth made good his pledge by granting the township of Landaff some 25,000 acres. Ex-Governor Benning Wentworth granted 500 acres in Hanover which he had promised. Approximately 20,000 acres remained of the original endowment and this came from private benefactors. The Governor had assured Wheelock of assistance from the Assembly, but aside from a grant of sixty pounds in 1773, that body was unresponsive—despite repeated memorials by the Governor. Chase, *Dartmouth College*, 272-77.

18. The Minutes of the Trustees of Dartmouth College, DCA, make no mention of this resolve, but Wheelock does in his 1771 *Narrative*. This *Narrative* aimed principally toward the easing of tension in England. See also McClure, *Memoirs of Wheelock*, 65.

19. For the tortuous correspondence with the English trustees over incorporation see Wheelock to Lord Dartmouth, March 12, 1770, DCA, 770212.2; Robert Keen to Wheelock, July 30, 1770, DCA, 770430; John Thornton to Wheelock, Aug. 30, 1770, DCA, 770480; David McClure to Wheelock, May 21, 1770, DCA, 770321. The difficulty was not resolved by simply informing the English trust of the 1770 proceedings. Even after reconciliation, relations between Wheelock and the Trust remained strained. English Trust to Wheelock, April 25, 1771, DCA, 771275.

20. Notice to the Lebanon subscribers, Aug. 23, 1770, cited in Chase, *Dartmouth College*, 155.

21. McClure, *Memoirs of Wheelock*, 117.

22. Hofstadter, *Academic Freedom*, 125.

23. A copy of Wheelock's will is in Chase, *Dartmouth College*, 561-62. There is scant biographical information on John Wheelock. See S. C. Bartlett, "Dr. John Wheelock," *Proceedings of the New Hampshire Historical Society* (1895), 2, 408-26.

24. Frederick Hall to Nathaniel Shattuck, April 28, 1804, DCA, 804278.

25. Even those who applauded his hard work and sound judgment felt compelled to refer to less admirable qualities. "Piety and Learning raise him above the common level of man, but by penury and parsimony, he is degraded below the dignity of human nature. His covetiousness [sic] is notorious. . . . His appearance in public is scandalous, his clothes are unfit for a man of his standing, and would even do dishonor to the character of a beggar." John Sage to [no addressee], March 20, 1808, DCA, 808220.

26. Minutes of the Trustees of Dartmouth College, DCA. Wheelock did not actually serve during 1779-80. There was a minor controversy over the succession despite his father's will, and it appears that the Trustees finally chose John Wheelock because, in the state of the College finances, he was less likely to find a conflict of interests between Wheelock and College assets.

27. "An Act for Laying Out a Public Road or Highway to Dartmouth College," Nov. 11, 1784, *Laws of New Hampshire*, 5:34; and subsequent statutes, Feb. 13, 1786, *ibid.*, 107; Jan. 6, 1787, *ibid.*, 215-16; "An Act for Granting Liberty to Set Up and Carry On a Lottery to Raise Money for the Purpose of Erecting an Edifice in the Township of Hanover for the Use and Benefit of Dartmouth College," Nov. 3, 1784, *ibid.*, 20-21; and subsequent statutes, Jan. 12, 1787, *ibid.*, 226-27; Sept. 28, 1787, *ibid.*, 283-84.

28. In 1785 the College petitioned for lands formerly assigned to an English missionary society; it was denied. In 1789 the College sought an annuity of two hundred pounds; denied. The state refused a $600 loan in 1791 and similar requests in 1792, 1793, and 1795, the latter despite an elaborate memorial calling attention to the state's interest in the institution. "Memorial of the Trustees of Dartmouth College to the Legislature of New-Hampshire, December, 1795," (Manuscript Division, New York Public Library). The circumstances surrounding a 1790 grant of 361 pounds do not permit it to qualify as state support. A private individual donated 175 pounds for scientific apparatus in 1772. This donation was placed in the hands of Governor Wentworth and had not been paid. The state's 1790 grant was taken from the Governor's sequestered estate and covered no more than the original private donation plus interest.

29. This included the establishment of a public grammar school in 1780, which the College supported for over two years. Minutes of the Trustees of Dartmouth College, DCA.

30. The eastern portion of the state dominated the legislature and re-

sented the less prosperous Connecticut Valley region, especially after a long imbroglio with Vermont in which the College figured prominently. Chase, *Dartmouth College*, 434-527.

31. "An Act for a Grant of Land Equal to Eight Miles Square in the Northwest and Unlocated Territory within this State to the Trustees of Dartmouth College," Feb. 5, 1789, *Laws of New Hampshire*, 5:396-97; and subsequent statutes, Jan. 13, 1790, *ibid.*, 506; Dec. 20, 1792, *ibid.*, 6:96. An Act declaring that "It will be for the honour and Interest of the State to make a grant to that Seminary of some of the unlocated lands belonging to this State"—some 24,000 acres adjoining the 1789 grant—failed to pass Dec. 24, 1795, *Laws of New Hampshire*, 6:304. See also Wheelock to McClure, Feb. 9, 1793, DCA, 793159. The Trustees formally relinquished all claim to Landaff on Aug. 23, 1791, *ibid.*, 791473.1. Chase, *Dartmouth College*, 600-11, contains a thorough discussion of this dispute.

32. The state granted another lottery Dec. 31, 1795, *Laws of New Hampshire*, 6:294. In 1805 the legislature voted $900 on a petition from Wheelock, Memorial of John Wheelock to the General Court of New Hampshire and a certified copy of the vote, June 5, 1805, DCA, 805355. There was no action on additional proposals in 1806, but in June 1807 the state granted another tract of land. "An Act Granting a Certain Quantity of Land to Dartmouth College," June 18, 1807, *Laws of N.H.*, 7:601-02; DCA, 807368, 807368.1, 807590. On June 23, 1809 the state granted $3,450 for a medical school building, *Laws of N.H.*, 7:813-14; DCA, 809372.2. Additional resolutions in 1787 and 1804 asking committees to investigate the College management, at the Trustees' expense, came to nothing, *Laws of N.H.*, 5:272; DCA, 804624.

33. Chase, *Dartmouth College*, 577. The rationale for this request was that the society no longer existed; that its lands lay contiguous to the College; and that both the society and the College aimed at educating charity scholars in New Hampshire. Wheelock proposed that the state should forever elect and appoint the objects of the charity and that the recipients should be considered indebted to the state for their education. By its failure to act, the state passed up an opportunity to make inroads into the administration of the College.

34. Copies of the charter are in DCA, 785364, 785364.1.

35. The Scotch trust shared the views of the English trust on incorporation and had been unwilling to allow the elder Wheelock to draw on its funds. To reassure them and gain the funds, John Wheelock adopted his father's 1770 strategy. On May 7, 1789 the College trustees formally resolved that they had never used any of the money collected for Indian education for the benefit of the College, DCA, 789307.1. The bulk of John Wheelock's correspondence in the College Archives concerns this fund.

36. The Trustees were willing but sought to secure the arrangement through legislative action explaining the College charter in such a manner as to specify their responsibilities to the School. Wheelock demurred until a renewal of the old charges about the township of Wheelock forced a change of heart. Chase, *Dartmouth College*, 619-20; Whee-

lock to McClure, Aug. 12, 1802, Aug. 30, 1803, Jan. 15, 1805, DCA, 802462, 803480, 805115.

37. Wheelock and Stephen Jacob attended this session with a statement of facts on the history of the School. See Vote of the College Trustees empowering Wheelock and Jacob to attend any business concerning College lands in Vermont, Aug. 1805, DCA, 805490; other pertinent information is in *ibid.*, 806502 and 806528. Wheelock and Jacob presented an elaborate memorial to the Vermont legislature on Nov. 7, 1806, DCA, 806611.

38. A copy of the legislature's compromise offer is in *ibid.*, 806610; Wheelock's refusal of the following day, DCA, 806611.

39. "An Act More Effectually to Define and Improve the Charitable Establishment Known by the Name of the President of Moor's Charity School and the Powers and Duties of the President Thereof and to Constitute a Board to Assist in Directing the Expenditures of the Funds of Said School," June 10, 1807, *Laws of N.H.*, 7:556-57; and a subsequent act Dec. 21, 1808, *ibid.*, 736; DCA, 808671. Documents relative to the first act are in *ibid.*, 807360.5, 807360.6, 807360.8, 807360.10, 807360.11.

40. Wheelock to McClure, Dec. 12, 1808, DCA, 808662; Vermont had brought suit to revoke the grant after Wheelock's refusal to compromise. A certified copy of the act directing the suit, Nov. 10, 1807, is in DCA, 807900.4; on Oct. 10, 1808, Wheelock asked that the suit be brought in the U.S. Circuit Court, DCA, 808560; Vermont investigated and confirmed the grant, DCA, 808569, 808578, and after another Wheelock memorial on Nov. 2, 1808, DCA, 808602, passed an act cancelling the suit, Nov. 21, 1808, DCA, 808621. See also Wheelock to Stephen Jacob, Nov. 21, 1808, DCA, 808621.1 and Wheelock to Jedidiah Morse, Nov. 21, 1808, DCA, 808621.2.

41. A brief biographical sketch of Jacob is in John King Lord, *A History of Dartmouth College, 1818-1909* (Cambridge, 1913), 62-63.

42. Chase, *Dartmouth College*, 590; for biographical information see Lord, *Dartmouth College*, 63; John M. Shirley, *The Dartmouth College Causes and the Supreme Court of the United States* (St. Louis, 1879), 82-83; David McWilliams Ludlum, *Social Ferment in Vermont* (New York, 1939), 145.

43. A record of Niles's appointment is in DCA, 793478; for biographical information see Lord, *Dartmouth College*, 62; Shirley, *Dartmouth College Causes*, 82; Nathan N. Withington, "A Clergyman of Old," *New England Magazine* (1904-1905), N.S., 31, a reprint in the Niles Mss (Lilly Library, Indiana University, Bloomington).

44. Minutes of the Trustees of Dartmouth College, DCA.

45. Chase, *Dartmouth College*, 618; Minutes of the Trustees of Dartmouth College, DCA.

46. McFarland and especially Marsh later became strong opponents of the President. See Lord, *Dartmouth College*, 62-64; Shirley, *Dartmouth College Causes*, 83; Ludlum, *Social Ferment*, 67; and James Barrett, "Memorial Address on the Life and Character of the Hon. Charles Marsh LL.D," *Proceedings of the Vermont Historical Society* (Montpelier, 1871), 2:1-25, 32-41.

47. Parish to Wheelock, Oct. 18, 1810, April 29, 1811, DCA, 810568, 811279.

48. A thorough history of the church controversy is Benoni Dewey, James Wheelock, and Benjamin J. Gilbert, *A True and Concise Narrative of the Origin and Progress of the Church Difficulties in the Vicinity of Dartmouth College in Hanover. The same being the Origin of President Wheelock's Disaffection to the Trustees and Professors of the College, with documents relating thereto* (Hanover, 1815); see also Lord, *Dartmouth College*, 1-61; and the abundant material in the College Archives.

49. Dewey, *A True and Concise Narrative*, 4.

50. Minutes of the Trustees of Dartmouth College, DCA; this view was expressed by a student in 1804. "The President appears determined to have the government of the College under his controll [sic]. I fear this may injure the College." Samuel F. Dickinson to Tilton Eastman, Sept. 4, 1804, DCA, 804504.

51. Minutes of the Trustees of Dartmouth College, DCA; a draft of the resolution to relieve the President of his teaching duties is in DCA, 804611.2.

Notes for Chapter Two

1. David Hackett Fischer, *The Revolution of American Conservatism* (New York, 1965), 182-226; William A. Robinson, *Jeffersonian Democracy in New England* (New Haven, 1916), 95-127.

2. Robinson, *Jeffersonian Democracy*, 128-50; Charles B. Kinney, Jr., *Church & State: The Struggle for Separation in New Hampshire, 1630-1900* (New York, 1955), 90-108.

3. See above, Chapter One. This mixed motivation is evident in Parish's letter to Wheelock, Feb. 2, 1815, DCA, 815152. "You must not Judge of my *affections* by the *infrequency* of my letters. I *do* love you very much . . . I wish you would appoint me professor at some College, at Dartmouth, if you please; or President, (not of Dartmouth) of anything else . . . be assured that *no man* . . . would be happier in your company."

4. Wheelock to William Allen, Feb. 23, 1815, DCA, 815173.2.

5. *Ibid.*

6. [John Wheelock], *Sketches of the History of Dartmouth College and Moor's Charity School, with a Particular Account of Some Late Remarkable Proceedings of the Board of Trustees, From the Year 1779 to the Year 1815* ([Newburyport], [1815]).

7. [Elijah Parish], *A Candid, Analytical Review of the Sketches of the History of Dartmouth College and Moor's Charity School, with a Particular Account of Some Late Remarkable Proceedings of the Board of Trustees, From the Year 1779 to the Year 1815* ([Newburyport], [1815]).

8. Parish to Wheelock, March 7, 1815, DCA, 815207.

9. *Review*, 10.

10. Parish to Wheelock, March 7, 1815, DCA, 815207.

11. Parish to Wheelock, April 11, 1815, DCA, 815261.

12. Parish to Wheelock, May 15, 1815, DCA, 815304, 815313.

13. In his letter to Wheelock, April 26, 1815, DCA, 815276, Parish referred to an article in the Boston *Daily Advertiser*—an error attributable no doubt to his indignation. Thomas W. Thompson, in a letter to Ebeneezer Adams, July 13, 1815, DCA, 815413, refers to the article in the *Repertory*.

14. Cyrus Parker Bradley, *Biography of Isaac Hill of New Hampshire* (Concord, 1835).

15. Parish to Wheelock, May 15, 1815, DCA, 815315.

16. Parish to Wheelock, June 1, 1815, DCA, 815351.

17. *Patriot*, May 23, 1815. Having entered the fray, Hill devoted more than half his editorial material up to 1819 toward opposing the Trustees. He must have been unaware that Parish was Wheelock's accomplice, because, in reference to the *Repertory* article which listed Parish as a possible successor, Hill said that Parish's name could not be coupled with "anything but infamy and contempt."

18. *Patriot*, May 23, 1815.

19. Josiah Dunham to Wheelock, May 12, 1815, DCA, 815312.

20. Wheelock to McClure, June 16, 1815, DCA, 815366.

21. A copy of the memorial dated May 29, 1815 is in DCA, 815329; see also *Documents Relative to Dartmouth College* (Concord, 1816), published by order of the legislature. Wheelock accused the Trustees of misusing funds, overpaying professors, infringing on the President's prerogatives, and conspiring to subvert popular liberties.

22. *House Journal, June Session, 1815*, 29; *Senate Journal June Session, 1815*, 29.

23. *House Journal, June Session*, 1815, 134, 144-45; see also DCA, 815373, 815374. This action removed Wheelock's earlier doubts whether the legislature would act, and he rejoiced to his son-in-law, William Allen, July 1, 1815, DCA, 815401.2, "that there could not be better men found in New England" than those assigned to the investigating committee. For his earlier doubts see Wheelock to McClure, June 16, 1815, DCA, 815366.

24. Lord, Dartmouth College, 67-68.

25. Only Niles, of the Trustees present in Concord, favored the investigating committee. Marsh, in a letter to Francis Brown, April 13, 1816, DCA, 81623.1, said "that had it not been for him [Niles] no committee would have been appointed."

26. Thompson to Ebeneezer Adams, July 13, 1815, DCA, 815413. This letter, with its mention of Webster and its clear reference to putting down Wheelock, subsequently became the most infamous piece of correspondence in the entire controversy. Its seal was violated in the Hanover post office, and Josiah Dunham released its contents to the columns of the Boston *Repertory* in early September. Lord, *Dartmouth College*, 69. This use of the *Repertory* seems to confirm Thompson's suspicions about the earlier article. Hill used the letter repeatedly whenever he wished to blacken the Trustees. *Patriot*, Dec. 3, 1816, Feb. 16, April 27, June 22, 1819. Shirley, *Dartmouth College Causes*, 89-91, uses the letter to discredit Webster.

27. Unfortunately these papers discussed at length church affairs, college management, and personalities, and this discussion proved less ef-

fective than the *Patriot's* consistent attack on the Trustees as aristocratic bigots. Hill charged that the Trustees and their press were guilty of character assassination in their attempt to prove that "the father and patron of Dartmouth College is an *infidel* in league with the French Illuminati and with the Devil; and . . . the *Inquisition.*" *Patriot*, Aug. 1, 8, 1815. William G. North, "The Political Background of the Dartmouth College Case," *New England Quarterly*, 18 (June 1945), 194-96, provides thorough discussion of this newspaper duel.

28. Parish to Wheelock, July 21, 31, 1815, DCA, 815421, 815431.1. In a letter to Wheelock, Aug. 1, 1815, DCA, 815451, Josiah Dunham reported that Marsh was "raving mad" about the *Sketches*. See also Benjamin Hale to Joshua Hale, July 25, 1815, DCA, 815425, for a discussion of the increasing hostility between Wheelock and the Trustees. The *Patriot*, Aug. 8, 1815 announced that Niles's series would commence the following week. See *Patriot*, Aug. 15, 22, 29, 1815.

29. Judah Dana to Wheelock, Aug. 10, 1815, DCA, 815460.1. Dana believed that should any other doctrine prevail "vested charter rights & privileges, would become the sport of dominant parties & the reward of political victories." Ironically, this precise argument became the foundation of the Trustees' later position in the legal battles of 1817-1819. Equally ironic was Charles Marsh's assertion that the state had visitatorial power over corporations within its boundary. Jeremiah Mason to Charles Marsh, Aug. 15, 1815, DCA, 815465; Marsh to Mason, Sept. 1, 1815, DCA, 815501.1. This argument was later used by the state to justify its position.

30. Parish to Wheelock, July 31, 1815, DCA, 815431.1.

31. Wheelock requested Webster's assistance during the June session. Wheelock to William Allen, Aug. 11, 1815, DCA, 815461.

32. Wheelock to Webster, Aug. 5, 1815, DCA, 815455.1. Wheelock enclosed a twenty-dollar retainer with the promise of further remuneration.

33. Wheelock was not terribly upset by Webster's failure to appear. He wrote Peyton R. Freeman, Aug. 20, 1815, DCA, 815470, asking him to inquire into the matter. He feared the letter had been lost in the mail, "and my apprehension is increased, as $20—were enclosed. If Mr. Webster has received the letter, my mind will be relieved." Freeman replied that Webster had received the letter too late. Freeman to Wheelock, Sept. 11, 1815, *ibid.* It was after Webster's failure to appear that Dunham wrote about Thompson's letter and accused Webster of conspiring against Wheelock. Josiah Dunham to Webster, Aug. 16, 1815, DCA, 815466; Webster to Mr. [Josiah] D[unham], Aug. 25, 1815, James W. McIntyre, ed., *The Writings and Speeches of Daniel Webster*, 18 vols. (Boston, 1903), 17:251-53 (hereafter cited as *WS*). For other indictments of Webster on this count see Parish to Wheelock, Sept. 9, 1815, DCA, 815509; and Shirley, *Dartmouth College Causes*, 89-91.

34. Dunham to Wheelock, Aug. 1, 1815, DCA, 815451. Parish informed Wheelock, July 31, 1815, DCA, 815431.1, that "Old N[ile]s was lately in Port[smouth], & said, 'We must have a new P-dent.'"

35. Mason to Marsh, Aug. 15, 1815, DCA, 815465; Dunham wrote a medical professor at the College, Nathan Smith, Aug. 26, 1815, DCA, 815476, seeking confirmation that the Trustees had planned Wheelock's

removal one year before the *Sketches* appeared and that they had deliberately appointed professors who were not likely to cooperate with
the President. Smith replied, Aug. 31, 1815, *ibid.*, that Dunham's im-
pressions were agreeable to what he had heard. Marsh wrote Mason,
Sept. 1, 1815, DCA, 815501, that the only question in the Trustees'
minds in August was the timing of the removal, since it "seemed a
settled point on all hands that he ought be removed."

36. The committee's report is in *Documents Relative to Dartmouth
College*, 9-33. An interesting account of the committee's investigation
and related moves by both parties is a sworn deposition by Josiah Dunham, Sept. 27, 1815, DCA, 815527; the Trustees' reply to Wheelock's
charges is in *ibid.*, 815490.3.

37. Dunham's deposition, Sept. 27, 1815, DCA, 815527.

38. *Ibid.;* see also Parish to Wheelock, Oct. 7, 1815, DCA, 815557.

39. Extracts from the proceedings of the Dartmouth College Trustees
at the August meeting, 1815, relating to the removal of John Wheelock
from the presidency, Aug. 24-28, 1815, DCA, 815490.2.

40. Extracts of the Trustees' Minutes, Aug. 24-28, 1815, DCA,
815475.1, 815490.2.

41. Wheelock's two friends on the Board, Stephen Jacob and Governor John Taylor Gilman, voted against the investigation, but did not
deny jurisdiction. They admitted the Trustees' power to make such
inquiries, but felt that it was not in the interest of all parties to exercise
that power at that time.

42. John Wheelock to The Trustees of Dartmouth College, Aug. 26,
1815, DCA, 815476.3. The original draft of this letter denying the
Trustees' right to try him and claiming his right to appeal to the legislature was dated Aug. 22, 1815, DCA, 815472.2.

43. See Elijah Paine's statement for the Trustees of reasons why Wheelock should not be President, Aug. 26, 1815, DCA, 815476.2; Extracts
of the Trustees Minutes, Aug. 24-28, 1815, DCA, 815490.2.

44. Extracts of Trustees Minutes, Aug. 24-28, 1815, DCA, 815490.2.

45. Trustees to John Wheelock, Aug. 1815, DCA, 815490.1.

46. Vote to Remove Wheelock, *ibid.*, 815490; statement of Joseph
Perry that the resolution was served President Wheelock who replied
that the Trustees might act however and whenever they wished, Sept. 1,
1815, DCA, 815501.

47. Extracts of Trustees Minutes, Aug. 24-28, 1815, DCA, 815490.2.

48. *Ibid.;* Trustees to Francis Brown, Aug. 26, 1815, DCA, 815476.

49. *Ibid.;* Henry Wood, "Sketch of the Life of President Brown," *The
American Quarterly Register*, 7 (1834), 133-45; announcement of
Brown's appointment as tutor, William H. Woodward to Brown, Aug. 30,
1806, DCA, 806480. Wheelock still considered himself President and
said so in a letter, Sept. 23, 1815, DCA, 815523.1, advising Brown to
weigh the appointment carefully. But his warnings were of less consequence to Brown than the future of his parish. Only after an ecclesiastical council at North Yarmouth advised his acceptance did he feel
free to move. Vote of the ecclesiastical council, Sept. 19, 1815, DCA,
815519.

50. Vote of the Trustees of Dartmouth College appointing Francis

Brown president of the College, Aug. 28, 1815, DCA, 815478; Wheelock to William Allen, Sept. 16, 1815, DCA, 815516; Trustees vote to give Brown Wheelock's place on the Board of Trustees, Sept. 27, 1815, DCA, 815527.1; for further action consolidating Brown's position see *ibid.*, 815528, 815528.1, 815556. Amos Kendall congratulated Brown, Nov. 6, 1815, DCA, 815606.

51. Trustees of Dartmouth College, *A Vindication of the Official Conduct of the Trustees of Dartmouth College, in Answer to Sketches of the History of Dartmouth College, and A Candid Analytical Review of the Sketches* (Concord, 1815).

52. Marsh to Mason, Sept. 1, 1815, DCA, 815501.1.

53. Samuel Woodbury to Roswell Shurtleff, Dec. 9, 1815, DCA, 815659.1.

54. Parish to Wheelock, Oct. 7, 1815, DCA, 815557; Judah Dana to Tristram Gilman, Sept. 2, 1815, DCA, 815502. The Trustees, distressed by Hill's polemics and their pamphlet's meager circulation, exerted every effort to enlist support, even urging students to spread far and wide what they knew of Wheelock, "that the College could never flourish whilst he should be continued at its head." Woodbury to Shurtleff, Dec. 9, 1815, DCA, 815659.1.

55. The summer's events stirred others to publication. On June 26, Benoni Dewey proposed to the anti-Wheelock church in Hanover that it discuss the *Sketches.* Benoni Dewey to Congregational Church of Christ, June 26, 1815, DCA, 815376. On July 31, the church voted to publish an answer to the *Sketches,* DCA, 815431.2. The *True and Concise Narrative* appeared shortly thereafter, see above, Chapter One. Later Josiah Dunham published *An Answer to the Vindication of the Official Conduct of the Trustees of Dartmouth College, in Confirmation of the Sketches: with Remarks on the Removal of President Wheelock* (Hanover, 1816); and Peyton R. Freeman published *A Refutation of Sundry Aspersions in the Vindication of the Present Trustees of Dartmouth College, on the Memory of their Predecessors* (Portsmouth, 1816).

Notes for Chapter Three

1. Concord *Patriot,* March 5, Jan. 2, 1816.

2. *Patriot,* Sept. 5, 12, 1815.

3. Lynn W. Turner, *William Plumer of New Hampshire, 1759-1850* (Chapel Hill, 1962), 236; "Chronicle of the Federalites," *Patriot,* Jan. 16, 23, and Feb. 6, 1816; Josiah Dunham to Daniel Webster, Aug. 16, 1816, DCA, 815466; Peyton Randolph Freeman to Jonathan Freeman, Feb. 17, 1816, DCA, 816167; Jeremiah Mason to Mrs. Mason, Jan. 24, 27, 1816, George Stillman Hillard, *Memoir and Correspondence of Jeremiah Mason* (Cambridge, Mass., 1873), 130-31.

4. *Patriot,* March 5, 1816. This was Plumer's allegation.

5. *Ibid.,* Feb. 27, 1816; Turner, *Plumer;* William Plumer, Jr., *Life of William Plumer* (Boston, 1857).

6. William Plumer to Cyrus Perkins, Feb. 11, 1816, Plumer Papers (New Hampshire State Library, hereafter cited as NHSL).

7. *Patriot*, Feb. 13, 27, and March 5, 1816.

8. Turner, *Plumer*, 237.

9. See, for instance, Concord *Gazette*, March 9, 1816; Portsmouth *Oracle*, Feb. 10, 17, and 24, 1816; "Seventy-five," "Who is William Plumer?" Portsmouth *Oracle*, Feb. 17, 1816, a clipping in Plumer's scrapbook, Plumer Papers (NHSL).

10. P. R. Freeman to J. Freeman, Feb. 17, 1816, DCA, 816167.

11. Plumer carefully outlined these ideas in a series of essays in 1812, especially "Cincinnatus—No. XXXV," *Patriot*, April 23,1812.

12. In his 1812 inaugural Plumer advocated insertion of reserve power clauses in corporate charters. Such clauses later became an important modification of the *Dartmouth College* doctrine. *House Journal, June Session*, 1812, 87-91.

13. William Plumer, "Autobiography," 314, Plumer Papers (Manuscript Division, Library of Congress, hereafter cited as LC).

14. See Josiah Dunham to Wheelock, Aug. 1, 1815, DCA, 81541.

15. *Patriot*, March 5, 1816; Hill wrote Plumer, Jan. 9, 1816, Plumer Papers (NHSL), that the "immediate friends of President W. . . . [have] determined to support the Republican candidate." See also Thomas W. Thompson to Francis Brown, Feb. 28, 1816, DCA, 816178; Charles Marsh to Mills Olcott, Feb. 28, 1816, DCA, 816178.1.

16. Republicans received 52.9 percent of the vote with Plumer defeating Sheafe by more than 2300 votes. Turner, *Plumer*, 238.

17. With Republicans victorious, though not because of large Federalist defections, the Trustees believed Republican interest in Dartmouth College would end. Timothy Farrar to Francis Brown, April 8, 1816, DCA, 816258; Concord *Gazette*, April 2, 1816.

18. *Patriot*, April 9, 1816.

19. Isaac Hill to William Plumer, Jr., April 22, 1816, Plumer Papers (NHSL).

20. William Plumer to [Amos Brewster], March 22, 1816, DCA, 816222; writer's draft in Plumer Papers (NHSL); Plumer to Cyrus Perkins, Feb. 15, 1816, *ibid.*; Brewster to Plumer, March 13, 1816, *ibid.*

21. Plumer, "Autobiography," 318-19, Plumer Papers (LC).

22. Plumer to Brewster, March 22, 1816, Plumer Papers (NHSL).

23. *Patriot*, April 23, 1816.

24. Throughout May Hill examined the College charter and the legislature's right to interfere and cried for radical reforms. *Patriot*, May 14, 21, 28, 1816.

25. Charles Marsh to Francis Brown, April 13, 1816, DCA, 816263.1.

26. Brown felt that the "names of Judge Niles (who is supposed to have been the prime mover) of Dr. Parish & Capt. Dunham taken in connection with the part they have acted must satisfy every candid mind on this point." Brown to Daniel French, April 3, 1816, DCA, 816253. See French to Brown, May 23, 1816, DCA, 816323.1, and Chapter Two, above.

27. Brown to French, April 3, 1816, DCA, 816253.

28. Plumer, "Autobiography," 317, Plumer Papers (LC).

29. Turner, *Plumer*, 246 and Shirley, *Dartmouth College Causes*, 9-10 unduly emphasize New Hampshire's contributions to the College. The financial mainstay of Dartmouth thorugh the first decade of the nine-

teenth century was the income derived from the Vermont land grant of 1785, See above, Chapter One.

30. *Senate Journal, June Session*, 1816, 26.

31. *Ibid.*, 27-28.

32. See above, Chapter Two, for the circumstances surrounding the appointment of the investigating committee in 1815.

33. Plumer sent a copy of his address to Jefferson, who praised its "sound" and "truly republican" principles. Jefferson to Plumer, July 21, 1816, H.A. Washington, ed., *The Writings of Thomas Jefferson*, 9 vols. (New York, 1853-55), 7:18-19. In a letter to his old friend, John Quincy Adams, in London, July 30, 1816, Letter Book, 3 (LC), Plumer described his plans for the future of Dartmouth College as a serviceable state institution.

34. *House Journal, June Session, 1816*, 30, 45, 51-52; *Senate Journal, June Session*, 1816, 45-46.

35. Lord, *Dartmouth College*, 85; *Documents Relative to Dartmouth College* (Concord, 1816); *House Journal, June Session, 1816*, 104. Wheelock's partisans were still expecting the legislature to support the ousted President, so they endeavored to explain away the report's innuendoes and prevent its printing. Their efforts were of no avail, and the House voted to print 300 copies together with Wheelock's memorial.

36. *Senate Journal, June Session*, 1816, 104.

37. *Ibid.*, 107.

38. *Ibid.*, 105.

39. Plumer, "Autobiography," 318, Plumer Papers (LC); Plumer to Plumer, Jr., June 10, 1816, Plumer Papers (NHSL).

40. Plumer, "Autobiography," 318, Plumer Papers (LC); Plumer dined with Brown, Paine, Olcott, Ripley, and Thompson on June 14, but the College and politics were not discussed. *Ibid.*, 321.

41. Turner, *Plumer*, 248; this work contains an excellent treatment of the June session, and I rely heavily upon it in the present discussion.

42. Plumer, "Autobiography," 318, Plumer Papers (LC); Eleazar Wheelock Ripley to John Wheelock, Dec. 6, 1815, DCA, 815656; Plumer to Plumer, Jr., June 10, 1816, Plumer Papers (NHSL); Plumer, Repository, 4:667, *ibid.*; Plumer, Jr., Journal 2 (1814-1816), 314, *ibid.*

43. Plumer, "Autobiography," 318, Plumer Papers (LC).

44. A requirement of state citizenship would have removed the four Vermont members of the Octagon and permitted appointment of thirteen out of a possible twenty-one.

45. Turner, *Plumer*, 250, says that ninety copies of this bill were printed and distributed.

46. Plumer, "Autobiography," 318-19, Plumer Papers (LC).

47. *Ibid.*, 322.

48. Webster to Brown, June 4, 1816, *WS*, 17:295-60; Webster to Phineas Handerson, June [no date], 1816, DCA, 816390.1.

49. *House Journal, June Session, 1816*, 119, 121; Timothy Farrar, *Report of the Case of the Trustees of Dartmouth College against William H. Woodward* (Portsmouth, 1819), 385-88.

50. Turner, *Plumer*, 251.

51. Levi Woodbury to William Plumer, June 21, 1816, Plumer Papers (NHSL).

52. *Ibid.;* T. W. Thompson to Mills Olcott, June 21, 1816, DCA, 816371.

53. Turner, *Plumer,* 252; Plumer to Plumer, Jr., June 24, 1816, Plumer Papers (NHSL), gives his opinion of the legislative battles of June 1816.

54. Farrar, *Report of the Case,* 385-88.

55. "An Act to Amend the Charter and Enlarge and Improve the Corporation of Dartmouth College," *Laws of N.H.,* 8:505-08.

56. Plumer, "Autobiography," 323, Plumer Papers (LC); Plumer to Plumer, Jr., June 24, 1816, Plumer Papers (NHSL).

57. Thompson to Olcott, July 1, 1816, DCA, 816401; Charles Marsh to Brown, July 4, 1816, DCA, 816404.

58. Reuben D. Mussey to Francis Brown, July 3, 1816, DCA, 816403; see also Boston *Columbian Centinel,* Sept. 14, 1816, cited in Gerald T. Dunne, "Joseph Story: The Great Term," *Harvard Law Review,* 79:889; Elmer Ellsworth Brown, *The Origin of American State Universities* (Berkeley, 1903); on the difficulties at Transylvania College see Hofstadter, *Academic Freedom,* 248-51, and Niels H. Sonne, *Liberal Kentucky, 1780-1828* (New York, 1939), 135-60. Influential New Hampshire supporters also exhorted the Octagon to legal action for maintenance of their corporate rights. Thompson to Brown, July 15, 1816, DCA, 816415.1; Asa McFarland to Brown, July 5, 1816, DCA, 816405; Thompson to Timothy Farrar, July 5, 1816, Farrar Papers (New Hampshire Historical Society, hereafter cited as NHHS).

59. Marsh to Brown, July 4, 1816, DCA, 816404.

60. Marsh to Brown, July 17, 1816, DCA, 816417.2.

61. Some of these appointments are preserved at Dartmouth, *ibid.,* 816403.1, 816410; an official list of all trustees and overseers is filed under 816427; Wm. Plumer to Joseph Story, July 3, 1816, Story Papers (LC). Plumer to Brown, July 17, 1816, DCA, 816417.1; Plumer to Niles, July 17, 1816, DCA, 816417.

62. Marsh to Brown, July 26, 1816, DCA, 816427.1.

63. Acknowledgements from Paine, Farrar, Thompson, Smith, McFarland, Brown, and Payson, *ibid.,* 816429.1, 816429.2, 816429.3, 816455, 816459, 816470.

64. Levi Woodbury to William Plumer, Jr., Aug. 7, 1816, Plumer Papers (NHSL).

65. *Ibid.*

66. John Taylor Gilman and Stephen Jacob, the recalcitrant Trustees of 1815 were absent. Gilman had withdrawn from active participation in the controversy, though not resigning his seat. Jacob had decided to cooperate with the new board.

67. Brown to William H. Woodward, Aug. 23, 1816, DCA, 816473.

68. Woodward to Brown, Aug. 23, 1816, DCA, 816473.1.

69. Brown to Woodward, Aug. 27, 1816, DCA, 816477.2; Extract of the Minutes of the Trustees of Dartmouth College, *ibid.,* 816477.3; Woodward to Brown, Aug. 27, 1816, DCA, 816477.4; Brown to Woodward, Aug. 29, 1816, DCA, 816479.1.

70. Brown received advice from Parker Noyes and Arthur Livermore, but the most important advice came from Daniel Davis, Solicitor General of Massachusetts and one of the leading Republican lawyers of Boston. Davis wrote Brown a sixteen-page evaluation of the legal status of the controversy between the College and the state, Aug. 14, 1816, DCA,

816464. His recommendations were remarkably prescient and contained, in essence, the arguments of the College counsel later in the controversy. See below, Chapter Four.

71. Plumer asked Brown if he had provided a place for the meeting in his capacity as president. Brown replied that he lacked authority. Plumer then asked the College librarian for the key. The librarian replied that Brown had the key, and Brown, in turn, said the librarian had the key. The pertinent letters are in DCA, 816475 through 816476.11.

72. Plumer to Brown, Aug. 27, 1816, DCA, 816477.

73. Brown to Plumer, *ibid.*, 816477.1.

74. DCA, 816900. Davis had advised such a formal refusal.

75. Minutes of the Trustees of Dartmouth University, DCA; it is interesting to notice that the minutes of the Trustees of both institutions are in the same manuscript volume in the DCA.

76. DCA, 816900; Plumer to Brown, Aug. 29, 1816, DCA, 816479.2.

77. Woodbury to Eleazar Wheelock Ripley, Sept. 28, 1816, DCA, 816528.

78. Plumer, Jr., advised his father, Sept. 3, 1816, Plumer Papers (NHSL), that Judge William M. Richardson doubted the legality of the August meeting and cautioned against a second failure which the Octagon could prove illegal in Plumer's own court. See also Plumer, "Autobiography," 333, Plumer Papers (LC).

79. Plumer, "Autobiography," 335, Plumer Papers (LC).

80. William M. Richardson and Samuel Bell were appointed; see Charles H. Bell, *Life of William Richardson, LL.D., Late Chief Justice of the Superior Court in New Hampshire* (Concord, 1839), and Charles Henry Bell, *The Bench and Bar of New Hampshire* (Boston, 1894), 79-81.

81. Copies of the request in DCA, 816540.1 and 816900; see also Ebeneezer Adams to Benjamin J. Gilbert, Oct. 19, 1816, DCA, 816567.

82. Woodbury to Ripley, Sept. 28, 1816, DCA, 816528. In a letter to Woodward, Oct. 11, 1816, Letter Book, 3 (LC), Plumer expressed his confidence that the legislature would amend the June act in November.

83. Adams to Gilbert, Oct. 19, 1816, DCA, 816567.

84. Plumer, Jr. to Plumer, Oct. 25, 1816, Plumer, Jr., Letter Book, III (NHSL).

85. Samuel Batchelder to Reuben D. Mussey, Dec. 6, 1816, DCA, 816656; Plumer to William Richardson, Sept. 28, 1816, Letter Book, 3 (LC).

86. Batchelder to Mussey, Dec. 6, 1816, DCA, 816656.

87. Adams to Gilbert, Oct. 19, 1816, DCA, 816567.

88. Mills Olcott to Woodward, Sept. 29, 1816, DCA, 816529. Davis had advised dismissing Woodward.

89. Adams to Gilbert, Oct. 19, 1816, DCA, 816567; Minutes of the Trustees of Dartmouth College, *ibid.*; Shirley, *Dartmouth College Causes*, 117.

90. *Senate Journal, November Session, 1816*, 13; *Patriot*, Nov. 26, 1816.

91. "An Act, in Addition to and in Amendment of an Act, Entitled 'An Act to Amend the Charter and Enlarge and Improve the Corporation of Dartmouth College,'" *Laws of N.H.*, 8:555-56.

92. "An Act in Addition to an Act Entitled 'An Act in Addition to and in Amendment of an Act Entitled an Act to Amend the Charter and Enlarge and Improve the Corporation of Dartmouth College,' " *Laws of N.H.*, 8:584-85.

93. Plumer's notice is in DCA, 816670; see also Plumer to Woodward, Jan. 9, 1917, Letter Book, 3 (LC); Plumer to Thomas Searle, Jan. 13, 1817, *ibid.*

Notes for Chapter Four

1. Brown to Farrar, Jan. 3, 1817, Farrar Papers (NHHS); Marsh to Brown, Jan. 6, 1817, DCA, 817106.1; Thompson to Brown, Jan. 9, 1817, DCA, 817109.1.

2. Marsh to Brown, Jan. 6, 1817, DCA, 817106.1; Paine to Brown, Jan. 27, 1817, DCA, 817127.

3. Farrar to Brown, Jan. 26, 1817, DCA, 817126.1; Jeremiah Smith to Brown, Feb. 12, 1817, DCA, 817162.1.

4. Thompson wrote specifically to Webster and urged him to advise Brown, Thompson to Brown, Jan. 9, 19, 1817, DCA, 817109.1, 817119. Thompson to Farrar, Jan. 21, 1817, Farrar Papers (NHHS).

5. Farrar to Brown, Jan. 26, 1817, DCA, 817126.1; Marsh to Brown, Jan. 26, 1817, DCA, 817126.3; Thompson to Brown, Jan. 26, 1817, DCA, 817126.4; McFarland to Brown, Jan. 29, 1817, DCA, 817129; in a letter to Plumer, Dec. 28, 1816, Plumer Papers (NHSL), Woodward said he expected the penal act to undermine the Octagon's opposition, but events proved the Octagon correct—it was never invoked. The Octagon grew slightly more perturbed over Hamilton College's offer of the presidency to Brown. Marsh wrote Brown, Jan. 21, 1817, DCA, 817121, that should the President abandon Dartmouth the remaining hope of the institution would expire. Brown did not decline the invitation until summer, but his adherence to Dartmouth helped insure the stability of the College cause.

6. Daniel Davis to Brown, Aug. 14, 1816, DCA, 816464; see above, Chapter Three.

7. In a letter to Brown, Jan. 6, 1817, DCA, 817106, Paine said that so many "revolutionary opinions have entered the heads of the best men of late years" that the pronouncement of even a competent tribunal could not be predicted. He had never perceived "that the Supreme Court of the U.S. have embraced any revolutionary doctrines." See also Thompson to Brown, Jan. 19, 1817, DCA, 817119, for Thompson's discussion of probable state court action; Smith to Brown, Feb. 12, 1817, DCA, 817162.1; Smith to Olcott, Jan. 26, 1817, DCA, 817126.

8. Smith to Olcott, Jan. 26, 1817, DCA, 817126.

9. Writing to Brown, April 21, 1817, DCA, 817271, Farrar said he wished the questions discussed in Justice Brockholst Livingston's Circuit Court in Vermont and before state courts there and in Massachusetts. He thought an action of trespass against any member of the University boards for taking possession of the College library would suffice. The form of action to give the circuit court jurisdiction became an im-

portant question later in the collateral cases in the New Hampshire Circuit Court. See below, Chapter Eight.

10. The College later decided to initiate actions in the Circuit Court that would raise all the questions. See below, Chapter Eight.

11. Woodward to Plumer, Feb. 11, 1817, Plumer Papers (NHSL).

12. The special verdict constituted one of the most important and vexing problems throughout the litigation. Had University counsel devoted more attention to the facts there included, the outcome in 1819 might have been different.

13. Plumer to Plumer, Jr., Jan. 14, 1817, Plumer Papers (NHSL).

14. Proceedings of the Meetings of the Trustees of Dartmouth University held at Concord, N.H. on Feb. 4, 6, 7, 22, 1817, DCA, 817154; see also 817154.1, 817154.7, 817157, 817157.1, 817157.2; *Patriot*, March 18, 1817; Plumer, "Autobiography," 345-47, Plumer Papers (LC); Plumer to Plumer, Jr., Feb. 11, 1817, Letter Book, 3 (LC).

15. Copy of Reply to Specifications, DCA, 817170.3, 817170.4; *Patriot*, Feb. 26, March 18, 1817; Plumer, "Autobiography," 346, Plumer Papers (LC).

16. Vote for Brown's removal, Feb. 22, 1817, DCA, 817172; Proceedings of University Trustees, DCA, 817172.6 through 817172.11; Plumer was acting on Richardson's advice, Plumer, Jr. to Plumer, Jan. 18, 1817, Plumer Papers (NHSL); Plumer to Plumer, Jr., March 4, 1817, *ibid.;* Plumer "Autobiography," 346, Plumer Papers (LC); Lord, *Dartmouth College,* 112, says that for some unexplained reason no action was taken against the remaining trustees until June. Yet Plumer said that "actions against Payne & Smith not being personal, the consideration of their cases were postponed to the annual meeting [August], There being no return of notice against Niles, & no citation having issued against Tompson & Marsh, the secretary was directed to summon them to attend the next annual meeting." Plumer, "Autobiography," 347, Plumer Papers (LC).

17. Plumer to Plumer, Jr., March 4, 1817, Plumer Papers (NHSL); in a letter to Plumer, Jan. 13, 1817, *ibid.*, Allen had requested Wheelock's restoration at the February meeting.

18. In a letter to Plumer, April 5, 1817, *ibid.*, Woodward said that Wheelock "bade us a very serene adieu." Wheelock willed the University five farms in Vermont and two houses in Hanover plus his existing claims. He estimated the value of this bequest at $20,000. Plumer to Plumer, Jr., Feb. 11, 1817, Letter Book, 3 (LC). Together with property for the endowment of two professorships, this bequest was sufficient to prompt Plumer's remark. The bequest was conditioned to become void should the 1816 acts be declared invalid, and this was good reason for the University's vigorous exertions in the courts. A registered copy of the will is in DCA, 817173; see also Allen to Woodward, March 4, 1817, DCA, 817204.1; Proceedings of the Trustees of Dartmouth University, *ibid.*, 817363, for the board's confirmation of Allen as president at their June meeting.

19. "An address of the Executive Officers of Dartmouth College to the Public"; one of the printed handbills is in Minutes of the Trustees, 2, DCA; *Patriot*, March 18, April 1, 1817; in a letter to Plumer, March 8,

1817, Plumer Papers (NHSL), Woodward called this a "public declaration of their determined devotedness to Martyrdom."

20. Minutes of the Trustees of Dartmouth College, 2, DCA.

21. For an account of this quarrel see Lord, *Dartmouth College*, 120-22; also Brown to Cyrus Perkins and Amos Brewster, Feb. 23, 1817, DCA, 817173; Brown to Allen, Feb. 28, March 1, 1817, DCA, 817178.1, 817201, 817201.3; Rufus Choate to David Choate, March 12, 1817, DCA, 817212; in letters to Plumer, March 8, 13, 1817, Plumer Papers (NHSL), Woodward said that the students were told that if they joined the University they could never be received into the College should it prevail, but if the College failed, the University would accept them "en masse." He also said the University had only ten students.

22. Woodward to Plumer, Feb. 11, 1817, Plumer Papers (NHSL).

23. Woodward to Plumer, March 8, 13, 29, April 5, 26, 1817, *ibid.*

24. Woodward to Plumer, March 8, 1817, *ibid.*

25. Plumer to Woodward, March 21, 1817, Letter Book, 3 (LC); Woodward to Plumer, March 29, 1817, Plumer Papers (NHSL).

26. Plumer to Woodward, April 5, 1817, Plumer Papers (NHSL).

27. For Bartlett's acceptance see Bartlett to Plumer, May 10, 1817, *ibid.;* Plumer's son was enlisted in the search for lawyers which extended into Massachusetts where Timothy Bigelow and Judge Dana were suggested; and Nicholas Emery, Prentice Mellen, and John Holmes, all from Maine, were suggested. See Woodward to Plumer, March 29, April 5, 1817, Plumer to Woodward, April 5, 1817, Plumer, Jr. to Plumer, April 26, 1817, Plumer to Woodward, April 5, 1817, Plumer, Jr. to Plumer, April 26, 1817, Plumer to Plumer, Jr., April 28, 1817, and Woodward to Plumer, April 26, 1817, Plumer Papers (NHSL).

28. J. W. Putnam to Brown, April 11, 1817, DCA, 817261; Bartlett to Plumer, May 10, 1817, Plumer Papers (NHSL).

29. Putnam to Brown, April 11, 1817, *ibid.*, 817261.

30. Thompson to Olcott, April 25, 1817, *ibid.*, 817275. Woodward wrote Plumer, April 5, 1817, Plumer Papers (NHSL), that Smith and Webster were spoken of as representing the College.

31. Brown to Farrar, May 28, 1817, Farrar Papers (NHSL).

32. Allen to Plumer, July 31, 1817, Plumer Papers (NHSL); Plumer to Plumer, Jr., March 4, 1817, *ibid.;* Bartlett wrote Plumer on May 10, 1817, *ibid.*, that he was uncertain about the College's points.

33. Farrar to Brown, Sept. 28, 1817, DCA, 817528.

34. Smith to Brown, Feb. 12, 1817, DCA, 817162.1.

35. Webster to Jeremiah Mason, June 28, 1817, Webster Papers, 1 (NHSL).

36. Farrar to Brown, April 21, 1817, DCA, 817271; these documents would have included the charter of 1769, the 1816 acts, the College board's August resolutions, the Extract from the Cambridge Remonstrances, published in the newspapers as Chief Justice Parson's opinion—this was an argument about similar legislative changes at Harvard, see above, Chapter Three, Parson's manuscript on the same subject, and an extract from *Fletcher* v. *Peck* (1810).

37. Brown to Farrar, May 28, 1817, Farrar Papers (NHHS); these early discussions of a pamphlet eventually bore fruit in the publication of

Farrar's *Report of the Case of the Trustees of Dartmouth College Against William H. Woodward* in 1819. See below, Chapter Nine.

38. Woodward to Plumer, Oct. 2, 1817, Plumer Papers (NHSL); *Patriot*, Nov. 11, 1817.

39. Charles Warren, "An Historical Note on the Dartmouth College Case," *American Law Review*, 46 (Sept.-Oct. 1912), 667, quoting the Salem *Gazette*. For biographical information see George S. Hillard, *Memoir and Correspondence of Jeremiah Mason* (Cambridge, Mass., 1813); John Chipman Gray, "Jeremiah Mason," William D. Lewis, ed., *Great American Lawyers: A History of the Legal Profession in America*, 8 vols. (Philadelphia, 1890), 3:3-36.

40. Mason's argument is printed in 65 New Hampshire Reports 473-502, and in Farrar's *Report*, 28-69. Two manuscript drafts of his brief plus his notes on the arguments of opposing counsel are in "Briefs in the Dartmouth College Case," DCA.

41. *Terrett* v. *Taylor*, 9 Cranch 43 (1815).

42. 65 New Hampshire Reports 492.

43. Mason cited Coke's *Institutes* and cases in South Carolina and Massachusetts. For a thorough treatment of this concept see Edward S. Corwin, "The Doctrine of Due Process before the Civil War," *Harvard Law Review*, 24 (1911), 366-85, 460-95.

44. 65 New Hampshire Reports 494.

45. In addition to *Fletcher* v. *Peck* (1810) and *New Jersey* v. *Wilson* (1812), Mason was here referring to *Terrett* v. *Taylor* (1815) as a contract clause decision. The exact grounds for this decision are still disputed, but it did not invoke the contract clause. It rested instead on principles of natural justice. Since the case came from the District of Columbia, there was no need for the Court to confine itself to constitutional clauses as there would have been, had the case come on appeal from a state supreme court under Section 25 of the Judiciary Act of 1789.

46. Bell, *Bench and Bar*, 58-64; John Hopkins Morison, *Life of the Hon. Jeremiah Smith* (Boston, 1845); Smith's argument is in 65 New Hampshire Reports 524-63.

47. I Lord Raymond 5, printed in 91 English Reports 90. See below, Chapter Five.

48. 65 New Hampshire Reports 540.

49. Bell, *Bench and Bar*, 671-72; Sullivan's argument is in 65 New Hampshire Reports 502-24.

50. In fact, as Smith had pointed out, English law did not distinguish between private and public corporations, and the quasi-private classification held true only within the general category of eleemosynary corporations.

51. 65 New Hampshire Reports 506.

52. Bell, *Bench and Bar*, 173-78; in a letter to Plumer, May 10, 1817, Plumer Papers (NHSL), Bartlett outlined his argument; the argument is in 65 New Hampshire Reports 563-93.

53. See Chapter One.

54. 65 New Hampshire Reports 591.

55. Webster to Mason, Sept. 4, 1817, *WS*, 17:265-66; Warren, "An Historical Note," 668, quoting the Salem *Gazette*.

56. Woodward to Plumer, Oct. 2, 1817, Plumer Papers (NHSL).

57. Shirley, *Dartmouth College Causes*, 186; *Patriot*, Oct. 7, 1817.

58. Plumer, "Autobiography," 340, Plumer Papers (LC).

59. When Richardson became Chief Justice, he began the practice of publishing reports of the actions of the Superior Court. See Bell, *Life of Richardson*, 33.

60. Bell, *Bench and Bar*, 79-81.

61. *Ibid.*, 81-84; Charles L. Woodbury, ed., *Writings of Levi Woodbury, LL.D.: Political, Judicial and Literary. Now First Selected and Arranged*, 3 vols. (Boston, 1852). Woodbury had been appointed a trustee of Dartmouth University but resigned to become a judge. He was an avid Republican and hostile to the Octagon; see Woodbury to Plumer, Aug. 7, 1816 and Jan. 18, 1817, Plumer Papers (NHSL). A minor controversy has arisen over whether he participated in the decision of the case. The docket entries in the case state that Woodbury did not sit at the May argument and the November decision, but that he was present for the September argument, 65 New Hampshire Reports (Parsons, 1888-89), 624-25. These items coupled with correspondence in the Plumer Papers, NHSL, leave no doubt that Woodbury heard the argument and played some part in the decision. See Plumer, Jr. to Plumer, Sept. 11, 1817, Woodbury to Plumer, Sept. 19, 1817, Plumer to Woodbury, Sept. 22, 1817, Plumer, Jr. to Plumer, Sept. 27, Oct. 4, 1817, and Plumer to Plumer, Jr., Sept. 30, 1817, Plumer Papers (NHSL); Thompson to Smith, Nov. 3, 1817, cited in Shirley, *Dartmouth College Causes*, 193.

62. In a letter to Plumer, Sept. 19, 1817, Plumer Papers (NHSL), Woodbury advised that a decision would not be rendered until the Plymouth term. Plumer replied, Sept. 22, 1817, *ibid.*, that this would cause no inconvenience.

63. Brown to Farrar, Sept. 23, 1817, Putnam to Farrar, Oct. 2, 1817, Farrar Papers (NHHS). Still favoring the pamphlet, Brown urged Farrar to call upon the judges without delay and inform them of the intended publication. He felt this would operate "as an additional motive to them to do justice."

64. Plumer, Jr. to Plumer, Sept. 27, Oct. 4, 1817; Plumer to Plumer, Jr., Oct. 7, 1817, Plumer Papers (NHSL); in a letter to Woodward, Sept. 27, 1817, Letter Book, 8 (LC), Plumer indicated that he had received no intimation of the court's decision.

65. 65 New Hampshire Reports 626; the opinion is in *ibid.*, 624-43.

66. *Bank of the United States* v. *Deveaux*, 5 Cranch 57 (1809).

67. 65 New Hampshire Reports 628.

68. *Ibid.*, 630.

69. *Ibid.*, 638-39.

70. *Ibid.*, 640.

71. *Ibid.*, 643.

72. See Horace Hagan, "The Dartmouth College Case," *Georgetown Law Journal*, 19 (May 1931), 415.

73. *Patriot*, Nov. 4, 11, and 25, 1817.

74. Parish to Plumer, Nov. 14, 1817, Plumer Papers (NHSL).

75. Portsmouth *Oracle*, Nov. 15, 1817.

76. Plumer to Parish, Nov. 29, 1817, Letter Book, 9 (LC).

77. Webster to Brown, Nov. 15, 1817, DCA, 817615.3.

78. Brown to Mason and Smith, Aug. 7, 1817, DCA, 817457; Brown to Farrar, Nov. 15, 1817, Farrar Papers (NHHS).

79. Rufus Choate to David Choate, Nov. 8, 1817, DCA, 817608.

Notes for Chapter Five

1. Brown wrote President Francis Kirkland of Harvard that the appeal would entail an expense the College would be unable to meet without the assistance of friends in other states. "Our friends in N.H. have already taxed themselves somewhat severely. . . ." Brown to Kirkland, Nov. 15, 1817, quoted in Charles Warren, *History of the Harvard Law School and of Early Legal Conditions in America*, 3 vols. (New York, 1908), 1:336-37. One notable New Hampshire friend was John B. Wheeler, a merchant of Orford, N.H., who donated $1000 to the College. J. Wheeler of Orford, Citizen of New Hampshire to the Trustees of Dartmouth College, 1816, DCA, 816900.3; *Patriot*, April 1, 1817.

2. Brown to Kirkland, Nov. 15, 1817, quoted in Warren, *Harvard Law School*, 1:336-37.

3. Webster to Brown, Nov. 15, 1817, DCA, 817615.3; Marsh to Brown, Nov. 22, Dec. 5, 1817, DCA, 817622, 817655; Webster to Mason, Nov. 27, 1817, *WS*, 17:266. Hopkinson later received five hundred dollars, not paid out of Webster's thousand-dollar fee.

4. Burton A. Konkle, *Joseph Hopkinson, 1770-1842* (Philadelphia, 1931); Warren, "An Historical Note," 666.

5. Thompson to Olcott, Nov. 17, 1817, DCA, 817617; Webster to Brown, Nov. 27, 1817, DCA, 817627. Edward Hopkinson noted on a letter from Webster to Joseph Hopkinson, Jan. 21, 1818, Hopkinson Papers (Historical Society of Pennsylvania, hereafter cited as HSP), that Webster wrote Hopkinson for his assistance but that he could not find the letter. Hopkinson agreed and, with Brown's approval, became Webster's associate. Hopkinson to Webster, Nov. 20, 1817, DCA, 817260.3.

6. Webster to Brown, Nov. 27, 1817, DCA, 817627; Marsh to Brown, Dec. 8, 1817, DCA, 817658.6.

7. In a letter to Brown, Feb. 14, 1818, DCA, 818164, Webster said he had a copy of the Court's opinion. "It is not quite so formidable as I expected."

8. Webster to Smith, Dec. 8, 1817, Jan. 9, 1818, *WS*, 17: 268-69; Webster to Mason, Dec. 8, 1817, Jan. 9, 1818, Jan. [no date indicated], 1818, *WS*, 16:39; 17:269-71. There is a close similarity between the arguments of Mason and Webster as a comparison of the manuscript drafts in "Briefs in the Dartmouth College Case" shows. But this similarity is insufficient ground to charge Webster with plagiarism as does W. S. G. Noyes, "Webster's Debt to Mason in the Darmouth College Case," *American Law Review* (May-June 1894), 359-67. See Maurice G. Baxter, *Daniel Webster and the Supreme Court* (Amherst, 1966), 77.

9. A copy of Bartlett's verdict is in Shirley, *Dartmouth College Causes*, 196-99.

10. Smith forwarded the documents on December 25, 1817, Smith to Olcott, Dec. 25, 1817, DCA, 817675.1; a copy of the record is in *ibid.*, 817675. Included in these documents was an agreement by both parties that the Trustees would accept delivery of the College records and seal in full satisfaction if they were successful. *Ibid.*, 817675.2; see also Marsh to Brown, Dec. 29, 1817, DCA, 817679.2.

11. Webster to Brown, Feb. 14, 1817, DCA, 818164; in a letter to Hopkinson, Jan. 21, 1818, Hopkinson Papers (HSP), Webster said that "our record in the College Cause is prepared." The record was received and filed on February 12, 1818, Supreme Court Docket, Vol. C. 892, National Archives (Washington, D.C., hereafter cited as NA).

12. There was some doubt whether the College would appeal, Plumer to Plumer, Jr., Nov. 25, 1817 and Plumer, Jr. to Plumer, Nov. 29, 1817, Plumer Papers (NHSL); Plumer to Parish, Nov. 29, 1817, Letter Book, 9 (LC); Plumer to Hale, Dec. 8, 1817, *ibid.*; Plumer wrote Hale, Jan. 15, 1818, Plumer Papers (NHSL), that he was confident the Supreme Court's decision would affirm the "judgment of our own court, & settle the question for other states as well as this," See also Woodward to Plumer, Nov. 20, 1817, Letter Book, 9 (LC).

13. *Patriot*, Jan. 27, 1818. Hill wanted young Plumer to write a history of the entire controversy and to include it in the pamphlet and asked counsel on both sides for their arguments. Hill to Plumer, Jr., Dec. 16, 1817, Plumer Papers (NHSL); Hill to Webster, Dec. 10, 1817 and Webster to Hill, Dec. 27, 1817, Webster Papers (NHHS). Webster declined to give a copy while the cause was still pending.

14. Plumer to Plumer, Jr., Jan. 6, 13, 1818, and Plumer to Hale, Jan. 15, 1818, Plumer Papers (NHSL); Hill sent copies to Washington and reported that many lawyers and members of Congress "have examined this performance, and pronounce it an able, learned and sound opinion." *Patriot*, Feb. 1818.

15. Plumer to Hale, Feb. 5, 1818, Plumer Papers (NHSL).

16. Records of the Dartmouth University Trustees, DCA, 817681; Allen to Hale, Jan. 1, 1818, DCA, 818101.1.

17. Woodward to Hale, Jan. 18, 1818, DCA, 818118.

18. Plumer to Hale, Jan. 15, 1818, Plumer Papers (NHSL).

19. Holmes to Allen, Jan. 8, 1818, DCA, 818108; Holmes also requested some gentlemen of the bar to prepare a brief and send it to him.

20. Perkins to Hale, Jan. 24, 1818, DCA, 818124.

21. Woodward to Hale, Jan. 18, 25, 1818, DCA, 818118, 818125.

22. Hale to Plumer, Jan. 20, 1818, DCA, 818120; Hale to Plumer, Jan. 25, 1818, Letter Book, 9 (LC).

23. Hale to Allen, Feb. 15, 1818, DCA, 818165.

24. *Ibid.;* Feb. 27, 1818, DCA, 818177.

25. These included Secretary of Navy, Benjamin W. Crowninshield, whom Hale said "insists, almost, upon my engaging Mr. Wirt," and the old lobbyist, General Eleazar Wheelock Ripley, Hale to Plumer, Jan. 20, 1818, DCA, 818120; Woodward asserted that Holmes would not mind and that Bartlett felt it was essential, Woodward to Hale and Woodward to John Harris, Jan. 25, 1818, DCA, 818125, 818125.3. Hale assumed

the responsibility and retained Wirt. Initially Allen said that the trustees had not provided for other counsel. "Another meeting cannot be called; & I do not distrust the result of the trial in the hands of Mr. Holmes, burdened as he is with the business of Congress." Allen to Hale, Feb. 5, 1818, DCA, 818155. Later he rejoiced in Hale's action, Allen to Hale, Feb. 18, 1818, DCA, 818168.2. Plumer supported the action, Plumer to Hale, Feb. 5, 1818, Plumer Papers (NHSL); later he commended Hale declaring that "sound policy" required it and assuring Hale the trustees would provide compensation, Plumer to Hale, Feb. 16, 1818 and Plumer to Clement Storer, Feb. 23, 1818, Letter Book, 9 (LC); *Patriot*, Feb. 17, 1818.

26. *The Fortuna*, 2 Wheaton 161 (1817) and *U.S.* v. *Bevans*, 3 Wheaton 336 (1818). These encounters impressed both men with Wirt's ability. See Webster to Mason, Feb. 22, 1818, *WS*, 17:271; in a letter to his wife Emily, Feb. 17, 1817, Hopkinson Papers (HSP), Hopkinson called Wirt "a new antagonist of great celebrity." On Wirt see Joseph C. Burke, "William Wirt: Attorney General and Constitutional Lawyer," Ph.D. diss., Indiana University, 1965.

27. See Burke, "William Wirt," 53-56, 129.

28. Hale to Plumer, Feb. 7, 1818, Letter Book, 9 (LC); Plumer to Clement Storer, Feb. 23, 1818, *ibid.;* Hale to Plumer, Feb. 24, 1818, *ibid.;* Allen to Hale, Jan. 1, 1818, DCA, 818101.1; Woodward to Hale and Woodward to John Harris, Jan. 25, 1818, DCA, 818125, 818125.3; Hale to Allen, Feb. 15, 1818, DCA, 818165.1; Woodward to Hale, Feb. 18, 1818, DCA, 818168.1; Allen to Hale, Feb. 18, 1818, DCA, 818168.2; Hale to Allen, Feb. 27, 1818, DCA, 818177.

29. Woodward to Hale, Feb. 18, 1818, DCA, 818168.1; Allen to Hale, *ibid.*, 818168.2.

30. Hale to Allen, Feb. 27, 1818, DCA, 818177.

31. Hale to Plumer, Feb. 7, 1818, Letter Book, 9 (LC).

32. Supreme Court Docket, Vol. C, 892 (NA); Webster's argument is in 4 Wheaton 551-600; it is also reprinted in *WS*, 10: 195-233. There are two manuscript drafts of the argument in DCA. One is a rough outline of ten pages including notes on Mason's and Smith's arguments, "Briefs"; the other is a smoother draft of fifty-five pages used in the preparation of the printed report of the case, DCA, 8181210.2.

33. Warren, "An Historical Note," 668; Baxter, *Daniel Webster*, 1-16, 80.

34. Story's description of Webster's argument is in the Webster Papers, 12, 1809-1815 (LC).

35. Section 25 of the 1789 act provided for appeals to the United States Supreme Court on a writ of error whenever the state supreme court ruled against the constitutionality of a federal treaty or law; ruled in favor of a state statute which had been challenged as contrary to the Constitution, treaties, or laws of the United States; or ruled against a right or privilege claimed under the Constitution or federal law.

36. 4 Wheaton 557; in a letter to Mason, Dec. 8, 1817, *WS*, 16:39, Webster said: "This point [the contract clause], tho' we trust a strong one, is not stronger, than that derived from the character of these acts, compared with the Constitution of New Hampshire."

37. 6 Cranch 143-48; see also Donald G. Morgan, *Justice William Johnson, The First Dissenter; The Career and Constitutional Philosophy of a Jeffersonian Judge* (Columbia, 1954), 211.

38. The tendency in early efforts to provide constitutional protection for corporate charters was to appeal first to the "due process" and "law of the land" clauses in the state constitutions and second to the contract clause of the national Constitution. See Howard Jay Graham, "The 'Conspiracy Theory' of the Fourteenth Amendment," *Yale Law Journal*, 47 (1938), 172-73.

39. Webster to Marsh, Dec. 8, 1817, DCA, 817658.7. Jurisdiction in the Circuit Court would be in the nature of the parties, diversity of citizenship, rather than on the nature of the question, a conflict between a state statute and a clause of the national Constitution.

40. See below, Chapter Eight, for a discussion of these cases.

41. 1 Lord Raymond, printed in 91 English Reports. This is a summary of the case. The arguments and opinion are in 87 English Reports 289; 100 English Reports 186 contains a note of Holt's opinion taken from his own manuscript. Holt had declared that a consideration of the types of corporations would facilitate understanding of the nature of the visitor. There were, he said, "in law two sorts of corporations aggregate; such as are for public government, and such as are for private charity." There were no private founders for the former and, consequently, no particular visitor. "But private and particular corporations for charity, founded and endowed by private persons, are subject to the private government of those who erect them . . . the founder is patron, and, as founder, is visitor. . . . So patronage and visitation are necessary consequents upon one another." 100 English Reports 189-90.

42. 4 Wheaton 569. It is noteworthy that Marshall was familiar with *Philips* v. *Bury* and had used it as authority in *The Reverend John Bracken* v. *The Visitors of Wm. & Mary College*, 3 Call 573, printed in 3 Virginia Reports 607 (1790). This was a case involving only the visitatorial power, and Marshall, as attorney for the visitors, proclaimed William and Mary to be an eleemosynary corporation. "It comes completely within the description of Chief Justice Holt, in the case of *Philips* v. *Bury*," 3 Va. Rep. 609.

43. *Calder* v. *Bull*, 3 Dallas 394 (1798).

44. Coke's *Institutes* 46.

45. This is the statement of Thomas M. Cooley, *A Treatise on Constitutional Limitations*, 5th. ed. (Boston, 1883), 432-40.

46. 4 Wheaton 581-82.

47. The evidence indicates that the framers intended to protect only private contracts. But the Supreme Court had included public contracts within the scope of the clause and so supported Webster's argument.

48. 4 Wheaton 591.

49. *Terrett* v. *Taylor*, 9 Cranch 43 (1815). The decision was not based on the contract clause, but Webster was not citing the case as a decision based on the contract clause. See above, Chapter Four.

50. It is important to remember that there was no well-established contract law in 1818. Questions of what constituted a contract and its obligation were unsettled in almost every case. It seems therefore, unfair to criticize Webster, and later Marshall, for failing to consider what

constituted the obligation of this contract and what in the New Hampshire statutes impaired it.

51. 4 Wheaton 598.

52. 4 Wheaton 598-600.

53. See Samuel G. Brown, *Works of Choate,* 2 vols. (Boston, 1862), 1:187-88; John W. Black, "Webster's Peroration," *Quarterly Journal of Speech,* 23 (1937), 636-42.

54. Ripley to Allen, March 10, 1818, DCA, 818210.1.

55. Hale to Plumer, April 2, 1818, DCA, 818252.2.

56. Shirley, *Dartmouth College Causes,* 236-40, and Henry Cabot Lodge, *Daniel Webster* (Boston, 1891), 81, have made much of these "political remarks."

57. Baxter, *Daniel Webster,* 85, says that Webster's insistent assertion that Dartmouth had operated through the years as a private institution could have been challenged. Had this been done, he argues in "Should the Dartmouth College Case Have Been Reargued," *New England Quarterly,* 33 (1960), 19-36, lawyers and justices would have been directed to the realistic question of the relation of this school to the public.

58. *North Carolina* v. *Foy,* 5 North Carolina Reports 58 (1805); and *The Reverend John Bracken* v. *The Visitors of Wm. & Mary College,* 3 Virginia Reports 607 (1790).

59. American precedents supported Webster. In *Foy* the North Carolina court construed the state "law of the land" clause as a restriction on legislative power and held that it prevented the legislature from depriving either members of corporations or individuals of property rights. Although the University trustees were a corporation "established for public purposes, yet their property is as completely beyond the control of the Legislature as the property of individuals or that of any corporation," 5 North Carolina Reports 88.

60. Supreme Court Docket, Vol. C, 892 (NA).

61. Hale to Allen, March 10, 1818, DCA, 818210; Holmes' argument is in 4 Wheaton 600-06.

62. Webster to Mason, March 13, 1818, *WS,* 17:275; Webster to Smith, March 14, 1818, *ibid.,* 277.

63. Webster to Brown, March 11, 1818, *WS,* 16:39-40.

64. Hale to Allen, March 11, 1818, DCA, 818211; Hale to Levi Woodbury, March 11, 1818, Levi Woodbury Papers, 1807-1819, Correspondence, Box 1 (LC); in a letter to Plumer, March 12, 1818, Letter Book, 9 (LC), Hale wrote that "I have been occupied day and night during this week in searching for facts and am almost exhausted. Mr. Wirt could not find time to reflect on the case till Monday evening." To Allen he wrote, March 12, 1818, DCA, 818212.1, that the "point insisted on here was not taken at Exeter. We have therefore been taken by surprise—which has thrown great labor on myself and Mr. Wirt," See also Hale to Woodbury, March 17, 1818, Woodbury Papers (LC). Wirt's argument is in 4 Wheaton 606-15.

65. Webster noted the apology in a letter to Mason, March 13, 1818, *WS,* 17:275-76; the Boston *Daily Advertiser,* March 23, 1818, reported that before Wirt concluded "he became so exhausted . . . that he was obliged to request the Court to indulge him until the next day." Quoted

in Charles Warren, *A History of the American Bar* (Boston, 1911), 373-74.

66. Hale to Allen, March 11, 1818, DCA, 818211.

67. 4 Wheaton 609.

68. *Ibid.* There is a widespread rumor initiated by Shirley, *Dartmouth College Causes*, 235, that while Wirt was arguing that Wheelock was not the founder, Webster had his attention called to the clause in the charter reciting that Wheelock was founder. "Wirt had no knowledge that such a clause was in the charter, and knowing nothing of the history of Moor's Charity-School, was 'dumbfounded,' and, as Webster says, 'abandoned' the 'point.' " Shirley continues that this greatly impressed the Court. But there is no evidence to substantiate this. Webster did say that Wirt "undertook to make out one legal point on which he rested his argument, namely, that Dr. Wheelock was not the founder. . . . He abandoned the first point [the matter of bills of attainder], recited some foolish opinions of Virginians on the third, but made his great effort to support the second, namely, that there was no contract." Webster to Mason, March 13, 1818, *WS*, 17:275-76.

69. Hale to Allen, March 13, 1818, DCA, 818212.1.

70. Hale to Plumer, March 12, 1818, Letter Book 9 (LC).

71. Plumer to Hale, March 26, 1818, Plumer Papers (NHSL); the *Patriot*, March 24, May 5, 1818, praised Wirt's argument.

72. Allen to Hale, April 2, 1818, DCA, 818252.1; Hale to Wirt, April 10, 1818, DCA, 818260; Hale to Allen, April 8, 1818, DCA, 818258.

73. Wirt to Hale, April 11, 1818, DCA, 818261; Hale to Allen, April 13, 1818, DCA, 818263. Webster wrote Wirt in refutation of the rumor that he had said Wirt's inferior argument had helped the College more than the University. He assured the Attorney General that he had spoken of the argument as a "*full, able,* and most *eloquent* exposition of the rights of the Defendant." To have said otherwise would have been to diminish the luster of his own argument. "In victory, or in defeat, none but a fool could *boast* that he was warring, not with giants, but with pigmies." There is ample evidence that Webster had been sincere in praising Wirt's professional talents. Webster to Wirt, April 5, 1818, quoted in Everett P. Wheeler, *Daniel Webster: The Expounder of the Constitution* (New York, 1905), 33. He did privately inform Mason that Wirt "seemed to treat this case as if his side could furnish nothing but declamation." Webster to Mason, March 13, 1818, *WS*, 17:275-76.

74. Hopkinson to Brown, Aug. 27, 1818, DCA, 818477.4; Hopkinson's argument is in 4 Wheaton 615-24; a manuscript brief of the argument is in DCA.

75. Webster was satisfied with Hopkinson's performance. Webster to Brown, March 13, 1818, *WS*, 17:274; Webster to Mason, March 13, 1818, *ibid.*, 276; Webster to Smith, March 14, 1818, *ibid.*, 277.

76. Hale to Allen, March 11, 12, 1818, DCA, 818211, 818212.1; Holmes to Allen, March 12, 1818, DCA, 818212.2; Hale to Plumer, March 12, 1818, Letter Book, 9 (LC); Plumer to Hale, Feb. 5, 1818, Plumer Papers (NHSL); Hale to Plumer, Dec. 19, 1817, DCA, 817669.

77. Webster to Brown, March 13, 1818, *WS*, 17:274; Holmes informed

Allen that a decision was doubtful in 1818. "It has been urged as far
as *delicacy* would permit." Holmes to Allen, March 12, 1818, DCA,
818212.3.

78. Supreme Court Docket, Vol. C, 892 (NA); Hopkinson to Brown,
March 13, 1818, DCA, 818213; Webster to William Sullivan, March 13,
1818, *WS*, 16:40-41; Webster to Smith, March 14, 1818, *WS*, 17:276-
77; *Patriot*, March 31, 1818.

79. Plumer to Hale, March 26, 1818, Plumer Papers (NHSL); Hale to
Plumer, April 2, 1818, DCA, 818252.2; Hale to Allen, April 8, 1818,
DCA, 818258; Hopkinson to Brown, March 13, 1818, DCA, 818213;
Webster to Smith, March 14, 1818, *WS*, 17:276-77; Webster to Brown,
April 12, 1818, *ibid.*, 280; *ibid.*, July 16, 1818, *ibid.*, 284-85; Webster
to Brown, March 13, 1818, *ibid.*, 274-75; Webster to Mason, March 13,
1818, *ibid.*, 275-76.

Notes for Chapter Six

1. Hale to Allen, April 2, 1818, DCA, 818252.2.

2. Hale to Allen, April 8, 1818, *ibid.*, 818258.

3. Plumer to Hale, March 26, 1818, Plumer Papers (NHSL); Allen to
Plumer, March 26, 1818, Letter Book, 9 (LC); Allen to Hale, April 2,
1818, DCA, 818252.1; a loan was requested from the legislature, Proceedings of the Trustees of Dartmouth University, June 6, 1818, DCA,
818356; the legislature loaned four thousand dollars, *Laws of N.H.*
8:744; in a letter to Allen, Aug. 14, 1818, DCA, 818464, Hale suggested
that $1500 ought to be provided to pay counsel at Washington; a photo-
static copy of the original subscription list to pay Wirt, devised and circulated by Hale, is in the Montague Collection (Manuscript Division,
New York Public Library).

4. Moses Eastman to Allen, April 7, 1818, DCA, 818257.

5. Webster to Smith, March 14, 1818, *WS*, 17:276.

6. In a letter to Webster, Sept. 19, 1818, DCA, 818519, Brown wrote:
"We are under obligations to Dr. Kirkland for his civilities & proffers
of aid." Marsh to Brown, Nov. 22, 1817, DCA, 817622; David A. White
to Brown, Nov. 26, 1817, DCA, 817626; Farrar to Brown, Dec. 29,
1817, DCA, 817679.3; Benjamin J. Gilbert to Brown, Dec. 29, 1817,
DCA, 817679.1; a subscription list is in DCA, 817900.2; Jeremiah Day
to Brown, Jan. 10, 1818, DCA, 818110.1.

7. E. Porter to Brown, April 14, 1818, DCA, 818264.

8. Brown to Kirkland, Nov. 15, 1817, quoted in Warren, *Harvard Law
School*, 1:336. Webster made similar remarks in concluding his argument
before the Supreme Court, 4 Wheaton 598-99. The Boston *Columbia
Centinel*, Sept. 2, 1818, quoted in Dunne, "Story," 901, referred to the
gathering as a "Congress of Divines"; Hill commented on the congress:
"It is believed that the governors of nearly every College north of the
Delaware, as soon as they ascertained this question was to be tried before the U.S. Court, entered the combination and exerted all their influence to procure a decision which should forever place them beyond
the control of the people." *Patriot*, Feb. 16, 1819.

9. Webster to Mason, April 23, 1818, *WS*, 17:280-81; Webster to Hopinson, July 3, 1818, Hopkinson Papers (HSP); Judges Tapping Reeve and Gould of the Litchfield Law School were interested in the case and desirous of reading Webster's argument, White to Brown, Sept. 7, 1818, DCA, 818507.

10. Isaac Parker to Webster, April 28, 1818, quoted in Warren, *Harvard Law School*, 1:338.

11. Webster to Mason, April 23, 1818, *WS*, 17:280-81.

12. Webster to Brown, July 16, 1818, *ibid.*, 284-85.

13. Webster to Story, Sept. 9, 1818, *ibid.*, 287; Webster to Jacob McGraw, with Webster a former law student of Christopher Gore, July 27, 1818, *WS*, 16:42; Webster to Hopkinson, July 3, 1818, Hopkinson Papers (HSP). Initially Brown could see no benefit in publication. In a letter to Webster, Sept. 19, 1818, DCA, "Briefs," 818519, he said that the scarcity of the argument and the secret method of distribution stimulated curiosity and increased the document's value. It has been read "by all the *commanding* men of New England and New York" and had united them in support of the College. Disturbing news changed his attitude. Cyrus Perkins had seen the argument and wrote Brown that friends of the University had made copies. Brown wrote Webster, Sept. 26, 1818, DCA, 818526, that if any part of the argument were to be published in the *Patriot,* then "unquestionably the argument ought to be published and circulated." Within a month, one hundred and fifty copies had been distributed. Webster to Hopkinson, July 3, 1818, Hopkinson Papers (HSP); Webster to Story, Sept. 9, 1818, *WS*, 17:287.

14. Webster to Story, Sept. 9, 1818, *WS*, 17:287.

15. Ironically, the Chancellor said that after some search he was enabled to purchase a copy of the opinion. Kent to Marsh, Aug. 26, 1818, DCA, 818476.1.

16. Kent to Marsh, Aug. 26, 1818, DCA, 818476.1; Kent's Journal, 1; Kent to William Johnson [of New York], Aug. 22, 1818, and Kent to Isaac Hone, Aug. 8, 1818, Kent Papers, 4 (LC); Brown to Webster, Sept. 8, 1818, Farrar Papers (NHHS).

17. Kent to Marsh, Aug. 26, 1818, DCA, 818476.1.

18. In a letter to Webster, Sept. 15, 1818, DCA, "Briefs," 818515, Brown said that he regarded the visit to Albany "as of no small importance to our cause. The Court of Errors being in session, the greatest legal talents of the State were convened there; & so far as any impression has been given, it is unquestionably in our favour."

19. Brown to Webster, Sept. 8, 1818, Farrar Papers (NHHS); the information on Kent's meeting with Johnson is in the Kent Collection (New York State Law Library, Albany). On page xi of his copy of 1 Wheaton, Kent placed an asterisk alongside Johnson's name and in a footnote added, "August 27-1818 I had the pleasure of seeing Judge Johnson at Albany."

20. Brown to Webster, Sept. 15, 1818, DCA, "Briefs," 818515.

21. The Council of Revision was established by the New York Constitution of 1777. It was composed of the Governor, the Chancellor, and the Justices of the Supreme Court or any two of them. It was a nonjudicial body whose function was to see that the laws passed by the legislature were consistent with the public good and the spirit of the

constitution. A bill could be passed over a veto by a two-thirds vote of each house of the legislature. From 1798 to 1804 Kent was Associate Justice of the state supreme court, then Chief Justice to 1814, and Chancellor until his retirement in 1823. The Council was abolished by the new constitution of 1821. See John T. Horton, *James Kent, A Study in Conservatism* (New York, 1939).

22. Alfred B. Street, *The Council of Revision of the State of New York* (Albany, 1859), 328-29; see also Edwin M. Dodd, *American Business Corporations Until 1860* (Cambridge, 1954), 21-25; Mark DeWolfe Howe, "A Footnote to the 'Conspiracy Theory,'" *Yale Law Journal,* 48 (1939), 1007; Graham, "The 'Conspiracy Theory' of the Fourteenth Amendment," *ibid.,* 47 (1938), 171.

23. Street, *Council of Revision,* 328.

24. *Ibid.,* 425; it is interesting that Kent did not distinguish between public and private corporations or even civil and eleemosynary.

25. *Ibid.,* 345.

26. Section 13 of the 1777 constitution provided that "no member of this state shall be disfranchised, or deprived of any rights or privileges secured to the subjects of this state by this Constitution, unless by the law of the land, or the judgment of his peers." Charles Poletti, *New York Constitutions Annotated* (New York, 1938), Part 2:13; Kent was surely aware at this time that Coke and others had equated Magna Charta and "law of the land" with "due process of law," Kent, *Commentaries,* 3 vols. (Boston, 1884), 2:13. In *Gardner* v. *Village of Newburgh,* 2 Johnson 162 (1816), Kent gave a statute of 1787 providing that "no Citizens of this State shall be . . . disseised of his or her Freehold, or liberties . . . but by lawful Judgment of his or her Peers, or by Due Process of Law," a position of importance comparable to the "law of the land" in section 13 of the 1777 constitution.

27. Webster to Brown, Sept. 20, 1818, DCA, 818520.

28. See Street, *Council of Revision,* 191-93, for a biographical sketch of Livingston. In a letter to Brown, Oct. 11, 1818, DCA, 818561.1, Marsh said: "Judge Livingston intimates to me that the court would not hear another argument unless it might be to some new point not before urged—he also inquired whether these cases [cognate cases] would present the question of the constitutionality of the acts of N.H. under the constitution of the State. On the whole I feel much encouraged as to our eventual success." In a letter to Brown, Feb. 12, 1819, DCA, 819162.2, Paine abstracted the contents of a letter Livingston had sent him. "Each of the Judges, who united in the judgment without any previous consultation at the last term of the Court, or at any time since had formed & written his opinion & the views which were taken of the subject were not essentially different."

29. See above, Chapter Five; also Johnson's concurring opinion in *Fletcher* v. *Peck,* 6 Cranch 143-48, and in *Ogden* v. *Saunders,* 12 Wheaton 271-92 (1827).

30. Shirley, *Dartmouth College Causes,* 252-72, but it is interesting that he does not mention the 1807 veto. For more balanced accounts see Lord, *Dartmouth College,* 143, and Baxter, *Daniel Webster,* 98.

31. White to Brown, Nov. 26, 1817, DCA, 817626.

32. J. W. Putnam to Brown, Dec. 12, 1817, DCA, 817662.

33. Murdock to Brown, Dec. 27, 1817, DCA, 817677.

34. Hopkinson to Marsh, Dec. 31, 1817, quoted in Shirley, *Dartmouth College Causes*, 274.

35. See below, Chapter Eight, for a discussion of the Circuit Court cases.

36. Albert J. Beveridge, *The Life of John Marshall*, 4 vols. (New York, 1919), 4:221, 223; Benjamin J. Gilbert had attempted unsuccessfully to see Marshall on a fund-raising trip in December 1817. He did manage to place a copy of the charter and other papers into the Chief Justice's hands. Gilbert to Brown, Dec. 29, 1817, DCA, 817679.1.

37. Ripley to Allen, March 10, 1818, DCA, 818210.1; Cyrus Perkins to Levi Woodbury, May 3, 1818, Woodbury Papers, 4 (LC).

38. Hale to Allen, April 2, 1818, DCA, 818252.2.

39. Vote of the Trustees of Dartmouth University, Aug. 26, 1818, DCA, 818476; Allen to Plumer, Oct. 15, 1818, Letter Book, 9 (LC).

40. Pinkney to Allen, Aug. 29, 1818, Gratz Collection (HSP).

41. Pinkney to Allen, Sept. 2, 1818, *ibid.*

42. *Ibid.*

43. Allen to Pinkney, Sept. 10, 1818, DCA, 818510.1; the abstract was made from one of the University copies Perkins had spoken of.

44. Allen to Hale, Oct. 15, 1818, DCA, 818565; Allen to Pinkney, Sept. 10, 1818, DCA, 818510.1; Allen to Plumer, Oct. 15, 1818, Letter Book, 9 (LC).

45. These were the "new facts" which the University would present on reargument at Washington and which Allen would later attempt to introduce in the Circuit Court cases. Arguing from them was largely a matter of letting them fit the desired position. The *fact* was that Wheelock's design from the beginning envisioned an expanded School— a College. See above, Chapter One. For the Circuit Court cases see below, Chapter Eight.

46. Hale to Allen, Oct. 16, 1818, DCA, 818566.

47. Allen to Hale, Nov. 12, 1818, DCA, 818612; Hale to Allen, Nov. 23, 1818, DCA, 818623.

48. Allen to Hale, Jan. 23, 1819, DCA, 819123.

49. Perkins to Allen, Jan. 28, 1819, DCA, 819128; Allen to Hale, Nov. 12, 1818, DCA, 818162; the papers used by Perkins are in DCA, 818510 and have the College seal attached; see also the historical and explanatory statement of the origins of the College with reference to documents, which was the basis for the University's proposed appeal for reargument, DCA, 818900.5; Allen to Hale, Dec. 6, 1818, DCA, 818656; DCA, Nov. 26, 1818, DCA, 818626; Hale to Allen, Dec. 4, 1818, DCA, 818654.

50. Perkins to Allen, Jan. 28, 1819, DCA, 819118; Hale to Woodbury, Jan. 13 [1819], Woodbury Papers, 5 (LC).

51. Perkins to Allen, Jan. 28, 1819, DCA, 819128; see above, Chapter Five, on the preparation of the special verdict.

52. Dismay over the special verdict in *Woodward* persisted even after the decision and had been a principal reason for gathering the new facts.

The University planned to introduce them into the special verdict in the "cognate cases" and get them before the Supreme Court in that manner. Bartlett's 1817 special verdict, which had said that the greater part of the money and land held by the College since its origin had been donated by the state, contained the substance of the new facts. The *Patriot* exclaimed immediately after the decision: "It is easy to see that the question of contract may depend wholly on the facts relating to the origin of the College. If the Trustees were its founders and owners, then a contract might be made with them by the government; but if the State founded the College, then probably there was no contract within the meaning of the Constitution, as the Trustees could have no private interest in the seminary." *Patriot,* Feb. 16, 1819. On March 12, 1819, Hill called Webster's assertion that Dartmouth College was a private charity "new and extraordinary ground," and bemoaned the fact that the special verdict did not admit facts to disprove this by showing the distinction between the College and Moor's Indian Charity School.

53. Perkins to Allen, Jan. 18, 1819, DCA, 819118; Hopkinson to Webster, Nov. 17, 1818, *WS,* 17:288-89; Hale to Woodbury, Jan. 13, [1819], Woodbury Papers, 5 (LC).

54. Burke, "William Wirt," 140; Story to Henry Wheaton, Dec. 9, 1818, William W. Story, *Life and Letters of Joseph Story,* 2 vols. (Boston, 1851), 1:312-13.

55. Webster to Brown, Sept. 20, 1818, DCA, 818520.

56. Brown to Webster, Sept. 26, 1818, DCA, "Briefs," 818526; in a letter to Brown, Dec. 18, 1818, DCA, 818668.1, Smith also summarized these points as the object of the Circuit Court cases.

57. In letters to Brown, Sept. 28, 1818, DCA, 818528, and Dec. 6, 1818, *WS,* 17:289-90, Webster admitted that English colleges were eleemosynary and universities civil institutions. But the only particular in which Dartmouth resembled an English university was in its granting of degrees, and this could not change the nature or rights of a college. Webster read the charter literally, and common-law principles applied to that charter made Dartmouth an eleemosynary corporation subject to the exclusive superintendence of the founder. It was possible, he believed, that Pinkney might argue that even though the King could not alter charters at common law, Parliament, in its omnipotence, could. This point, which University counsel had argued briefly before the Superior Court, did not disturb Webster.

58. Brown to Webster and Marsh to Brown, Nov. 14, 1818, DCA, 818604 and 818604.1; Hopkinson, who had learned of Pinkney's intentions while traveling with him, wrote Webster, Nov. 17, 1818, *WS,* 17: 289, that it "cannot be expected that we shall repeat our argument merely to enable Mr. Pinkney to make a speech, or that a cause shall be re-argued, because, after the argument had been concluded, either party may choose to employ new counsel." He agreed with Brown that a reply would be necessary if Pinkney were allowed to speak, but he did not think the Court would want the College argument repeated. See also, Webster to Farrar, Feb. 1, 1819, Farrar Papers (NHHS).

Notes for Chapter Seven

1. In a letter to Allen, Jan. 28, 1819, DCA, 819128, Perkins wrote: "Our cause, which was argued last winter, stands on the docket No. 25 the new action No. 75." See also Webster to Farrar, Feb. 1, 1819, Webster Papers (NHHS).

2. There is some question concerning Pinkney's failure to reargue. Tradition says that while the Marylander was requesting a reargument, Marshall turned a "blind ear" and began reading the opinion. Webster wrote Mason, Feb. 4, 1819, WS, 16:43-44, that Pinkney was in Court that morning, but, significantly, made no mention of a request for reargument. Perkins informed Allen, Feb. 2, 1819, DCA, 819152, that he accidently went into Court while the opinion was being read. "And even our counsel was not there, till just the close of the opinion!! They had no intimation that it was to have been delivered without a new argument." See also *Patriot,* Feb. 16, 1819. Despite these contradictory reports, it is safe to assume that Marshall was aware of the intent to reargue, whatever his reason for not allowing it. In a letter to Hale, Feb. 13, 1819, Plumer Papers (NHSL), Plumer complained of the haste of the decision. He said that "it was known to Judge Story that Pinkney was engaged to argue it again, & he said 'the engaging of Pinkney was the only wise thing the University had done.'" Moody Kent informed Farrar, Jan. 31, 1819, Farrar Papers (NHHS), that the decision would probably be made known early in February. Thompson had told Kent that "the cause would certainly be again argued—that the Court would not refuse to hear an argument—and that the counsel recently engaged, if told that the Judges had formed, & drawn up their opinion, & were ready to declare it, would nevertheless argue it."

3. Webster to Mason, Feb. 4, 1819, WS, 16:43-44; Marshall's entire opinion is in 4 Wheaton 624-54.

4. 4 Wheaton 627.

5. The number of commentators who have seized this paragraph out of context is legion, and so is the number of distortions. This is as true of an early work such as Shirley, *Dartmouth College Causes* (St. Louis, 1879), 412-25, as of a more recent work such as Charles G. Haines, *The Role of the Supreme Court in American Government and Politics, 1789-1835* (Berkeley, 1944), 405. Both belabor the "fact" that the charter was granted by the Governor of the Province of New Hampshire and not the crown and use this to impugn Marshall's technique. But the *fact* is that most colonial corporate charters were granted in the name of the crown and sealed with the provincial seal. This method was not specifically sanctioned by the common law, but it was presumed to have been delegated by the ultimate source of the power to incorporate, the sovereign. The common law did sanction this delegation, and royal governors, colonists, and English officials never doubted the propriety of such procedure. See Joseph S. Davis, *Essays in the Earlier History of American Corporations,* 2 vols. (Cambridge, Mass., 1917), 1:7-10. On the status of corporations at common law see Clarence P. Denham, "An Historical De-

velopment of the Contract Theory in the Dartmouth College Case,"
Michigan Law Review, 7 (Jan. 1909), 201-25; Warren B. Hunting, *The Obligation of Contracts Clause of the United State Constitution* (Baltimore, 1919), 58-110.

6. 4 Wheaton 629.

7. *Ibid.*, 634; Marshall expands this point at 640-41.

8. Benjamin F. Wright, *The Contract Clause of the Constitution* (Cambridge, Mass., 1938), 42-43, believes that this point is of little significance when compared with the ruling that a corporate charter was a contract. But it was the notion that certain corporate charters were private property which enabled corporations to use the due process clause of the Fourteenth Amendment when the contract clause began to decline as a protection for private property at the turn of the twentieth century.

9. 4 Wheaton 636; for Marshall's earlier rulings on corporations see *Bank of the United States* v. *Deveaux*, 5 Cranch 57 (1809).

10. 4 Wheaton 636.

11. *Ibid.*, 637-38; here certainly is an early statement of Taney's doctrine that "nothing passes by implication." A clearer statement of the same is in Story's concurring opinion.

12. 4 Wheaton 647.

13. *Ibid.*, 641; Marshall later qualified this denial with the statement that "it is not clear, that the trustees ought to be considered as destitute of such beneficial interest in themselves, as the law may respect." He found a beneficial interest in the freehold right to be the tutors with salaries and the freehold right to the powers granted them by the charter, *ibid.*, 653-54.

14. *Ibid.*, 642.

15. *Ibid.*, 654.

16. *Bank of the United States* v. *Deveaux*, 5 Cranch 57 (1809); but Marshall's personal views tended to equate private rights with corporate rights. In a letter to Greenhow, Oct. 17, 1809, Washburn Collection (Massachusetts Historical Society), Marshall said: "I consider the interference of the legislature in the management of our private affairs, whether those affairs are committed to a company or remain under individual direction, as equally dangerous and unwise."

17. *Bank of the United States* v. *Deveaux*, 5 Cranch 87 (1809).

18. 4 Wheaton 644-45.

19. Bartlett was the only lawyer to stress the power of Parliament to annul corporate charters. The precedents he used are thoroughly discussed in Hunting, *The Obligation of Contract*, 75-89. Hunting's analysis is unfavorable to Bartlett. For a different view see Clement Hugh Hill, "Dartmouth College Case," *American Law Review*, 8 (Jan. 1874), 189-239. It should be noted that "the crown lawyers repeatedly pointed out that the exercise of certain powers by Parliament implied nothing as to the colonial powers of legislation." How much truer this would be for the states. George Chalmers, *Opinions of Eminent Lawyers on Various Points of English Jurisprudence* (London, 1814), 1:263-64, 296, quoted in Davis, *Earlier History of American Corporations*, 1:29.

20. 4 Wheaton 650.

21. *Ibid.*, 653.

22. The mandate, reversing the decision, which was sent to the Superior Court is in DCA, 819152.6; see also Webster to Smith, Feb. 28, 1819, *WS*, 16:45.

23. Webster to Mason, Feb. 4, 1819, *WS*, 16:43-44; Webster to Smith, Feb. 2, 1819, *WS*, 17:299-300; Webster to Farrar, Feb. 2, 4, 1819, Farrar Papers (NHHS); Moody Kent to Farrar, Jan. 31, 1819, Farrar Papers (NHHS).

24. Henry Wheaton to Story, May 13, 1819, Wheaton Papers (The Pierpont Morgan Library, New York); Wheaton to Farrar, Aug. 2, 1819, Farrar Papers (NHHS).

25. Story to Wheaton, Dec. 30, 1818, quoted in Dunne, "Story," 904; Livingston to Story, Jan. 24, 1819, Story, *Story*, 1:323-24; William Prescott to Story, Jan. 9, 1819, *ibid.*, 324; Story's opinion is in 4 Wheaton 666-713.

26. 9 Cranch 43 (1815); see above Chapter Five.

27. 4 Wheaton 671.

28. *Ibid.*, 669; it was coincidental that Story was president of the Merchant's Bank of Boston.

29. Story makes several references to this reserved power. See 4 Wheaton 675, 708, 712. To support this assertion, he cited two decisions of the Massachusetts court. In *Wales* v. *Stetson*, 2 Mass. 143 (1806), the court declared that rights legally vested in a corporation "cannot be controlled or destroyed by any subsequent statute, unless a power for that purpose be reserved to the legislature in the act of incorporation," *ibid.*, 146. The other case was *Ellis* v. *Marshall*, 2 Mass. 269 (1807). See also Dodd, *American Business Corporations*, 20-22.

30. 4 Wheaton 708; see Story's argument in *Fletcher* v. *Peck* that the state could not reclaim what it had granted.

31. 4 Wheaton 712; see also Story's Circuit Court decision in *Society for the Propagation of the Gospel* v. *Wheeler*, 22 Federal Cases 763 (1814), which had voided a New Hampshire statute on similar grounds.

32. Washington's opinion is in 4 Wheaton 654-66.

33. *Ibid.*, 659.

34. Hill, "Dartmouth College Case," 217-20; Hunting, *Obligation of Contracts*, 64-75.

35. See above Chapter Five.

36. *The King* v. *Passmore*, 100 English Reports 531.

37. Webster to Brown and Hopkinson to Brown, Feb. 2, 1819, *WS*, 17:300-01.

38. Brown to Farrar, Feb. 11, 1819, Farrar Papers (NHHS); Webster to Farrar, Feb. 2, 4, 7, 1819, *ibid.*; Thompson to Olcott, Feb. 8, 1819, DCA, 819158.1; Paine to Brown, Feb. 12, 1819, DCA, 819162.2; Webster to Mason, Feb. 4, 15, 23, 1819, *WS*, 16:43-44, 49-52; Webster to Smith, Feb. 2, 1819, *WS*, 17:299-300; Webster to Ezekiel Webster, Feb. 2, 1819, *ibid.*, 300; Webster to Brown, Feb. 23, 25, 1819, *ibid.*, 301-03.

39. Webster to Farrar, Feb. 7, 1819, Farrar Papers (NHHS).

40. Perkins to Allen, Feb. 2, 1819, DCA, 819152; see also Perkins to Allen, Feb. 7, 11, 1819, DCA, 819157.2, 819161, in which Perkins expresses the tired lament over the bad management and inadequate preparation of the case in New Hampshire in 1818.

41. Perkins to Allen, Feb. 14, 1819, DCA, 819164.1.

42. *Patriot*, Feb. 16, 1819; Perkins had transcribed the opinion and had forwarded a copy to Allen. Hill's use of Perkins' phrases, notably the "monkery" in the case, makes it seem likely that he obtained his knowledge of the opinion from this source.

43. *Patriot*, Feb. 16, 23, 1819.

44. *Ibid.*, April 20, May 4, 1819.

45. Plumer to Hale, Feb. 13, 1819, Letter Book, 8 (LC); a slightly different copy of this letter is in the Plumer Papers (NHSL); Plumer to Clement Storer, Feb. 15, 1819, Letter Book, 9 (LC); Plumer to Allen, March 17, 1819, *ibid.;* Plumer to Hale, April 8, 1819, Plumer Papers (NHSL).

46. Hale to Plumer, Feb. 26, 1819, Letter Book, 9 (LC).

47. Plumer to Allen, March 17, 1819, *ibid.;* Plumer to Hale, April 8, 1819, Plumer Papers (NHSL).

48. Plumer to Hale, Feb. 13, 1819, Plumer Papers (NHSL).

49. Webster to Farrar, Feb. 7, 1819, Farrar Papers (NHHS); Perkins to Allen, Feb. 2, 14, 1819, DCA, 819152, 819164.1.

50. Webster to Brown, Feb. 23, 1819, *WS*, 17:301; Webster to Mason, Feb. 24, 1819, *WS*, 16:44; Webster to Smith, Feb. 28, 1819, *ibid.*, 45. These letters indicate that the Court entered judgment on February 23, but the Supreme Court Docket, Vol. C, 892 (NA), says February 27. The Minutes of the Supreme Court of the United States, Feb. 1, 1790-Aug. 14, 1828 (NA), says February 25.

51. Plumer to Hale, Feb. 13, 1819, Plumer Papers (NHSL).

52. Webster to Mason, Feb. 23, 1819. *WS*, 16:51-52.

53. Webster to Brown, Feb. 23, 1819, *WS*, 17:301-02.

54. Perkins to Allen, Feb. 11, 1819, DCA, 819161; see also Perkins to Allen, Feb. 2, 14, 1819, DCA, 819152, 819164.1.

55. Supreme Court Docket, Vol. C, 943-45 (NA); Webster to Mason, Feb. 24, 1819, *WS*, 16:44; Webster to Smith, Feb. 28, 1819, *ibid.*, 44-45; the records of these cases are in the Federal Records Center (Waltham, Mass., hereafter cited as FRC). Plumer remained confident and Pinkney continued to talk of a more powerful argument. Plumer to Allen, March 17, 1819, Letter Book, 9 (LC); Plumer to Amos Brewster, April 21, 1819, DCA, 819271; Plumer to Hale, April 8, 1819, Plumer Papers (NHSL). Webster wrote Mason, April 13, 1819, *WS*, 16:49, that "Pinkney sent back this cause to get rid of it. He talked, however, and blustered, because among other reasons the party was in a fever and he must do something for his fees. As he could not talk in court, he therefore talked *out* of court. I believe his course is understood." See also Webster to Hopkinson, March 22, 1819, *ibid.*, 46-47.

Notes for Chapter Eight

1. In a letter to Marsh, attached to a letter to Brown, Dec. 8, 1817, DCA, 817658.7, Webster said of the objection based on the contract clause: "This point, tho' we trust a strong one, is not perhaps stronger, than that derived from the character of these acts, compared with the Constitution of New Hampshire." See above, Chapter Five.

2. Webster to Smith, Dec. 8, 1817, *WS*, 17:267-68; Webster to Mason, Dec. 8, 1817, *WS*, 16:39; Webster to Brown, Dec. 8, 1817, DCA, 817658.7. Webster included a letter to Marsh of the same date and subject and asked Brown to forward it. The broad grounds of Story's concurring opinion in *Woodward* and his conversations with Webster support Webster's assertion. See Webster's letter to Mason, Jan. [no date] 1818, *WS*, 17:270-71, where Webster reported that Story had told him of conversations with Mason about "things"; Webster to Story, Aug. 16, 1818, *ibid.*, 286.

3. Farrar had casually mentioned actions in the Circuit Court of Vermont in August 1816, but Smith advised against bypassing the state court. See above, Chapter Four, especially Daniel Davis to Brown, Aug. 14, 1816, DCA, 816464. For weaknesses in the College's new strategy see Baxter, "Should the Dartmouth College Case Have Been Reargued," *The New England Quarterly*, 33 (March 1960), 29-31.

4. Brown to Olcott, Jan. 10, 1818, DCA, 818110.

5. Webster concentrated on preparing his argument in *Woodward*, though he maintained a lively interest in the progress of the new action. Webster to Mason, Jan. [no date] 1818, *WS*, 17:270-71; Webster to Brown, Feb. 14, 1818, DCA, 818164.

6. Farrar to Brown, Feb. 7, 1818, DCA, 818157.1; Brown to Farrar, Feb. 19, 1818, Farrar Papers (NHHS). Farrar continued to act as intermediary. Brown and the Trustees felt that the nature of the actions rendered it "prudent to avoid direct discourse with counsel as much as possible." Brown to Farrar, April 22, 1818, *ibid.*

7. The difficulties lay in executing the suits in the forms Mason suggested. Marsh did not wish to tax Mason's patience but had "no inclination to try 'experiments,'" and continually appraised Mason about these difficulties. Brown to Farrar, Feb. 19, 1818, Farrar Papers (NHHS), contains a note from Marsh to Farrar; Marsh to Farrar, Feb. 27, 1818, *ibid.;* attached to this letter was a note to Farrar in which Brown wrote that Olcott had sold some College land to Horace Hatch of Vermont and that other suits would be initiated in due time. In a letter to Brown, Feb. 27, 1818, DCA, 817177.1, Marsh specifically questioned Mason's recommendation for a writ of entry. He asked whether Mason meant the process in Vermont "vulgarly called ejectment." If not, he pointed out that a writ of entry was an action for real property and that there was scarcely a piece of real property in the College holdings which could be used for the action. Moreover, he noted correctly, the writ had never been used in Vermont and seldom in any of the states. In fact, ejectment had replaced it even in England. In a letter to Brown, March 13, 1818, *WS*, 17:274-75, Webster expressed his particular satisfaction "that an ejectment is brought. It is just what should be done." It was, indeed, what he had suggested in December 1817.

8. William Blackstone, *Commentaries on the Laws of England*, 2 vols. (Philadelphia, 1864), 2:199-204; ejectment developed in England because of the confusion and injustice attending the use of real writs such as entry.

9. Webster to Brown, Dec. 8, 1817, DCA, 817658.7.

10. This and the other cases are not reported in the *Federal Cases*, but the complete record is in the FRC; see also Marsh to Farrar, Feb. 27,

1818, Farrar Papers (NHHS); Gilbert to Farrar, April 23, 1818, *ibid.;*
Smith to Farrar, Dec. 7, 1818, *ibid.;* Allen to John Harris, April 5, 1818,
DCA, 818255; Copy of Lang's summons to the Circuit Court, April 22,
1818, *ibid.,* 818272; Lang to Allen, April 22, 1818, *ibid.,* 818272.1;
Allen to Pinkney, Sept. 10, 1818, *ibid.,* 818510.1; Allen to Plumer,
March 26, 1818, Letter Book, 9 (LC); Farrar to Smith, Dec. 11, 1818,
Shirley, *Dartmouth College Causes,* 283-85.

11. Lang was never actually dispossessed. Smith wrote Farrar, Dec. 7,
1818, Farrar Papers (NHHS), that it was unnecessary. The entry of
either Dartmouth College or Hatch did not imply Lang's expulsion.

12. *Charles Marsh* v. *William Allen, Henry Hutchinson, and Ahimaaz
B. Simpson* (FRC); in a note appended to Marsh to Farrar, Feb. 27,
1818, Farrar Papers (NHHS), Brown wrote that there was no proper
tenant of the College buildings. "But Mr. Hutchinson is the Inspector
. . . could the inspector be sued in ejectment." See also Smith to Farrar,
Dec. 7, 1818, *ibid.;* Copy of Trustees' lease to Charles Marsh, *ibid.;*
Allen to Hale, April 2, 1818, DCA, 818252.1; Allen to Harris, April 5,
1818, DCA, 818255; Allen to Pinkney, Sept. 10, 1818, DCA, 818510.1;
Allen to Plumer, March 26, 1818, Letter Book, 9 (LC); Farrar to Smith,
Dec. 11, 1818, Shirley, *Dartmouth College Causes,* 283-85.

13. *Pierce ex dem. Lyman* v. *Gilbert* (FRC); see also Smith to Farrar,
Dec. 7, 1818, Farrar Papers (NHHS); Copy of Trustees' deed to Lyman,
ibid.; Copy of Gilbert's summons to the Circuit Court, *ibid.;* Allen to
Harris, April 5, 1818, DCA, 818255; Allen to Pinkney, Sept. 10, 1818,
DCA, 818510.1; Allen to Plumer, March 26, 1818, Letter Book 9 (LC);
Farrar to Smith, Dec. 11, 1818, Shirley, *Dartmouth College Causes,*
283-85.

14. Gilbert's letter is part of the record in the case (FRC); the University trustees did appear, and at the October term the Court substituted them as defendants in the action. The case then became *Pierce ex
dem. Lyman* v. *The Trustees of Dartmouth University.* Correspondence
between Smith and Farrar expressed concern that "poor G." should not
be the defendant, even in the special verdict. Smith to Farrar, Dec. 7,
1818, Farrar Papers (NHHS), Farrar to Smith, Dec. 11, 1818, Shirley,
Dartmouth College Causes, 283-85.

15. Farrar to Brown, Feb. 7, 1818, DCA, 818157.1; Brown, in his
note to Farrar, Marsh to Farrar, Feb. 27, 1818, Farrar Papers (NHHS),
said: "I wish you would say nothing to Dr. Hatch about the Library.
That business will require a little time, but it must not take air."

16. Allen to Plumer, March 26, 1818, Letter Book, 9 (LC).

17. Webster to Brown, March 11, 1818, *WS,* 16:39-40; Webster to
Brown, March 13, 1818, *WS,* 17:274-75.

18. Webster to Brown, Feb. 14, 1818, DCA, 818164.

19. Webster to Mason, March 22, 1818, *WS,* 17:278.

20. Allen to Plumer, March 26, 1818, Letter Book, 9 (LC).

21. Webster to Brown, April 12, 1818, *WS,* 17:280; Webster to Brown,
March 30, 1818, *ibid.,* 279; Brown to Farrar, April 23, 1818, Farrar
Papers (NHHS); Mason to Marsh, April 14, 1818, DCA, 818264.1;
Marsh to Brown, April 20, 1818, DCA, 818270.

22. Webster to Mason, April 23, 1818, *WS,* 17:280-81; in a letter to

Mason, April 28, 1818, *ibid.*, 282-83, Webster wrote that "the question which we must raise in one of these actions, is, 'whether, by the general principles of our governments, the State legislatures be not restrained from divesting vested rights?' This, of course, independent of the constitutional provision respecting contracts."

23. Allen to Plumer, March 26, 1818, Letter Book, 9 (LC); Allen to Hale, April 2, 1818, DCA, 818252.1.

24. Moses Eastman to Allen, April 7, 1818, DCA, 818257.

25. In a letter to William Plumer, Jr., May 5, 1818, Plumer Papers (NHSL), Richard Ela reported that Bartlett wanted to appear as amicus curiae "but did not want to appear as counsel." Ela, together with young Plumer and Bartlett, had studied law under Chief Justice Richardson.

26. Marsh to Brown, May 18, 1818, DCA, 818138; Allen to Pinkney, Sept. 10, 1818, DCA, 818510.1.

27. Marsh to Brown, May 2, 1818, DCA, 818302.1; in a letter to Plumer, Jr., May 19, 1818, Plumer Papers (NHSL), Ela said that Story's dismissal of the fictitious nature of the suits was an assumption of power equivalent to French despotism. But, he added, the action was consistent with Story's favorite topic, the extension of the jurisdiction of the national courts. Writing to Hopkinson, July 3, 1818, Hopkinson Papers (HSP), Webster said, "The new actions are brought; & are in a fair way to go up in a favorable shape the next term. There was a good deal of ingenious painstaking effort to defeat the suit by abatement, &c. &c., but without success. The *Judge* said it was important that a cause should go up embracing all the questions. I should not have great doubt of *his*, opinion, when we get the question *fairly & broadly up.*"

28. Mason to Marsh, Sept. 9, 11, 1818, DCA, 818508, 818511.

29. Webster to Brown, Sept. 20, 1818, DCA, 818520.

30. Brown to Webster, Sept. 26, 1818, DCA, "Briefs," 818526.

31. Allen to Plumer, Oct. 15, 1818, Letter Book, 9 (LC); Allen to Pinkney, Sept. 10, 1818, DCA, 818510.1; see also Chapter Six, above.

32. In a letter to Mason, April 23, 1818, *WS,* 17:280-81, Webster had suggested a special verdict. "A special verdict is the most convenient mode, I think. The verdict in the other case [*Woodward*] I think very right, and from the same minutes one can be drawn in the present case."

33. These agreements are part of the record in the case (FRC), but the agreements to admit copies of the 1807 New Hampshire grant to the College, Wheelock's 1815 memorial to the legislature, Wheelock's will, and a letter from the English trustees to Eleazar Wheelock, April 25, 1771, are in DCA, 818590.1, 818590.2, 818590.3. Hale to Allen, Oct. 16, 22, 1818, DCA, 818566, 818572.

34. Marsh to Olcott, Oct. 3, 1818, Lord, *Dartmouth College,* 159.

35. In a letter to Hale, Oct. 15, 1818, DCA, 818565, Allen said that John Wheelock's will contained express sanction of the 1816 legislation.

36. Marsh to Brown, Oct. 11, 1818, DCA, 818561.1; Webster to Brown, Dec. 6, 1818, *WS,* 17:289-90.

37. Smith to Farrar, Dec. 7, 1818, Farrar Papers (NHHS); most of the correspondence concerning the special verdicts dealt only with *Marsh v. Allen* and *Pierce ex dem. Lyman* v. *The Trustees of Dartmouth University*, Lang seems to have been abandoned, since his case did not directly involve the University.

38. Farrar to Smith, Dec. 11, 1818, Shirley, *Dartmouth College Causes,* 283-85; Mason's note to Smith is appended.

39. Smith to Brown, Dec. 17, 18, 1818, DCA, 818667, 818668.1.

40. The cases were received and filed at the Supreme Court on February 1, 1819, Supreme Court Docket, Vol. C, 943-45 (NA); Farrar to Webster, Jan. 8, 1819, Farrar Papers (NHHS); Smith to Farrar, Jan. 9, 1819, *ibid.;* Farrar to Webster, Jan. 2, 1819, DCA, 819102.

41. Hale to Allen, Oct. 16, 1818, DCA, 818566.

42. Allen to Hale, Dec. 6, 1818, DCA, 818656.

43. Hale to Allen, Dec. 16, 1818, DCA, 818666.

44. Allen to Hale, Jan. 23, 1819, DCA, 819123; after forwarding the papers, Allen heard nothing from Bartlett and Sullivan either regarding the use made of them or the result of the hearing at Exeter. Allen to Plumer, Oct. 15, 1818, Letter Book, 9 (LC).

45. Perkins to Allen, Feb. 11, 1819, DCA, 819161.

46. Pinkney did not assist in the final handling of the cases. See Webster's letter to Mason, April 13, 1819, *WS,* 16:49 and Chapter Seven, above.

47. Perkins to Allen, Feb. 14, 1819, DCA, 819164.1.

48. Plumer to Hale, April 8, 1819, Plumer Papers (NHSL); Plumer to Allen, March 17, 1819, Letter Book, 9 (LC); Plumer to Amos Brewster, April 21, 1819, DCA, 819271.

49. Webster to Farrar, Feb. 7, 1819, Farrar Papers (NHHS).

50. Webster to Brown, Feb. 23, 1819, *WS,* 17:301-02; Webster to Smith, Feb. 28, 1819, *WS,* 16:45.

51. The cases were remanded by consent for further proceedings on February 25, 1819, Supreme Court Docket, Vol. C, 943-45 (NA); Webster to Smith, Feb. 28, 1819, *WS,* 16:45.

52. Webster to Brown, Feb. 23, 1819, *WS,* 17:301-02; Webster to Brown, Feb. 25, 1819, *ibid.,* 303; Webster to Mason, Feb. 24, 1819, *WS,* 16:44.

53. Webster to Mason, March 23, 1819, Mason Papers (NHHS); Webster to Mason, March 22, 1819, *WS,* 16:47-48.

54. Webster to Mason, April 6, 1819, *ibid.,* 52; Webster to Mason, April 10, 1819, *ibid.,* 48-49.

55. Webster to Mason, April 13, 1819, *ibid.,* 49; Webster to Brown, April 14, 1819 (two letters), *WS,* 17:303-04.

56. Allen to Marsh, April 15, 1819, Lord, *Dartmouth College,* 165.

57. Marsh to Allen, April 22, 1819, DCA, 819272; Marsh also noted that in passing the acts the legislature had assumed the broad principle that, allowing the corporation to be such as the charter seemed to make it, they had a right to alter the charter. How then, he asked, since this principle had been denied by the Supreme Court, "can you reasonably desire to have the controversy decided upon an entirely different principle," drawn from antiquated papers which were not even considered by the legislature. Allen filed an affidavit with the Court, April 27, 1819, DCA, 819277.

58. Boston *Columbian Centinel,* May 8, 1819, quoted in Dunne, "Story," 910; *Patriot,* May 11, 1819; Webster to Hopkinson, May 9, 1819, copy in Personal Papers Miscellaneous (LC); the record of the

case (FRC) does not contain the opinion, but it can be assumed that it closely followed Story's concurring opinion in *Woodward*.

59. Webster to Hopkinson, May 9, 1819, copy in Personal Papers Miscellaneous (LC).

60. Webster to Mason, May 27, 1819, *WS*, 16:53; Webster to Brown, May 30, 1819, *WS*, 17:306-07.

61. Webster to Brown, May 30, 1819, *ibid.*

62. *Patriot*, June 8, 1819.

63. *Ibid.*

64. The College had repossessed the buildings on February 28, and the University was forced to suspend operations. In a notice of suspension printed in the *Patriot*, March 9, 1818, Allen called attention to the ironic circumstances of the repossession. He left it to the public to decide "the motives which induced this determination to outstrip the steps of the law and to retake by force the buildings for the recovery of which a suit against me by way of writ of ejectment has been brought by Charles Marsh Esq. of Vermont (the lessee of this very property under 'The Trustees of the College' so-called) and is still pending in the Court of the United States." See also Webster to Hopkinson, March 22, 1819, DCA, 819222.

Notes for Chapter Nine

1. Marshall's dissent in *Ogden* v. *Saunders*, 12 Wheaton 346 (1827).

2. A vested right is a legal claim to ownership which comes to exit or "vest" in one party through a legitimate contract with another. See Robert Kenneth Faulkner, *The Jurisprudence of John Marshall* (Princeton, 1968), 3-44; James Willard Hurst, *Law and Conditions of Freedom in Nineteenth-Century United States* (Madison, 1956), 11-18, 22-29, 39-45.

3. Faulkner, *Jurisprudence of John Marshall*, 3-44; Charles Grove Haines, *The Revival of Natural Law Concepts* (Cambridge, Mass., 1930), 79-88; Edward S. Corwin, "The Basic Doctrine of American Constitutional Law," *Michigan Law Review*, 12 (1914), 246-76; Nathan Isaacs, "John Marshall on Contracts: A Study in Early American Juristic Theory," *Virginia Law Review*, 7 (1921), 413-28. During Marshall's tenure nine states adopted contract clauses of the federal model. When added to the three states already possessing such contract clauses this indicates popular suspicion of legislative tyranny over legitimate property rights. See Wright, *Contract Clause*, 60-61.

4. 6 Cranch 139. In addition to natural law and the contract clause, Marshall also referred to the prohibitions in Article I, section 10 against bills of attainder and *ex post facto laws*—the latter despite Justice Chase's ruling in *Calder* v. *Bull*, 3 Dallas 386 (1798), that *ex post facto* applied only to accusations of crime and not to civil suits. On *Fletcher* v. *Peck* see C. Peter Magrath, *Yazoo; Law and Politics in the New Republic; The Case of Fletcher* v. *Peck* (Providence, 1966).

5. 4 Wheaton 650.

6. *Ibid.*, 636.

7. George H. Evans, Jr., *Business Incorporations in the United States,*

1800-1943 (New York, 1948), 21; Oscar and Mary Handlin, "Origins of the American Business Corporation," *Journal of Economic History*, 5 (1945), 22; see also Davis, *American Corporations*, 1; and Samuel Williston, "History of the Law of Business Corporations Before 1800, "*Harvard Law Review*, 2 (1888), 105-66. The existence of such an attitude was evident in Hopkinson's statement in his argument in *Dartmouth College* that "there may be supposed to be an ultimate reference to the public good in granting all charters of incorporation; but this does not change the property from private to public." 4 Wheaton 616-17. Even Richardson shared this attitude for he included turnpikes and canals under the heading "private." In the late nineteenth century these would have been labelled public or at least "affected with a public interest." The term "public" for Richardson meant an agency of government. Williard W. Smith, "The Relations of College and State in Colonial America," (Ph.D. diss., Columbia University, 1950), shows a large amount of state aid to colleges.

8. For criticism of Marshall's statement about the objects of incorporation see Norman J. Small and Lester S. Jayson, eds., "The Constitution of the United States of America, Analysis and Interpretation, Annotations of Cases decided by the Supreme Court of the United States to June 22, 1964," 88 Cong., 1st sess., *Senate Document No. 39* (Washington, 1964), 391. This is a revision of the 1952 edition by Edward S. Corwin. Henry J. Friendly, "The Dartmouth College Case and the Public-Private Penumbra," *Texas Quarterly*, 12 (1969), 7-41, criticizes Marshall's dichotomy between public and private. Story's specific reference to banks in his concurring opinion in *Dartmouth College* was intended only to bolster his distinction between the popular and strictly legal meanings of the term "public."

9. *Allen* v. *McKean*, 1 Fed. Cas. 489 (1833).

10. Wood, "Life of President Brown," 143.

11. It must be noted that the 1816 reforms, much to Plumer's chagrin, did not remake Dartmouth College into a state college. The Governor grew continually more disappointed with the University and, in 1818, had despaired of its ever approaching his liberal goals. Plumer to Hale, Dec. 28, 1818, Letter Book, 9 (LC).

12. Charles Warren, *The Supreme Court in United States History*, 2 vols. (Boston, 1926), 1:488-91; Warren, "An Historical Note," 671-75. Hill's protest that the Supreme Court had subordinated the public welfare to the benefit of a privileged few forecast the criticisms of the decision during the Granger Movement.

13. *McCulloch* v. *Maryland*, 4 Wheaton 316, and *Sturges* v. *Crowninshield, ibid.*, 122.

14. An unsuccessful attempt was made in *Benjamin Foster and Another, Executors, &c.* v. *The President, Directors and Company of the Essex Bank*, 16 Massachusetts Reports 244 (1819) to apply the *Dartmouth College* rule to a bank charter. The Essex Bank was incorporated on July 1, 1799 for a term of twenty years. Before expiration of the charter, the legislature passed a law on June 19, 1819 extending the lives of coprorations three years beyond charter expiration for purposes of suing and being sued and settling and closing their affairs; but not for

continuing the business for which they were established. Using the *Dartmouth College* doctrine that a law which altered any part of a contract contained in a corporate charter was of no effect, the Bank protested the act's constitutionality on the ground that it continued the existence of the corporation without the consent of the members. Interestingly, Webster argued for the state and against the attempt to use the *College* precedent. He argued that the purpose of the law was to protect creditors' rights, not to violate rights—an interesting switch from the *Dartmouth College* case where the purpose of the law was not germane. Webster distinguished the cases by pointing out that in the *College* Case the legislature, by a special act, had undertaken to abolish a private corporation and give its property to others. This 1819 statute was general, and its provisions beneficial to all parties, and hence within the proper exercise of legislative power. The Court, through Chief Justic Parker, concurred.

15. Timothy Farrar, *Report of the Case of the Trustees of Dartmouth College Against William H. Woodward* (Portsmouth, 1819); on the preparation of the *Report* see Baxter, *Daniel Webster,* 104-06; Shirley, *Dartmouth College Causes,* 290-98; Farrar's *Report* was used by Henry Wheaton in preparing his report of the Supreme Court decision and by the New Hampshire reporters in preparing their later report of the case.

16. Story to Kent, Aug. 21, 1819, Story, *Life and Letters,* 1:330.

17. Kent, *Commentaries,* 1:419; on Kent's refusal to review the book see Kent to Story, Aug. 3, 1819, *Proceedings of the Massachusetts Historical Society,* Second Series, 14 (190), 413.

18. Eleemosynary corporations have been involved in six contract cases before the Supreme Court, excluding *Dartmouth College,* and only three of these concerned colleges: *Vincennes University* v. *Indiana,* 14 Howard 268 (1852); *Pennsylvania College Causes,* 13 Wallace 190 (1872); and *Bryan* v. *Board of Education,* 151 U.S. 639 (1894). The other cases involved a church, a hospital, and a benevolent association. See Wright, *Contract Clause,* 129.

19. Hofstadter, *Academic Freedom,* 219-20; Donald G. Tewksbury, *The Founding of American Colleges and Universities Before the Civil War* (New York, 1932), 64-5, *passim;* Lester Bartlett, *State Control of Private Incorporated Institutions of Higher Education* (New York, 1926); Gordon L. Clapp, "The College Charter," *Journal of Higher Education,* 5 (1934), 79-87.

20. *The State, ex rel. Robinson* v. *Carr, Auditor of State,* 111 Ind. 335 (1887); *Trustees of the University of Alabama* v. *Winston,* 5 Stew. and P. (Ala.) 17 (1833). For a thorough discussion of these and related cases see Edward Charles Elliott and M. M. Chambers, *The Colleges and the Courts: Judicial Decisions Regarding Institutions of Higher Education in the United States* (New York, 1936), 115-18, *passim.*

21. Hofstadter, *Academic Freedom,* 219-20.

22. Thomas M. Cooley, *Constitutional Limitations,* 338, says that under the protection of the *College* doctrine, "the most enormous and threatening powers in our country have been created. . . . Every privilege granted or right conferred—no matter by what means or on what pretence—being made inviolable by the Constitution, the government is

found frequently stripped of its authority in very important particulars, by unwise, careless, or corrupt legislation; and a clause of the federal Constitution, whose purpose was to preclude the repudiation of debts and just contracts, protects and perpetuates the evil." Hugh E. Willis, "The Dartmouth College Case—Then and Now," *St. Louis Law Review*, 19 (1934), 185, is critical of Marshall for not ruling that even though a charter was a contract, it was subject to the state's sovereign powers of eminent domain, police, and taxation. Between Cooley and Willis, the number of such commentators and of grounds upon which they criticize the decision is legion.

23. 4 Wheaton 636, 675, 708, 712.

24. *Wales* v. *Stetson*, 2 Mass. 143 (1806); Dodd, *American Business Corporations*, 141, refers to a Pennsylvania charter of 1784 containing such a reservation.

25. Dodd, *American Business Corporations*, 141; Wright, *Contract Clause*, 169-70.

26. 12 Wheaton 213.

27. In *Greenwood* v. *Freight Co.*, 105 U.S. 13 (1881) the Supreme Court ruled this way. In *Allen* v. *McKean*, 1 Fed. Cas. 489 (1833), Story invalidated a Maine statute altering the charter of Bowdoin College, despite a reserved power to amend, on the ground that the statute went beyond mere alteration. Nearly all cases involving reserved power arose after the Civil War, and in all of them, except those involving public utilities, the Court ruled for the state. See *Pennsylvania College Cases*, 13 Wallace 109 (1871). The Court has stated, but never ruled, that reserved powers must be exercised reasonably and that alteration must be consistent with the object of the grant. See *Phillips Petroleum Co.* v. *Jenkins*, 297 U.S. 629 (1936).

28. 4 Peters 514.

29. *Ibid.*, 535.

30. *Ibid.*, 561.

31. In *Beaty* v. *Lessee of Knowler*, 4 Peters 168 (1830), Marshall concurred in McLean's opinion that "a corporation is strictly limited to the exercise of those powers which are specifically conferred on it. . . . The exercise of the corporate franchise, being restrictive of individual rights, cannot be extended beyond the letter and spirit of the Act of Incorporation." Marshall made a similar statement in *Dartmouth College*, 4 Wheaton 636 (1819).

32. 6 Howard 301 (1848). This was not the first contract case to involve a commercial corporation. It was the first involving state regulation of a commercial corporation in which the decision was for voiding the state legislation. An earlier decision of unconstitutionality involving a bank tax exemption was *Gordon* v. *Appeal Tax Court*, 3 Howard 133 (1845).

33. Wright, *Contract Clause*, 63, 245, notes that there were eight such cases in Marshall's thirty-four years and eighteen in Taney's twenty-eight years.

34. 11 Peters 420 (1837).

35. *Ibid.*, 547-48.

36. Wright, *Contract Clause*, 65-66.

37. *Bridge Proprietors* v. *Hoboken Co.*, 1 Wallace 116 (1864).

38. 11 Peters 455, 466, 505, 515, 535.

39. *Dartmouth College* v. *Woodward,* 4 Wheaton 629 (1819).

40. *Providence Bank* and *New Jersey* v. *Wilson* are conclusive on this point.

41. 6 Howard 507.

42. *Ibid.,* 532-33.

43. The Court continually stressed this point in dicta throughout the century. In 1917 it went so far as to apply the rule to a case involving an express contract not to exercise the right of eminent domain. See *Pennsylvania Hospital* v. *Philadelphia,* 245 U.S. 20 (1917). An interesting development from the inalienability of eminent domain was the decision in *Illinois Central Railway Co.* v. *Illinois,* 146 U.S. 387 (1892) that a state may revoke an improvident grant of public property without recourse to eminent domain—especially interesting in view of *Fletcher* v. *Peck.*

44. In view of subsequent taxation cases, *Providence Bank* looms as an important precedent upholding the state tax.

45. 16 Howard 369 (1853).

46. See the other Ohio Bank Cases; *Home of the Friendless* v. *Rouse,* 8 Wallace 430 (1869); in *Given* v. *Wright,* 117 U.S. 648 (1886) the exemption at issue in *New Jersey* v. *Wilson* was ruled invalid, but this did not affect the precedent which still binds. See *Georgia R. Co.* v. *Redwine,* 342 U.S. 299 (1952).

47. 8 Wallace 439; for a discussion of the dissenting opinions in the tax cases during the Taney period see Robert L. Hale, "The Supreme Court and the Contract Clause," *Harvard Law Review,* 57 (1944), 642-52.

48. 8 Wallace 442.

49. Small and Jayson, "Constitution Annotated," 395-96.

50. Wright, *Contract Clause,* 127; Wright also discusses the different kinds of corporations affected in this litigation, 128-30. For a statistical breakdown of cases under the contract clause after 1865 see Small and Jayson, "Constitution Annotated," 409-10.

51. Small and Jayson, "Constitution Annotated," 410, believe that the subordination of public grants to the police power and the expansion of due process contributed to the decline of the contract clause. In his chapter on the later history of the contract clause, Wright, *Contract Clause,* 91-100, believes the reserved power was more important.

52. Marshall suggested the idea that was later designated as "police power" with his statement in *Dartmouth College* that the contract clause was not intended to restrain the states in the regulation of their internal affairs, 4 Wheaton 629. The idea became more explicit in *Gibbons* v. *Ogden,* 9 Wheaton 1 (1824); *Brown* v. *Maryland,* 12 Wheaton 419 (1827); and in *Wilson* v. *The Blackbird Creek Marsh Co.,* 2 Peters 245 (1829). See also Webster's argument in *Wilkinson* v. *Leland, ibid.,* 627. Taney implied such a power with his statement about the state promoting the public happiness in *Charles River Bridge* v. *Warren Bridge,* 11 Peters 420 (1837); he was more succinct in *The License Cases,* 5 Howard 504 (1847).

53. 27 Vt. 140 (1854).

54. *Ibid.*, 155; Redfield also doubted the state's right to alienate its taxing power.

55. 94 U.S. 113 (1877).

56. In view of late nineteenth-century criticisms of Marshall for his lack of understanding of common law and his selective choice of precedent, it is instructive to note the manner in which Waite arrived at the "public interest" doctrine. He borrowed from a treatise by the seventeenth-century English jurist Lord Chief Justic Hale. The treatise, *De Portibus Maris*, was not published until 1787, and it is not representative of Hale's jurisprudence. The synthesis of Hale's position was his *Analysis of the Civil Part of Our Law*, which was the foundation for Blackstone's *Commentaries*. It was not coincidental that Waite did not use Blackstone and that Blackstone never mentioned anything being "affected with a public interest." Waite chose the antiquated *De Portibus Maris* and quoted a phrase pertaining to the regulation of fees charged by enterprises in public ports: "For now the wharf and crane and other conveniences are affected with a public interest, and they cease to be *juris privati* only." By translating the particulars—"the wharf and crane"—into the generic term "private property," Waite completely transformed the quotation's meaning. Moreover, there were five cases involved, and all but *Munn* concerned railroad corporations. *Munn* concerned a grain elevator partnership and so did not raise the question of a corporate charter. Yet Waite decided the other cases on the basis of *Munn*. See Breck P. McAllister, "Lord Hale and Business Affected with a Public Interest," *Harvard Law Review*, 43 (March, 1930), 759-91; Walton H. Hamilton, "Affectation with Public Interest," *Yale Law Journal*, 34 (June, 1930), 1089-1112.

57. 101 U.S. 814 (1880).

58. The other cases involved reserved power or grants which, if strictly construed, warranted abolition of the grant. See *Boyd* v. *Alabama*, 94 U.S. 645 (1877); Bradley's definition of the police power in *Beer Co.* v. *Massachusetts*, 97 U.S. 25 (1878); and *Fertilizing Co.* v. *Hyde Park, ibid.*, 659.

59. 101 U.S. 814.

60. In *Butchers Union Co.* v. *Crescent City*, 111 U.S. 476 (1884), the Court applied both the *Fertilizing Company* and *Stone* rulings in striking down the New Orleans slaughterhouse monopoly which it had sustained in the *Slaughterhouse Cases*, 16 Wallace 36 (1873).

61. Aldace F. Walker, "A Legal Mummy, or the Present Status of the Dartmouth College Case," *Proceedings of the Vermont Bar Association* (1885), 32; William P. Wells, "The Dartmouth College Case," *American Bar Association Report*, 9 (1886), 229-56. See also Justice Stephen Field's dissent in *Munn* v. *Illinois*, 94 U.S. 148 (1877).

62. *Santa Clara County* v. *Southern Pacific Railroad*, 118 U.S. 394 (1886).

63. *Chicago &c. Railway Co.* v. *Minnesota*, 134 U.S. 418 (1890). See also Charles Wallace Collins, *The Fourteenth Amendment and the States* (Boston, 1912), 126-38, 188-207.

64. 169 U.S. 526 (1898).

65. 290 U.S. 398 (1934). The *Blaisdell* decision insofar as it affected due process must be considered together with *Nebbia* v. *New York*, 291

U.S. 502 (1934). The death blow for economic due process came in
West Coast Hotel v. *Parrish,* 300 U.S. 379 (1937).

66. 290 U.S. 435.

67. In *Sturges* v. *Crowninshield,* 4 Wheaton 200 (1819), Marshall said:
"Without impairing the obligation of the contract, the remedy certainly
be modified as the wisdom of the nation shall direct."

68. 290 U.S. 442.

69. This was particularly true of the decisions facilitating corporate
transactions on an interstate scale and those giving corporations standing in federal courts. See *Bank of Augusta* v. *Earle,* 13 Peters 519 (1839)
and *Louisville Railroad Co.* v. *Letson,* 2 Howard 497 (1844).

A Note on Sources

The principal source for a study of the *Dartmouth College* case is the Dartmouth College Archives. The manuscript collection in the Archives covers the entire history of the College and contains a wealth of information on the College controversy and cases from 1815 to 1819: correspondence of Eleazar and John Wheelock, of Daniel Webster, William Plumer, and the other principals involved in the controversy, copies of the briefs of the counsel in the cases, and letters of students and alumni giving personal anecdotes and descriptions of the officers and faculty of the College.

One could write a good account of the College controversy from the collection of papers of William Plumer and his son, William, Jr., at the New Hampshire State Library at Concord. In addition to drafts, copies, and originals of the letters of William Plumer concerning the College difficulties, the Letter Books, Memoirs, and Journals of Plumer, Jr., and various other items by both men, the Plumer Collection includes letters from Salma Hale, Cyrus Perkins, Levi Woodbury, William H. Woodward, and lesser figures in the controversy. A calendar of the Plumer Collection, prepared by Lynn W. Turner, assists the researcher in finding relevant materials.

The Library of Congress in Washington, D.C. also has some Plumer Papers. The most important Plumer manuscript there is his "Autobiography," a folio volume of 419 handwritten pages. In addition the Library has seven volumes of Plumer Correspondence, which complement the holdings of the New Hampshire State Library and contain informative material on the Dartmouth controversy. Small pieces of information can be obtained in the James Kent Papers, Levi Woodbury Papers, Joseph Story Papers, and the Daniel Webster Papers at the Library.

Another storehouse of information is the library of the New Hampshire Historical Society at Concord. The Society has a comprehensive Webster collection containing many letters relevant to the College difficulty. Information obtained in the papers of Timothy Farrar, Jr., Jeremiah Mason, Isaac Hill, and Samuel Bell sheds further light.

Fragments of evidence are scattered through collections in other libraries. The Historical Society of Pennsylvania has important letters between William Allen and William Pinkney in its Gratz Collection and some correspondence between Webster and Joseph Hopkinson in the Hopkinson Papers. Henry Wheaton's letters to Joseph Story in the Wheaton Papers at the Pierpont Morgan Library in New York help clarify Justice Livingston's part in the litigation. The Manuscript Division of the New York Public Library has a memorial of the Trustees of Dartmouth College to the New Hampshire legislature, which helps demonstrate the College's early desire for state assistance and the state's unwillingness to lend aid. There are scattered pieces of information in the Public Library's Montague Collection, a melange of letters, pamphlets, and miscellaneous items by or about Daniel Webster. Chancellor James Kent commented on various Justices of the Supreme Court and cases decided by that Court in his copies of the Supreme Court reports. Kent's copies of the Court reports are in the Kent Collection at the New York State Law Library in Albany. His comments in 1 and 4 Wheaton were helpful. Occasional items can also be uncovered in the Washburn Collection at the Massachusetts Historical Society in Boston and in the Niles Manuscripts at the Lilly Library of Indiana University.

The study of any legal controversy necessarily implies the use of Court reports and other official documents. The set of official reports of cases argued and decided before the Supreme Court of the United States is indispensable. Before 1875 these reports were issued under the names of the reporters (Dallas, Cranch, Wheaton, Peters, Howard, Black, and Wallace); after 1875 they were issued simply as the *United States Reports*. These volumes state the facts, indicate the proceedings in lower courts, and report the arguments of counsel. In addition, factual information concerning the dates of hearings, decisions, and judgments can be obtained from the Docket of the Supreme Court of the United States and the Minutes of the Supreme Court of the United States. Both are located at the National Archives.

The set of *Federal Cases* contains a valuable selection of cases argued and decided in the circuit and district courts of the United States. Unfortunately, the Circuit Court cases which composed an integral part of the Dartmouth College controversy are not recorded in this set. The records of these cases are located in the Federal Records Center at Waltham, Massachusetts and at the United States District Court at Concord, New Hampshire. The reports of the state courts, especially New Hampshire, but also Virginia, North Carolina, and Massachusetts are necessary tools. The most complete record of the *Dartmouth College* case is Timothy Farrar, *Report of The Case of the Trustees of Dartmouth College Against William H. Woodward* (Portsmouth, 1819). This volume was used in the preparation of Wheaton's report of the case and for the full report in 65 New Hampshire Reports. Since lawyers and judges of the early nineteenth century frequently cited English precedents, the comprehensive *English Reports* is also indispensable.

The Journals of the House and Senate of New Hampshire and the set of *Laws of New Hampshire* cannot be overlooked, since they not only give the text of the various pertinent statutes but furnish corroboration for many of the statements made in letters by the persons involved in the controversy. Moreover, only a search of these records can furnish the crucial information about the extent of the state's support of Dartmouth College. The New Hampshire legislature published *Documents Relative to Dartmouth College* (Concord, 1816), a pamphlet containing Wheelock's 1815 memorial and the report of the 1815 investigating committee.

Published memoirs and correspondence always aid the researcher, and several were of particular importance to this study. The standard edition of Webster's works is James W. McIntyre, ed., *The Writings and Speeches of Daniel Webster*, 18 vols. (Boston, 1903). Volumes 17 and 18 contain many letters pertaining to the College case. University Microfilms, in collaboration with the Dartmouth College Library, *Microfilm Edition of the Papers of Daniel Webster* (Ann Arbor, 1971), will replace McIntyre. Reel 3, covering Webster's correspondence from January 2, 1815 through 1821, and Charles M. Wiltse, ed., *Guide and Index to the Microfilm* (Ann Arbor, 1971), were pertinent to this study. The Marshall Papers Project sponsored by the College of William and Mary and the Institute of Early American History and Culture has uncovered nothing relevant to the *Dartmouth College* case. George Stillman Hillard, *Memoir and Correspondence of Jeremiah Mason* (Cambridge, Mass., 1873), and William W. Story, ed., *Life and Letters of Joseph Story*, 2 vols. (Boston, 1851), are useful.

No account of the Dartmouth College controversy can neglect the pamphlets of 1815-1816: [John Wheelock], *Sketches of the History of Dartmouth College and Moor's Charity School* ([Newburyport], [1815]); [Elijah Parish], *A Candid, Analytical Review of the Sketches* ([Newburyport], [1815]); Benoni

Dewey, Banjamin J. Gilbert, and James Wheelock, *A True and Concise Narrative* (Hanover, 1815); Trustees of Dartmouth College, *A Vindication of the Official Conduct of the Trustees of Dartmouth College* (Concord, 1815); Peyton Randolph Freeman, *A Refutation of Sundry Aspersions in the Vindication* (Portsmouth, 1816); and Josiah Dunham, *An Answer to the Vindication* (Hanover, 1816). It is impossible to read these pamphlets and not be impressed with the emotion generated by these hortatory and denunciatory works. In most cases these publications only amplify material which has already appeared in the popular press, but occasionally, as with the *True and Concise Narrative,* they furnish facts which are not available elsewhere.

While early nineteenth-century newspapers intended more to excoriate their political opponents than to objectively report events, they do have historical value as propaganda pieces. This is particularly true of the College controversy in which the New Hampshire press not only jumped headlong into the fray but contributed to the transformation of the controversy from a personal feud to a political controversy. The most valuable paper for this study was the Republican Concord *Patriot,* but the Republican New Hampshire *Gazette* and the Federalist Portsmouth *Oracle* and Concord *Gazette* contain some relevant information. The decision gained little notoriety outside New England, especially New Hampshire, so newspapers such as the *National Intelligencer* of Washington, are less important than the New Hampshire papers.

Dartmouth College v. *Woodward* is one of the most frequently cited decisions of the Supreme Court and one of the most often discussed in articles and books. It would serve no useful purpose to list every history of the Supreme Court which mentions the case or every article or monograph which might have some bearing on the subject. Some are naturally more useful than others. Those listed below are especially useful, and those of less importance are fully cited in the notes.

With all that has been written on the *Dartmouth College* case, it is strange that there is no complete history of the controversy. No single work combines the significant features of the early history of the College, the origins and progress of the friction between Wheelock and the Trustees, the frenzied actions of 1815-1816, the litigation through the New Hampshire Superior Court and the United States Supreme Court, the Circuit Court cases, and the decision's impact on American colleges and American Constitutional theory. Frederick Chase, *A History of Dartmouth College and the Town of Hanover, N.H. to 1815,* 2nd. ed. (Brattleboro, 1928), is a thorough history of the origins and early development of the College. Chase's work is based on extensive research in original manuscripts which he collected and which now form much of the holdings in the College Archives. The companion volume, John King Lord, *A History of Dartmouth College, 1815-1909* (Concord, 1913) is based on Chase's research and exhibits the same thoroughness. Even so, the coverage of the litigation is weak from the standpoint of analysis and interpretation of counsels' arguments and judges' opinions. Leon Burr Richardson, *History of Dartmouth College,* 2 vols. (Hanover, 1932), is an abbreviated edition of Chase and Lord. The prose is smoother and more colorful, but Richardson's flowing style and flashes of insight are marred by an almost total absence of documentation. Eleazar Wheelock's *Narratives* furnish a complete history of the Indian Charity School and its removal to Hanover.

The chapter on "The Dartmouth College Case" in volume 4 of Albert J. Beveridge, *The Life of John Marshall,* 4 vols. (New York, 1919), is a thorough exposition of the legal portion of the controversy, but it is weak on the early history of the College. Much the same is true of the chapter on the case in Maurice G. Baxter, *Daniel Webster and the Supreme Court* (Amherst, 1966). These are not shortcomings, only the natural result of the College case being subordinate to the main purpose of the works. One attempt has been made at providing a monograph on the case, and this is the work of John M. Shirley, *The Dartmouth College Causes and the Supreme Court of the United States* (St. Louis, 1879). Unfortunately, Shirley's work reflects the late nineteenth-century bias against the College decision as an example of a conservative Supreme Court subordinating the public good to the benefit of a privileged few. Beveridge evaluated the volume as "crammed with the results of extensive research, strange conglomeration of facts, suppositions, inferences, insinuations, so inextricably mingled that it is with the utmost difficulty that the painstaking student can find his way." While the "painstaking student" can find much of value in Shirley's work, especially since some of the correspondence cited is no longer available, he must agree that Beveridge's evaluation is still accurate.

Shirley's criticism of the decision as an undue restriction of state power is echoed in numerous legal journals from the late nineteenth century to the 1930s. A review of "A New View of the Dartmouth College Case," *American Law Review,* 27 (Jan.-Feb. 1893), 71-75, labels the College decision as contrary to the Anglo-American legal tradition. Part of that tradition was a refusal to grant excessive power to the executive; and, the article claims, the *Dartmouth* decision vested excessive power in the judiciary. Ephraim A. Otis, "The Dartmouth College Case," *American Law Review,* 27 (July–August 1893), 525-39, lauds the decision in *Munn* v. *Illinois* for returning to the states some of the regulatory power over corporations which had been lost by the College decision. William Trickett, "The Dartmouth College Case Paralogism," *American Law Review,* 40 (March-April 1906), 175-87, calls the decision "pernicious" for exalting corporate power over state power. Arthur Twining Hadley, "The Constitutional Position of Property in America," *Independent,* 64 (April 1908), 834-38, bemoans the nineteenth century's preoccupation with property rights at the expense of human rights. Writing in the spirit of the *Blaisdell* decision Hugh E. Willis, "The Dartmouth College Case—Then and Now," *St. Louis Law Review,* 19 (April 1934), 183-200, criticizes Marshall for not allowing for a reserved state police power in his ruling that corporate charters were contracts.

Other articles in the same period were more balanced. Clement Hugh Hill, "The Dartmouth College Case," *American Law Review,* 8 (Jan. 1874), 189-239, disavows any hostile intent but says that with the consequences of corporate power beginning to weigh heavily, the *Dartmouth* decision threatened to make the strong stronger and the weak weaker, almost to helplessness. Chief Justice Charles Doe of the New Hampshire Supreme Court, "A New View of the Dartmouth College Case," *Harvard Law Review,* 6 (Nov. 1892), 161-83, reviews the legal aspects of the decisions in the Superior Court and the Supreme Court and he would reverse both decisions. Referring to the modifications of the College doctrine and stating that the historical interest in the case was greater than its practical consequences, Alfred Russell, "Status and Tendencies of the Dartmouth College Case," *American Law Review,* 30 (May-June 1896), 322-56, suggests that it was only necessary to further modify the doctrine with a just view toward both property rights and the general welfare. A similarly balanced evaluation is Horace H. Hagan, "The Dartmouth College Case," *George-town Law Journal*, 19 (May 1931), 411-26.

Two critics suggest that the *Dartmouth* decision should be recalled. James C. Jenkins, "Should the Dartmouth College Decision be Recalled," *American Law Review*, 51 (Sept.-Oct. 1917), 711-51, argues this from the viewpoint of a well-developed contract-law which did not exist in the early nineteenth century. A more credible argument is that of Maurice G. Baxter, "Should the Dartmouth College Case Have Been Reargued," *New England Quarterly*, 33 (March 1960), 19-36, that if Marshall had taken greater notice of the factual background of the case, a more satisfactory judicial standard for the disposition of later contract cases might have been devised.

Useful information on the transformation of the College quarrel into a political issue can be obtained in William Gwyer North, "The Political Background of the Dartmouth College Case," *New England Quarterly*, 18 (June 1945), 181-203. Charles Warren, *History of the American Bar* (Boston, 1911) and "An Historical Note on the Dartmouth College Case," *American Law Review*, 46 (Sept.-Oct. 1912), 665-75, furnish background information on the lawyers arguing the College case. William Draper Lewis, ed., *Great American Lawyers, A History of the Legal Profession in America*, 8 vols. (Philadelphia, 1907), provides some comprehensive information. A more detailed treatment of Webster's role in the litigation can be found in W. C. Noyes, "Webster's Debt to Mason in the Dartmouth College Case," *American Law Review*, 28 (May-June 1894), 359-67, and John W. Black, "Webster's Peroration in the Dartmouth College Case," *Quarterly Journal of Speech*, 23 (Dec. 1937), 635-42.

Biographies of many of the important persons connected with the College imbroglio are lacking. The only biography of Eleazar Wheelock is David McClure and Elijah Parish, *Memoirs of the Reverend Eleazar Wheelock* (Newburyport, 1811). This volume was written by two devoted followers of the College founder and under the direction of John Wheelock. For obvious reasons, therefore, the work resembles a piece of hagiography more than an historical appraisal of the elder Wheelock's life. Another short biography suffers the same defect, since it was written by his son-in-law, William Allen, "Eleazar Wheelock, D.D.," William Sprague, ed., *Annals of the American Pulpit*, 9 vols. (New York, 1857), 1:397. Sprague's *Annals* is a valuable biographical source on many otherwise obscure individuals. John Wheelock inspired even less biography than his father. The only important biographical piece on the irascible President is S. C. Bartlett, "Dr. John Wheelock," *Proceedings of the New Hampshire Historical Society,* 2 (1895), 408-26. There is no life of William Allen, the ill-fated president of Dartmouth University and Bowdoin College, and for President Francis Brown there is only Henry Wood, "Sketch of the Life of President Brown," *American Quarterly Register,* 7 (Nov. 1835), 133-45.

Fortunately for students of the College case, an exhaustive treatment of the election and legislation of 1815-1816 is available in Lynn W. Turner, *William Plumer of New Hampshire, 1759-1850* (Chapel Hill, 1962). Turner's biography, based on his intimacy with the Plumer Papers and thoroughly documented, is an invaluable aid. Six years after Plumer's death Andrew P. Peabody edited a *Life of William Plumer* (Boston, 1857), which had been prepared by Plumer's son. Peabody added a sketch of young Plumer's life, but the principle value of the work lies in its manifestation of the close relation between father and son. Plumer, Jr. carefully, often completely, rewrote the excerpts from his father's papers which are included in his biography.

Sketches of the lives and contributions of many of the lawyers and judges are found in Charles Henry Bell, *The Bench and Bar of New Hampshire* (Boston, 1894). In addition, John Hopkins Morison, *Life of the Hon. Jeremiah Smith* (Boston, 1845); Burton Alva Konkle, *Joseph Hopkinson, 1770-1842* (Philadelphia, 1931); and Joseph C. Burke, "William Wirt: Attorney General and Constitutional Lawyer," (Ph.D. diss. Indiana University, 1965), can be profitably consulted. The flamboyant William Pinkney still awaits his biographer. A thorough discussion of Webster's part in the case is Maurice G. Baxter, *Daniel Webster and the Supreme Court* (Amherst, 1966). R. Kent Newmyer, "Daniel Webster as Tocqueville's Lawyer: The *Dartmouth College* Case Again," *American Journal of Legal History,* 11 (April 1967), 127-47, sees Webster in 1819 as a broker between the professional-economic elite and the Court.

Besides Beveridge's biography of John Marshall, useful information can be obtained in Joseph Story, *A Discourse on the Life, Character, and Services of the Honorable John Mar-*

shall (Boston, 1835). Marshall's colleague stresses the Chief
Justice's belief in the importance of the contract clause. Edward S. Corwin, *John Marshall and the Constitution* (New
Haven, 1921), presents a balanced view of the consequences
of the Dartmouth decision and criticizes those who would
blame that decision for all the economic ills of the late nineteenth century. Robert Kenneth Faulkner, *The Jurisprudence
of John Marshall* (Princeton, 1968), may replace Corwin as
the standard introduction to Marshall's thought. Joseph
Dorfman, "John Marshall: Political Economist," W. Melville
Jones, ed., *Chief Justice John Marshall: A Reappraisal* (Ithaca,
1956), believes that John Marshall viewed economic matters
as paramount because he thought the Constitution was
created primarily to cope with problems of foreign and
domestic commerce. His contract-clause decisions were important because a basic condition for the expansion of business was the security of property and credit. Nathan Isaacs,
"John Marshall on Contracts: A Study in Early American
Juristic Theory," *Virginia Law Review,* 7 (March 1921), 413-
28, stresses the need to evaluate the judicial pronouncements
of the early nineteenth century in the context of the prevail-
ing juristic theories of that period. Isaacs advocates abandonment of modern concepts of contract law when evaluating
the contract decisions of the Marshall Court.

Joseph Story and James Kent merit attention not only because of their conservative views on the sanctity of private
property but because of the important roles they played in
the Dartmouth College drama. Gerald T. Dunne, *Justice
Joseph Story and the Rise of the Supreme Court* (New York,
1971), has supplied the badly needed biography of this important justice. Dunne's "Joseph Story: The Great Term,"
Harvard Law Review, 79 (March 1966), 877-913, can be
profitably consulted. Kent's views on the sanctity of vested
rights of corporations are evident in his work on the New
York Council of Revision. The only record of the Council's
activities is Alfred B. Street, *The Council of Revision of the
State of New York* (Albany, 1859). Street's volume not only
furnishes a complete documentary record of the Council's
vetoes but gives biographical information on its members.

Further information on the opinions of these eminent jurists on property rights can be obtained from their commentaries on the Constitution: Joseph Story, *Commentaries on*

the Constitution of the United States, 3 vols. (Boston, 1833); and James Kent, *Commentaries on American Law,* 2 vols. (Boston, 1884). Other legal treatises are equally important. No student of early American jurisprudence can neglect William Blackstone, *Commentaries on the Laws of England,* 2 vols. (Philadelphia, 1864). A discussion of the subsequent application of the *Dartmouth College* doctrine and its modifications is in Thomas M. Cooley, *A Treatise on the Constitutional Limitations Which Rest Upon the Legislative Power of the States of the American Union* (Boston, 1874).

The place of the *Dartmouth College* case in the history of the Supreme Court is discussed in almost any history of the Supreme Court. Charles Warren, *The Supreme Court in United States History,* 2 vols. (Boston, 1926), while weak regarding analysis of the decision and its historical importance, gives extensive treatment of the contemporary reception given the decision in the popular press. Charles Grove Haines, *The Role of the Supreme Court in American Government and Politics, 1789-1835* (Berkeley, 1944), presents a thorough discussion of the case, but is tainted with distortions of fact and a decided anti-Marshall bias. A provocative discussion of the dynamic role of property in the nineteenth century and of the relationship between legal protection of property rights and popular attitudes is James Willard Hurst, *Law and the Conditions of Freedom in the Nineteenth-Century United States* (Madison, 1956). Hurst concludes that the doctrine of "vested rights" was not mere "standpattism" and that the protection of private property helped create a framework for change.

The roots of the doctrine of "vested rights" are thoroughly explored in Charles Grove Haines, *The Revival of Natural Law Concepts* (Cambridge, Mass., 1930). Edward S. Corwin, "The Doctrine of Due Process of Law before the Civil War," *Harvard Law Review,* 24 (March, April 1911), 366-85, 460-95, discusses early English and American developments of the concept of due process which was set forth by Mason and Webster in the College case.

The principal study of the contract clause throughout United States history is Benjamin F. Wright, *The Contract Clause of the Constitution* (Cambridge, Mass., 1938). But Robert L. Hale, "The Supreme Court and the Contract Clause," *Harvard Law Review,* 57 (April, May, July 1944), 512-57, 621-74, 852-92, cannot be neglected. Warren B. Hunting, *The Obliga-*

tion of Contracts Clause of the United States Constitution (Baltimore, 1919), is particularly useful for its comprehensive examination of the English precedents relied upon by counsel on both sides of the College case. Other pertinent information is in Clarence P. Denham, "An Historical Development of the Contract Theory in the Dartmouth College Case," *Michigan Law Review,* 7 (Jan. 1909), 201-25.

Because of the emphasis on the relationship of the *Dartmouth College* decision to corporations, an acquaintance with the history of corporate development in the United States and of the development of corporation law is essential. Two works are absolutely indispensable: Joseph S. Davis, *Essays in the Earlier History of American Corporations,* 2 vols. (Cambridge, Mass., 1917), demonstrates the difference between English and American corporations in the eighteenth century and clarifies important points concerning the relationship between government and these corporations; Edwin Merrick Dodd, *American Business Corporations Until 1860; with Special Reference to Massachusetts* (Cambridge, 1954), is valuable as a study of the manner in which business corporations were fitted into the framework of American political society and the state and federal constitutions. The one vital area of American corporation law—that dealing with the power of the legislature to alter, amend, or repeal corporate charters—was one in which English law was of little assistance. American corporation law on this subject was an indigenous development, Dodd believes, and this makes his work particularly useful to a study of the *Dartmouth College* case. Information concerning the belief that prevailed in the United States prior to the Civil War, can be obtained in George H. Evans, *Business Incorporations in the United States, 1800-1943* (New York, 1948).

A comprehensive study of the College decision must assess the decision's impact on the subsequent development of colleges and universities in the United States. This entails some knowledge of the differences between the colonial colleges and those before and after the Civil War and a familiarity with the American system of lay government for college administration. Two surveys are helpful in these regards: Donald G. Tewksbury, *The Founding of American Colleges and Universities Before the Civil War* (New York, 1932), and Richard Hofstadter and Walter P. Metzger, *The Development of Aca-*

demic Freedom in the United States (New York, 1955). The question of the state's relation to Dartmouth College was a crucial one in the case, and a knowledge of the relation between state and college in early American history is essential to an understanding of the various solutions proposed in the College case. Lawrence E. Cremin, *American Education; the Colonial Experience, 1607-1783* (New York, 1970), which offers an historian's probe of the intimate connection between early American colleges and their communities, and Fred J. Kelly and John H. McNeely, *The State and Higher Education: Phases of Their Relationship* (New York, 1931), are of assistance. Richard Hofstadter and Wilson Smith, eds., *American Higher Education; A Documentary History*, 2 vols. (Chicago, 1961), is also useful. The impact of the College decision on the state's relation to colleges and universities is fully treated in Lester W. Bartlett, *State Control of Private Incorporated Institutions of Higher Education* (New York, 1926). A very useful compilation of judicial decisions in both state and federal courts pertaining to all types of colleges and universities is Edward Charles Elliott and M. M. Chambers, *The Colleges and the Courts; Judicial Decisions Regarding Institutions of Higher Learning in the United States* (New York, 1936). This is the first volume in a series which comprised six volumes in 1967.

Index